# NO GUARANTEES

DON
DIETRICH

## With Nadine Dietrich and Brad Bird

Trafford
PUBLISHING

Order this book online at www.trafford.com/07-1119
or email orders@trafford.com

Most Trafford titles are also available at major online book retailers.

Note for Librarians: A cataloguing record for this book is available from Library
and Archives Canada at www.collectionscanada.ca/amicus/index-e.html

Printed in Victoria, BC, Canada.

ISBN: 978-1-4251-3072-5

*We at Trafford believe that it is the responsibility of us all, as both individuals
and corporations, to make choices that are environmentally and socially sound.
You, in turn, are supporting this responsible conduct each time you purchase a
Trafford book, or make use of our publishing services. To find out how you are
helping, please visit www.trafford.com/responsiblepublishing.html*

*Our mission is to efficiently provide the world's finest, most comprehensive
book publishing service, enabling every author to experience success.
To find out how to publish your book, your way, and have it available
worldwide, visit us online at www.trafford.com/10510*

 www.trafford.com

**North America & international**
toll-free: 1 888 232 4444 (USA & Canada)
phone: 250 383 6864 ♦ fax: 250 383 6804 ♦ email: info@trafford.com

**The United Kingdom & Europe**
phone: +44 (0)1865 722 113 ♦ local rate: 0845 230 9601
facsimile: +44 (0)1865 722 868 ♦ email: info.uk@trafford.com

10 9 8 7 6 5 4 3

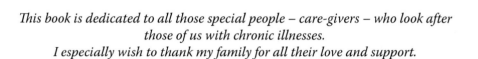

*This book is dedicated to all those special people – care-givers – who look after those of us with chronic illnesses.*
*I especially wish to thank my family for all their love and support.*

*Don Dietrich*
*December 2007*

# CONTENTS

# FORWARD

I FIRST MET Dieter in the fall of 1978 at the training camp of the Brandon Wheat Kings. We both made the team that year and would go on to be room-mates for two years, becoming life-long friends in the process. Over the years, during his professional career there would be times where we fell out of touch for a stretch, but in what is a measure of a great friend, we would always get caught up immediately and it would be like we had never been apart.

When Don moved backed to Deloraine with Nadine and the boys follow-ing his pro career, we began to see each other more often. I remember clearly the day he walked into my office to tell me he had been diagnosed with can-cer. By this time I was working with the Wheat Kings, and we had just re-turned from our annual West Coast trip. It was early in November. We were both young guys then, and it devastated me to see this happen to my friend. As time went on, it was determined he had a very rare cancer, with a very uncertain prognosis.

Since that time, my admiration for the man has grown continually. I have watched him go through numerous surgeries, different treatments, all the associated ups and downs, yet every step of the way he has made the effort to maintain a positive approach to life. Before the cancer, Don was also diag-nosed with Parkinson's disease, again at an early age for that type of disease which meant more challenges, more treatment and more hardship. Through it all he continues to battle with the support of Nadine, Tristan, Jacob and Nick. He should be extremely proud of all of them, and I know he is. They are a special family.

I don't want to dwell on Don's health challenges at the expense of talking about some of the endearing traits he has that make him a great friend to so many people. He is a natural athlete; he played many sports and always played them well. Whatever sport or activity he picked up, he had a great knack to do well, whether that was baseball, golf, pinball, cards, or of course hockey. As well, I can't think of Dieter without thinking of his great sense of humor and how much he loves a good laugh. He is a good friend of my wife Terry as well; they share a mutual admiration for golden retrievers and love to brag about their other "kids" when they see each other. More importantly, he has always been a kind and generous person who has time for anyone.

I consider it an honor to have Don Dietrich as a friend, I truly do. When I watch the strength he shows in his day to day life to be a husband, a father, and a friend I find it truly inspirational. There are times when a person feels life has dealt him a tough hand or you begin to succumb to the different stresses we all face and when this happens to me I often think of him to draw strength and help me through my own life. He means more to me than he'll ever know.

Kelly McCrimmon
Owner / General Manager / Coach
Brandon Wheat Kings
August, 2007

# INTRODUCTION

IN 2000 MY editor at the *Deloraine Times & Star*, Ben Kroeker, asked me to write a story about Don Dietrich. Don was a local man who had beaten the odds and become a pro hockey player. Few young prospects ever make it that far. But the reason I was asked to talk to him had little to do with hockey, or so I thought at the time. Don was a former athlete who was living with Parkinson's disease *and* cancer. The latter ailment – aggressive leiomyo sarcoma — had recently been diagnosed. The body Don had depended on, that had taken him to the top of professional sport, was failing him.

The man I met was big, friendly and determined. I realized this was no ordinary fellow. He had a stronger than usual will. Don, then 39, spoke in terms of surmounting his medical problems. Just as he had beaten the odds of making it to the NHL, so too would he beat them in terms of his illnesses. His cancer was being treated and the Parkinson's, though debilitating, was not preventing him from enjoying life.

Fast forward to summer 2004. I biked one day to Heather and Mike's All-Season Resort at Lake Metigoshe to buy groceries, when I came across Don and Lee Clark, our former Member of Parliament, talking on the deck. I sat there for an hour listening to Don reminisce with Lee about his medical and hockey experiences. I was reminded that here was a story that had to be told. Here was another book project. I had just seen the story of my father's air force career published by Pemmican of Winnipeg (*Nickel Trip*), and was looking for another.

It turned out that Don had been hoping to put his story in print. He was pleased when I approached him and Nadine about the idea of a book. (I had also written a news story about Nadine and her mother and the Guardian Angel dolls they made and sold.) We got down to business in October 2004, meeting once a week at their place. Four months later the bulk of the work was done.

Don made the job easy. He's a natural story teller. I simply placed the old ghetto blaster in front of him, turned on the record function and asked him what came next. His recall of places and stories was vivid and colourful. It helped that he had lived his hockey experiences with famous personalities such as Tony Esposito, Alan Eagleson, Denis Savard, Doug Wilson, Bob

Pulford, Dunc McCallum, Andy Murray, Kelly McCrimmon, Dave Semenko and Wayne Gretzky. Don wasn't a fighter, but his stories of scraps with John Wensink and others are thrilling; his experiences as a green prairie boy in the big city, hilarious. Nadine added essential memories and insights.

Here, then, is *No Guarantees*, a story of courage twice over — once, to carve out a career in a difficult and demanding business; twice, to confront and defy Parkinson's and cancer. This is an insider's story of pro hockey, a journeyman's story of being with "the guys," of the harsh business end of pro sport, of injuries, coaches, and self-motivation. It is also the story of a wife's love and support for her husband, and a community's appreciation for one of its own. With Nadine, three fine sons and good friends, Don has lots to live for. Surely that is also a measure of his success.

◼ ◼ ◼

Preparing a book is a big project. I wish to thank my brother-in-law Michael Kelly for his help with the cover and my wife, Karen Stewart, for her editing. I also thank Arthi Reddy of Trafford Publishing for her dedicated assistance. I remain responsible for any errors or shortcomings within these pages.

Most of the photographs herein are the property of Don and Nadine Dietrich. Some were taken by family members; others, by fans and media people who over the years gave them to Don. Unfortunately, as much as we would like to credit the photographers this is not possible because they were not identified. We do, however, thank them, and invite them to contact us so that we might credit them in future.

*Brad Bird, Editor*
*December 2007*

# PROLOGUE

IT WAS SEPTEMBER of 1981. I was 20. My second training camp with the Chicago Blackhawks had gone well, but I knew where I was heading. There were probably 15 of us who were going to the New Brunswick Hawks, Chicago's American Hockey League farm team in Moncton. Everyone had to see Jack Davidson, who was the assistant general manager to Bob Pulford, the GM. We also saw Pulford, who wasn't much for mincing words. You knew where you stood with him.

Before leaving home I got some fatherly advice from Dad. People with titles are just like the rest of us, he said, so don't be intimidated. Yet it was hard not to be a little in awe of Bob Pulford, who as well as being Chicago's GM had been a heck of a player with the Toronto Maple Leafs. He'd won four Stanley Cups. So I went in and Mr. Pulford, in a gruff kind of voice, said, "You've got to pass better, shoot better, skate better. You're going down."

He was right, I did have to do those things. At that point I realized that the pats on the back were coming fewer and farther between. That's part of the professional game. If you have a good game, they always want a little bit more. I remember going to camp in pretty decent shape, trying to show my best, but still being that guy who was on the outside looking in. Ninth round pick, three-way contract. I'm not saying this for anybody to feel sorry for me. Those were the facts.

The big hype at the time was an older Bruins guy by the name of John Wensink. He had played in Quebec the year before and had cleared waivers, so was sent down. The season is soon to start and we've got to go into Fredericton and apparently John Wensink's going to be there. He was about 29 at this time. Wensink played four seasons with the Boston Bruins in addition to his years with Quebec and Colorado. There's a website or two asking whether he was the toughest Bruin of all time. Wensink played for Don Cherry, and Cherry loved him.

We went into Fredericton and Wensink's mad. I'm sure he's protected a lot of guys in Quebec and they've abandoned him, and he's on the end of his career. He's not where he wants to be. The game gets under way and every time the whistle blows he beelines toward somebody, and everybody takes a wide swoop around him. You don't want to tick him off because

NO GUARANTEES | *Don Dietrich*

you never know what's going to happen.

At one point I got into a little scuffle in front of the net and got pushing with a guy. He threw his gloves off so I threw mine off but the linesmen were already between us. Nothing really came of it. I skated over to the penalty box with the official and all of a sudden I feel this tug on the back of my sweater. I turn around and it's John Wensink.

I'm out in the middle of the ice and he wants to dance. My heart was just pounding. I thought to myself, well. I didn't have my gloves on or anything. The linesman who was with me kind of let me go. I thought, OK. I'm standing there and I kind of faked like I was looking away from Wensink. Then I smoked him as hard as I could.

I know I punched a foot behind his head. When I trained with Rocky Addison the boxer in the summer, that's what he told us to do. It puts more into the punch. Well, Wensink just growled, literally, and grabbed hold of me and started throwing punches. I'm yelling "Help!" My hands are going, my face is getting peppered and I'm trying to hang on to him. I did kind of get him a little tied up. But I was done. I couldn't see, my eyes were watering. Wensink was this big head of hair and eyebrows standing out. I said that's it. I folded my knees to go down. He picked me right up.

Now I'm screaming for help. Dave Feamster jumps on Wensink and we all roll around. So we're sitting in the penalty box because we were the initial fight; everybody around us got thrown out. My face was swelling up and I'm thinking, I'd better learn to pass and shoot and skate better because this is a tough way to make a living!

I was fortunate to live my dream, 10 years of professional hockey, and most of it wasn't about fighting. Through hockey I met my wife, Nadine. Because of hockey I've seen some of the world, won awards, heard crowds chant my name, played with or against guys named Savard, Sutter, Esposito, Lafleur and Gretzky. I've always loved hockey, being with the guys, the camaraderie and competition, from the time I was a kid.

But it wasn't all roses. The business side of hockey can be harsh. Careers are in the hands of coaches and general managers who can make life tough. Hockey is a numbers game in many ways: jobs are limited, and if you're not putting up numbers you're gone. Then there are injuries and illnesses, of which I've had my share. My story shows what the game is like for hockey players who don't make a million bucks a year, and there are a lot of us. Maybe this book will inspire some of you kids to chase your dream of playing in the NHL anyway. I hope so.

I also hope that my experiences with Parkinson's and cancer are an encouragement to those of you in similar situations, because I've been fortunate in how things have gone. Good doctors, surgeons and support from family and friends have made the difference. Maybe, too, something my coaches said played a role: When you get knocked down, don't lash out. Put it aside. And whenever you can, get back in the game.

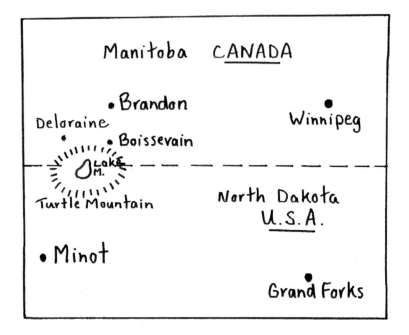

The area around my home, Deloraine, Manitoba.

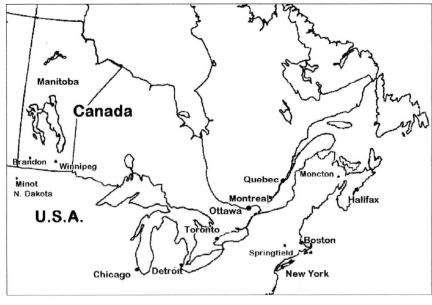

Eastern Canada and the United States, showing cities where I played.

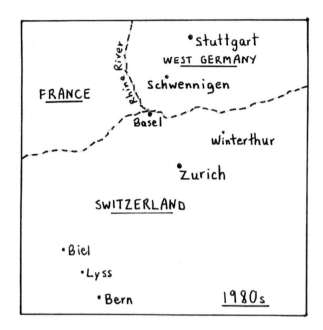

West Germany and Switzerland were home for a while.

The Sarajevo Olympics – an exciting but sad time.

# Chapter 1

## MY EARLY YEARS

*"Dennis Crowe and Cam King used to take us to games, because their sons Kevin King and Kenny Crowe were my age and playing too. To get me into the car, they bribed me with KitKat bars."*

I CAME INTO the world with a bang, as Dad would put it. I was screaming for food and have been ever since, I guess. I was born on April 5, 1961, in Deloraine, Manitoba, the son of Olive and Roland Dietrich. I have an older sister, Donna.

You never know the exact time a baby will be born. As a result, Mom and a nurse pretty much delivered me. Mom herself was a nurse. They had to get me out of the amniotic sac, as I was turning purple in the fluid. Dad said I was fine in the hospital but when I got into the car I started crying, and my sister wondered if they could take me back.

My mother, Olive Elizabeth Creaser, was from Clanwilliam, just north of Minnedosa, Manitoba. She was the eldest of four children. My mother is my hero. She's battled multiple sclerosis for countless years. MS is a disease of the nervous system that leads to poor control of your muscles. Mom's a calming influence on the family, and she was the backbone of us when we were growing up. She was six feet tall and very athletic.

Mom's people had come out of Ontario. Her Dad was Roy Creaser, who married Joyce Turner. They had a farm near Bethany, close to Clanwilliam, Manitoba. Mom, their first child, was born in Neepawa on Oct. 30, 1927. She was the eldest of three girls and a boy. Her father died young of a kidney disease, only 38, when Mom was 10. "It was tough," she said, "it was tough on my mother. She was only 28 with four kids." Mom had to work, and, being the eldest, was maybe leaned on a bit more. "I worked in Clear Lake at the Whitehouse Restaurant and bakery. I made maybe $25 a month." At 17 she went for nursing training at the Brandon Mental Health Centre because they paid $30 a month. She graduated as a psychiatric nurse two years later and worked to save money, then trained to become an RN.

My Dad, Roland Armond Jacob Dietrich, was an honest and hard-working man who had a business in Deloraine for 45 years, an auto body business. That was D & M Motors. He was somebody whose bark was worse than his bite. He had a hard-nosed exterior, but underneath it he was a kind man.

## A good third baseman

Dad was a tremendous ball player in his day, but he never played any hockey, never skated. He started out in Grandview, Manitoba, and then he continued on here in Deloraine with some pretty good ball teams. He was a third baseman. Mom always said he was pretty intense and tenacious. When we had Deloraine's 100th anniversary here they formed an old-timers' team and he was one of them, and I guess in that time, in the 1980s, he would have been 40-something years old. He played third base, Ron Amey's brother Ed played first, and there were other guys who aren't here anymore.

My father's parents, Philip Dietrich and Margaret Metz, were of Austrian-German descent. Both had grown up in Austria. From everything that I've researched they were from a small village in the Carpathian Mountains. While they were still children, their parents settled in Saskatchewan. They landed in New York, made their way up to Ontario and then settled in a German-type community in Saskatchewan. Eventually they moved to Grandview.

Dad was a twin and had eight siblings. He passed away Nov. 23, 1994. He had a problem with alcohol. He wasn't a bad alcoholic to us, but he'd had a heart valve replacement earlier in his life and maybe should have taken a little better care of himself. He had a massive heart attack in the hospital here, when he'd checked himself in to dry out.

Childhood was good. I can remember wanting to be at the shop with Dad. He always came home at lunch time and would leave us Juicy Fruit gum under our bowls of cereal and I could always smell it in his pocket. I remember being the little pain-in-the-butt little brother to my sister. She would always be the one who ended up in trouble, somehow.

Hockey came into my life early. I can remember Mom telling me a story of going to the rink and skating in the afternoons. I was three years old. I think it was the Catholic priest who had time to skate in the afternoons, and Mom would get me over there. She said I had a knack for skating or striding. I don't have much recollection of hockey before the age of 12.

My best memories up to that point are of the lake. My parents had a cabin at Lake Metigoshe on Turtle Mountain, a forested area with lakes in the southwest corner of Manitoba, on the North Dakota border. I was five years old the first time I got up on water-skis. I remember the feeling and the sensation. Betty and Louis Goodine, who were my god-parents, had a cabin right next door and a 15-horse Evinrude motor with a wooden boat. The first time I went off the dock I wiped out right away. They put the big skis on me and I made it up the second time and around I went. I kept pestering them for more and more.

One day we got up to the lake and there was a boat and a dock in front of our place, and I shouted for joy. I loved the lake. We used to have an old dog in those days. Of course it roamed all over town and kind of owned the lake a little bit, and when it came time to go home they'd have to pull me and the dog from underneath the trailer. When the summer was done I was hiding under there with him because I didn't want to leave either.

We caught a lot of perch off the dock. We used a stick with fishing line and a hook on it and we'd put some wiener on the end and catch perch. I was always too scared to take them off the hook so I'd be screaming for Mom to get them off, or whoever was with me. Fishing was a pastime that you did in those rare moments you were bored. My middle son, Jacob, loves it. I always used to say I couldn't hate golf bad enough to fish.

## 'You need stitches'

Dad made sure we kids had a swimming area. He would put sand in there and gravel and of course chemicals that you can't even go near nowadays. But they killed a lot of the weeds and we always had a nice swimming area. I remember jumping off the dock when I was a kid and cutting my left foot right down to the bone. Someone had broken beer bottles. I think I was nine. Mom wasn't there at the time; she was in town for morning surgery. I came racing out of the water and blood was kind of everywhere. Keith Maxwell, our neighbour (he was the postmaster here for years), had kids about our age, Danny and Kim. He could hear me yelling, and I lay down on the grass. He came over and picked my foot up and I could see his face as he recoiled.

"You've got to go in for stitches," he said. I didn't want to go to the doctor, so I said, "No, I'm OK." He wrapped me up in a towel and took me in the car and I remember coming down that gravel lake road over those hills and he's just flying and I'm in the back.

There was Mom coming out with a load for the summer. We met her on the road. So they transferred me to the old '61 Ford Comet that we had. In those days Gordon "Doc" Bonar was there on call and Mom was the surgical nurse. She had to give me the general anesthetic. She said it was the hardest things she'd ever done, put her own son under. But Doc said, "You're here, you're helping. Scrub up and put him under." I had about 10 stitches inside and 20 or 25 outside of my foot. It was shaped like a question mark.

It was a bad summer. I couldn't play baseball, couldn't go in the water. I had a couple of bad summers. I got covered one year with poison ivy from head to toe. I was just one big scab. That took me out of baseball and water-skiing.

But mostly I have good memories. I can remember trying to bare-foot ski behind our boat, and just about breaking my neck. I think I was 10 or 11 years old. Mom would fish me out of the water, and I couldn't even move or anything. There was Jim and Mildred Dando in the corner of the bay. Doug their son and Dale Peake were tremendous skiers and I would be sitting on the beach watching them go by. "I'll give that a try" I thought, because I was a good skier.

I'd try and wipe out. We had a 65-horse Johnson. Mom would open it up and away we'd go. There were lots of times she said she'd pull me out of the water, gasping for breath, neck all sore, but a week or two later I'd be begging to do it again.

Finally the Dandos showed me an easier way with a circular disk board. They told me to wear a pair of sneakers and I got up and I made it. I had lots of trial and error of things at the lake. Donna skied too, though not as much as I did. When I got to be 12 and 13 I'd spend my days over at Dandos, hoping they'd take me in the boat. Then the three of us went out and skied. Mildred and Jim were really good to me. I probably never thanked them enough for what they did for me. That was a big part of my life. Good people.

I can remember across the lake from us there was another Dando family, and they had the nicest boat. It was burgundy coloured with a brand new Merc motor on it. I think his name was Murray Dando. They had a daughter that was probably 19 or 20 years old and I was about 10. I was twitterpated with her. But my dream at that time was to ski behind their boat.

And it was a nice boat. It was one of the first ones to have a canopy over it. One day we were over at Charley McMechan's, and Murray and his daughter pulled up. I was sitting in the back of our boat, and she was in theirs. I was probably sitting there just staring at her the whole time. They went back out, and she says, "We'll see you guys." And then she says, "Bye cutie pie in the back seat." I remember going all red-faced; I thought she hadn't even seen me. Dad said I was red as a beet.

I was also playing ball and hockey. In a small town, that's what you had to do. We didn't have the golf course that is out here now until I was 17 or 18. We did have the course at the lake at Bill Rolston's campground. Your seasons consisted of baseball and hockey and time in between. Once the lake got going I wasn't really interested in playing ball. Baseball went through the summer in those days, so it was kind of a chore to get me in from the lake for baseball. But if you ask my Mom, I think she'd tell you I was a better ball player than hockey player.

I started playing ball at about age seven or eight, at about the same time as organized hockey. I was a good pitcher and loved hitting. Had a pretty consistent 90-mile-an-hour fastball in my late teens and early 20s. I went to a Cincinnati Reds rookie camp in South Dakota, which was common. There was a guy who scouted for them up here. They had a radar gun on me and I was pretty fired up, and threw one in there that clocked at 94 mph. They had guys that pitched, they had guys that could hit, and guys that could run 40 yards in four seconds. Those were the guys they were interested in. I would be 16 at the time. One of the coaches said, "You know, you might be interested in playing a little ball. We might get you into the University of Kentucky or something like that."

I just looked at him and said, "No, I'm going to play hockey." I had my mind made up that that was what I was going to do or try to do. I think it was almost every Canadian boy's dream to play in the National Hockey League. I remember Saturday nights and Hockey Night in Canada. It's always been one of my favourite theme songs.

Was there ever a time when I didn't like hockey? My parents told me this story and I've shared it with others. I was eight years old when I announced that I wasn't going to play hockey that year. Eight years old. I think it was the first or second practice of the season. Dad, he'd be down at the shop next door to the rink on Saturday morning, and he popped over to the rink and saw that I wasn't there. He came home in a tizzy because he'd just spent $30 on brand new equipment for me, which at that time was a lot of money. He was quite upset that I wasn't playing hockey.

## Bribed into the car

Dennis Crowe and Cam King used to take us to games, because their sons Kevin King and Kenny Crowe were my age and playing too. To get me into the car, they bribed me with KitKat bars. So I think I was the type of person who needed to get going, and once I got going in hockey I was fine. It just took a while.

It was the same story when I wasn't playing hockey: I had to get to a certain comfort level. I used to cry the nights before I had to go to school, for example, when summer holidays were over. But once I was in school for a week there was no better place to be. It was just initially getting started in things at that age that I found hard. Once I got to 11 or 12 years old it didn't seem to be a big deal anymore. I guess it was part of my personality not to like change a lot.

I can remember being 12 years old and if our team didn't play that Saturday, I'd walk down to the rink with my bag because that's where every team met, and I'd wait for the 13-year-olds to come in, because usually they'd be going to a tournament. If they had enough kids and didn't need me I'd wait for the 14-year-olds, and if they didn't have enough kids old Ivan Wilson always took me with the midget team. I didn't care whether I played one shift or 100 shifts, I was going to play hockey.

Mom tells the story of whenever I played with the midgets, she'd get the call to pick me up at the rink because I couldn't walk home because I'd got hit hard by somebody — a 12-year-old playing with 16-year-old guys. Or trying to. But I'd be back.

## No guarantees

What grabbed me about the game is that, like any sport, there are no guarantees. If I knew before every game that I'd score three goals and we'd win 5 to 2, I probably wouldn't play it. It's like if I went out for golf and shot 72 every time at the golf course no matter what, I probably wouldn't play it. I was a gifted athlete; anything that I did I could pick up and do. When we had a high school football team here I quarterbacked. Grade 9. You develop a competitive edge when you get to certain levels, but that more than anything appealed to me about sport, any sport — baseball, football, water-skiing, golf — it didn't matter, whatever it was, I tried it and usually did pretty well.

But with hockey being a team sport and players requiring various skills, there were no guarantees. You had to perform well each game. Life isn't a guarantee, either. You have to make it happen.

We always had a backyard rink. I still make them. I've got a 16-year-old son who still wants a rink in the backyard. And he can access a rink over here, the Doc Bonar Arena, half a block away. But that's where a lot of the little skills develop. I used to have a pair of Mom's skates that were probably 10 sizes too big for me but I put them on and went out there and we'd be out for hours. We'd go out to the creek here that led into the lagoon, or away from it, and we'd find a nice patch about 20 feet wide and 30 feet long and play out there for hours until it was dark.

We played road hockey endlessly. We shot pucks on each other and Jimmy Teetaert would drag his net down two or three blocks to my place and we'd set it up under a street light and shoot till midnight with sponge pucks. We'd put on snowmobile suits and mitts and mask and that would keep us warm and also protect us. You learned to hit the net because if you missed it you had to go and get it.

Jimmy Teetaert, he was my back catcher. I used to pitch to him endlessly while we were in town. When it came time to go to the lake I had my lake friends. Danny Maxwell was my best friend at the lake. He was two years older than I and of course when you came back to school, you didn't hang out with the younger kid, but when we were up there we were buds.

Geoff Bonar was somebody I hung around with a lot. In town there was Kevin Sorensen, Mike Olson, these were guys who I didn't even know existed when I was five years old. Then, the only kids I knew were Ross Roy and

Bruce Fraser because we lived in the same block. Then all of a sudden we got to be a little older and we ventured out to Broadway Street and found some other kids. Our worlds at first were pretty small in the confines of our yards.

There was an old bachelor named Pete Bissett who lived next door to us, and he let us run amuck through his yard. We would play catch over there and grass hockey and everything and he didn't mind. He was a great old guy. The odd time we'd have games of war and you'd get shot and have to count to 100 and then get up and keep going. I remember him saying one time, "I think I'm going to have to get a loader in here to get all the dead bodies out of the way."

Dad didn't coach me in hockey; he managed a lot of teams. I remember him coaching me in baseball, for sure. No man that I knew had more knowledge of baseball than he did. He even helped me in my late teens and early 20s, when I was playing. He wanted me to play ball. I don't know if he wanted me to play pro ball. That was never anything that my parents ever discussed. If it was something I was going to do, they would make every effort to get me there.

## *Clelland and Olson*

Roy Clelland and Johnny Olson were character type guys, good coaches. They always seemed to want the best for us as kids. Looking back, after having kids that went through minor hockey, and seeing the stuff that went on, I don't remember seeing it as a kid — politics, and people complaining about ice time, normal things that go on. I think you have to attribute a lot of that to them.

Good old "Doc" Bonar. I can remember being in the back of his station wagon and going all over the place. Of course with him being the doctor, we were always late, and he'd be flying down the road. He'd have the car full of hockey bags or baseball bags and kids, and we used to pile out of there like the clowns at the Shrine Circus. Every one of my minor hockey coaches or ball coaches was very influential in building the character that I have today. I know that I was an athlete that excelled at every level I participated in, and I think that's why no matter what I did, I wanted to be the best. They had something to do with that.

I know that through my own coaching experiences, when you have an elite athlete, you're just pretty much opening the door for them. You can offer certain things, but they have that drive and determination to excel. That's the way they were.

Our coaches were good honest people. I mean, I had Ivan Wilson at midget age, and Ivan had played the game at high levels. He played three years of minor pro hockey from 1947-48 to 1950, with Kansas City of the old United States Hockey League and Vancouver Canucks of the Pacific Coast Hockey

NO GUARANTEES | *Don Dietrich*

League. He was a winger who in his last two seasons in Vancouver scored 16 goals and 25 assists one year and 17 goals and 20 assists the next. He was born in Moose Jaw. You always knew where you stood with Ivan Wilson.

I was a defenceman who liked to carry the puck and score goals, and was allowed to do it. Mom tells the story that I started as a forward but got moved back to defence because I could skate backwards. It never stopped me. My parents never complained that I wasn't playing forward. I didn't mind playing defence because I loved Bobby Orr. He was incredible. No wonder some people, such as Don Cherry, consider him the greatest player ever.

Guys like Doc and my Dad and Ivan Wilson, Roy Clelland and Johnny Olson and Bob Caldwell, had a great influence on us. There's an arena with Doc's name on it over there. Dad put countless hours in at the baseball diamonds and both rinks installing artificial ice, hours that people don't know about, or wouldn't think of. Mind you, a lot of volunteers do the same thing today.

# Chapter 2
## Minor Hockey—
## And Up to the Wheat Kings

*"Dunc McCallum, God love 'im, was the best coach I ever had."*

WHEN I TURNED 12, that's when the scoreboard began to matter more to me than the act of playing. Dennis Crowe, Cam King and my mother were among the adults who always seemed to have us in a car on the way to games or practices.

The year I was 12 we had some pretty good accomplishments. We went to a Mile High Tournament in Colorado with teams from Dallas, San Diego, and all over the States. We came from a small town and we won that tournament. It was a big deal. We went down over Thanksgiving weekend, which meant we had to be out of school. We spent many hours on a bus. I still run into that bus driver, Jim Douglas, in Brandon at Wheat Kings games. Jim said that was one of his best trips.

Playing road hockey as much as we did, we could shoot the puck better than most kids. One of the things our coaches used to do was give each of us a puck in warm-up and we'd just hammer it on the boards. The other team would be standing there with their mouths open: "Look at these guys — they're 12 years old and they're hammering the puck!" They probably weren't into it as much as we were.

### Dallas Strachan

That tournament we picked up a guy by the name of Dallas Strachan from Hamiota, a curler and a good hockey player. He was a forward. I think Doc Bonar rustled him up for us. During one game Strachan was in front of the net and I took a slapshot and hit him right on the nose. I thought I'd killed him. He went down in a heap and they rushed him off the ice (but we ended up winning that game). I saw him afterwards and his face was all swelled up; and of course Doc Bonar got him back into the lineup the next day. He had a football mask on and a helmet and he played, and Strachan actually scored the winning goal in the final game for us.

My Dad got a trophy that tournament because the Zamboni broke down and he fixed it, right in the middle of the tournament.

When we got home, CKX TV of Brandon, Manitoba, north of Deloraine, had us in for an interview. Coaches Johnny Olson, Roy Clelland and myself were on the Noon Show. Cliff Jones was the sports man in those days, and I can remember being really nervous. I'd worn a white T-shirt that I'd got from the tournament and it was too white for TV and they were trying to get me to wear somebody's jacket.

Jones talked to the coaches a bit and then they said, we have a young fellow here, and I can remember Clones asking me, "Who's your favourite player?"

"Bobby Clarke."

"Your favourite team?"

"Montreal Canadiens."

"So what do you do when they're playing each other?"

I didn't know what to say, and he said, "You probably hope Montreal wins and Bobby Clarke scores a goal." I agreed with that, and then they cut back to the coaches.

Yes, we won a lot. I can remember going over to Killarney as an adult to help at a hockey school. Some of the Killarney guys we used to play against were there, and I'm in the dressing room getting my kids ready because they're in this hockey school too. They said, "Oh, Dietrich, I remember you beating the heck out of us when we were kids," and I said, "I just remember having fun." And he said, "Yeah, fun when you're beating us 10 nothing. It was fun for you guys."

At that age, that's also when we went out to Delta, B.C. for baseball, representing western Manitoba. We were the Deloraine Beavers. In hockey, we were the Little Royals. That's what we called ourselves, because we idolized the Royals, Deloraine's senior team. I used to go to Royals games hoping some day I'd play for them.

There were a lot of good Royals players. Bob Caldwell played on that team. Wayne Coxworth was somebody I idolized, and he played for the Wheat Kings as well. Bob Clelland, who knew hockey tremendously; Clark Tweed, a tenacious competitor; Dennis Olischefski, a heck of a hockey player and a good all-round athlete as well. Lyle Franklin, Neil Franklin, Don Morrison played then. There was a guy named Ken Onchalenko, who came out of Brandon. Gary Ewen, the goalie. Dale McKinnon when he first moved here was a 22-year-old teacher playing back-up goalie in those days.

Greg Morrison, Wayne Wilson. Roy Clelland coached them as well. Don

Coombs, Al Dyker. These are guys who, playing in a small town, made you want to play for the Royals some day. I'd get to their games about once a week. The NHL guys were on one level, somebody you saw on Saturday night on Hockey Night in Canada, but your senior team was real. The hockey was the same.

The Royals' biggest fan was Lee VanMackelbergh. His nickname was Heimer. We always had games of catch or whatever was going on. Actually, Heimer is probably the guy I miss the most in this town. He passed away in his early 50s. He loved sports. It makes me a little choked up thinking about him.

Heimer knew the Deloraine Royals by heart. If you said, "No. 2, Bob Caldwell," he'd tell you every Royals player from that era, from that point on, their number and their name. Heimer was mentally challenged and he lived on the next block over from me. When he passed away I was quite emotional. He said that I was one of his heroes. He died about three years after I moved back here, after I retired from hockey. I had to bring him a hat, a ball cap, from every place I played, when I came home. He collected them. When he passed away his mother showed me his hats, and there were too many to count. He was maybe 52 years old. I think he had the umbilical cord wrapped around his neck when he was born. He wasn't supposed to live past the age of eight or so, but he functioned quite well in this community. His picture is in the rink beside Doc Bonar's picture. He had the mind of an eight year old, and he bled Royals gold. He could be seen riding around on his bike with either a football or a ball glove. In winter he'd have a shovel on his shoulder as he headed to the rink to keep the doors clear of snow. He was a tremendous fan and a great man.

When Bob Caldwell moved to town he took over as coach of our minor bantam team for a couple of years. He'd been over to Russia to see how they did things, and he brought back a unique and different style. We were into it, including off-ice training. We played a pretty high calibre of hockey. We won the Tournament of Champions when we were 12 years old in Oak River, and we were keen.

## 1972 *Canada-Russia series*

Of course I watched the 1972 Canada-Russia hockey series and loved it. Dad went to the game in Winnipeg, and he had the programs and everything else involved. Like so many other Canadian kids I was glued to the TV when I could be, and in school we listened to it with a transistor radio in our ear. The final game, we all watched it in the auditorium at the elementary school. It was pretty neat. When they first started, I don't think the Canadian team was that serious about what their competition was, but I think the outcome overall was fantastic for us as a country and for our game, too.

NO GUARANTEES | *Don Dietrich*

I didn't grow a lot. When I was 13-14 I wasn't very big. Everybody sort of shot up past me. Bob Caldwell chose to move me up to a forward position. I'd played defence primarily to that point. I was a good skater and competed, so I didn't find that to be anything of a problem. I actually quite enjoyed it and had some good success in moving to that position for a couple of years. I think in today's day and age with this bantam draft that they have, size-wise I might have been overlooked, even though I had good skills and ability. That happens to kids who are later bloomers. I mean, I played professional hockey at 6 - 2, 195 pounds. I did eventually grow.

At 13, at the Tournament of Champions in Minnedosa I had a bad injury. I went in on a breakaway, made a move and tripped over the goalie and fell head first into the boards, breaking my collarbone. It was January, so there was still lots of hockey left to go and it even affected me for the next year starting out in baseball. I was still pretty sore. We had little knowledge of re-hab other than my mother, as an RN, telling me you have to lift a weight as soon as you can. Again, if it had been up to Doc Bonar he'd have put a sling or something on it to get me to play! That was Doc.

That was tough to handle, being put on the sideline. I'd had different injuries prior to that that put me on the sideline for hockey and baseball. For every playoff game or provincials or whatever was going on, I went with the team and watched. That was a tough pill to swallow, all that traveling and no playing. Looking back on it now, years later, it wasn't that big of a deal. But at the time it was.

I was told that from a very young age I was listed with the Brandon Wheat Kings. This was the local Junior A team in the Western Hockey League, which is only one step below pro. The story was, we were playing in a Mother-Son game, and then the Wheat Kings were going to play the Southwest All-Stars in an exhibition game. They came to the rink and we were playing our moms at 4:30 or whenever it was, and I must have been 10 or 11 years old.

We were beating the moms pretty handily, 15 to nothing or so. My coach John Olson said to me, "When you pick up the puck in your end why don't you go down into the moms' end, go behind the net and turn back and try to score on our goalie." Our goalie was Doug Hardy. I see all these Wheat King guys are watching the game, so I picked the puck up, took it down into their end, came back, made a move and put it in the net. Doug was quite upset because that would have been his first shutout of the year. But John Olson told me that's what I should do. The only thing I didn't like about it was that at the end all the moms were trying to kiss me, telling me thank you, thank you, for scoring a goal.

There was a write-up in the *Brandon Sun* the next day about the Southwest All-stars playing the Wheat Kings, and it mentioned me as a young prospect that Wheat Kings' coach Rudy Pilous had noted. Pilous, of Winnipeg, had been a pro scout and coach. One day he got a call from Bobby Hull and went on to coach and manage the Winnipeg Jets of the World Hockey Association.

## Wheat Kings camp

Then the letters started coming about going to camp when you're 15 or 16. I went to a Wheat Kings camp at 15, was there for just four or five days. It was like a rookie camp. I never had any inkling that I would stay on or would want to stay. I came back the next year at 16, and this time they talked about wanting me to stay for the full camp. Sixteen would have been my last year of midget. At 15 I'd played some games with the senior team, the Royals, and with my midget team, and we had a good team again. We'd won the Tournament of Champions that year. So I'd had a good first year of midget and been scouted.

I can remember sitting in the dressing room at Wheat Kings camp; I'm 16. Nearby are Dave Semenko and Mike Polonich, two pretty tough guys who were trying out for the team. I'm sitting there and I don't have a hair on my body and I'm petrified. These are big guys that I'd watched, that played with Dan Bonar, who was from Deloraine, and I was quite awestruck and a bit intimidated. They had a lot of hair.

Polonich and Semenko were buddies. They'd played together the year before and they're in the dressing room talking away and I had some tape that Dad had given me from the auto body shop. It was plastic stuff that they used for body work. I took it and ripped it and it made a big rrrriiiipppp! sound and everybody in the room was looking at me. I felt like crawling into my shoes!

We went out, and I'll never forget the first shift. Polonich and Semenko started fighting. He was a little right winger and Semenko was a big left winger and they fought. They were teammates the year before, and they were in the dressing room talking like buddies only minutes earlier. Semenko was an extremely tough character; so was Polonich. I mean, Semenko had hit him quite a few times and at the end of the fight, Polonich is sitting there going, "Is that all you've got? Is that all you've got?" I was standing on the ice thinking, what am I doing here?

As time went on the start of school got closer, and I knew I wasn't ready to stay that year. I was about six feet, maybe 180, but mentally I wasn't ready. I was about to go into Grade 11 and wasn't ready to move away from home. I knew I wasn't going to make the Wheat Kings. Andy Murray wanted me to stay for the Brandon Travelers, the Manitoba junior team they had in those days, the feeder system for the Wheat Kings. But I didn't want to do that.

I remember coming out every day and looking at the list on the wall, hoping that I would be cut. Geoff Bonar went in at the same time and had a lot of talent and he chose to stay. And he did stay. He was older. I talked to Andy Murray, and he really tried to sell me on staying, which was his job. He wanted the best available players, as he saw them. He tried to talk me into it, saying Brandon was a great town and everything, but I wasn't sold on the idea.

Staying meant being billeted and going to a different school. I didn't have a vehicle or anything, so getting around wouldn't have been easy. I just wasn't ready. I had it put to me that if hockey is something in your future, this is something you've got to do. You've got to stay. They may have been right, but I was quite upset. I walked out of the Murray Chev-Olds dealership that Andy Murray was running down on Rosser Avenue. I was upset that maybe I was going to blow something, so I phoned Dad at the shop.

I told him I didn't know what to do, I'm crying, and I'm afraid that if I don't stay I'm going to blow it. He said to me on the phone, well Don, you've got to do what your heart tells you. Because if you do what I tell you you'll blame me for the rest of your life. And he was right. If he'd told me to stay and it didn't work out, it'd be his fault. If he told me to come home and hockey didn't work out, it would still be his fault. So I had to make that decision. I swallowed the lump in my throat and decided to come back home and was still quite upset.

Then I got a call from their head scout Ron Dietrich, no relation. He wished me well in my last year of midget, and said you'll play on the senior team, have a good season and come back and make the Wheat Kings. Then into the driveway drove Roy Clelland and Bruce Stephens. I forgot to mention Stephens in senior hockey, the Royals, what a player. They said, you know, we'll make room for you on that team.

## Royals made sacrifices

There were players who made sacrifices. Bob Caldwell was then a defence-man as I was; he moved up and played forward to make room for me. They made some sacrifices and that was a tremendous year for me because they had a winning tradition, the Royals did in those days. Those guys were all winners. It was a neat year and a neat situation. I won Rookie of the Year with the Royals, played my final year of midget, and came back the next year to Brandon to make the Wheat Kings.

I also had a cracked ankle that year. I took a shot that put me out for about a month. I was playing midget in a tournament and a guy that I don't think could have shot it to the back of the net hit me at just the right spot on my ankle and gave me a hairline crack. It was tough for about a month. But I came back after I think three weeks and skated a bit, got into the playoffs and it was quite a good experience.

The senior league in that day was pretty good. As a 16 year old I com-peted with men. There were ex-Western Hockey League guys such as Wayne

Coxworth, and guys that played Brandon University hockey; there were the two Langs in Souris, and Russell had a tremendous team. There were guys who'd played in the International Hockey League, minor pro. Kelly Greenbank, who had played in the American Hockey League, played in Souris. It was quite an experience to play against him, at 16 years of age. Kelly Greenbank and I still are great friends. It's funny, because he ended up playing in Austria when I was over in Germany.

It ended up that the next year, I came to camp and my focus was completely on making the Wheat Kings. It turned out I was in the right place at the right time. My first year with the Wheat Kings was a really good year of learning. I played with some tremendous hockey players: Brian Propp, Brad McCrimmon, Laurie Boschman, Ray Allison. It was an amazing team; we lost only five games that year. At the same time we set a team penalty record. In net we had Rick Knickle, who played about 19 years of pro. Scott Olson was the other goalie; he invented roller blades.

I can remember them all. Mike Perovich, he was a second-round draft pick of the Atlanta Flames. Wes Coulson from Hamiota is still involved with hockey. Semenko could have played as an over-age, but it was the year the WHA, World Hockey Association, had its first draft. It was funny because he was on a line with Don Gillen, who was a monster of a man, and Bob Bidear who was from B.C., and Semenko was actually the smallest guy on the line. Gillen played right wing and Bidear played centre, but he tore his shoulder badly at camp and never played again. Semenko was 6 - 3, 218 or 220. Gillen was 6 - 4, 235, and Bidear was as big as Gillen. These guys were 18 years old.

My first year with the Wheat Kings was 1978-79. We also had Dave Stewart. I think there was only one guy on that entire team who didn't go on and play at least one season of professional hockey, which is unbelievable for a junior team. There was Dave Chartier, Steve Patrick, Dave McDonald, Kelly Elcombe, Kelly McCrimmon.

## Coach Dunc McCallum

We won the Western Hockey League and we went to the Memorial Cup. And we lost in the final in overtime to Peterborough that year. That was a blow. We were projected to be the ones to win it all. There was no doubt that we would. My coach was Dunc McCallum. Jack Brockest was GM.

Dunc McCallum, God love 'im, was the best coach I ever had. He was an old defenceman, played 15 years professionally and he'd played with the Wheat Kings. He taught me all the little things about playing defence: toes up ice all the time, little things that help you. Being a defenceman in my eyes is being able to make the best of the worst situation. You're the only guys back there and of course goalies are the last resort. You're always the one who has to figure out if it goes from a two on two to a two on one, how to handle it.

Dunc didn't teach us that winning was everything. He taught us the will to succeed. I remember a lot of his speeches. "It doesn't matter what you do in life, be sure to do your best." Whether you're a doctor, a hockey player or whatever. You've got to give it your best effort. That always stuck with me. He had quotes and things that seemed to jump out at you at different times in your life, you know. I think he taught a lot of life skills as well as hockey. That was important. I'm not saying I didn't have good coaches after Dunc; I did. Some really good coaches too. But I came from a senior hockey schedule — nothing against that — to a 72-game junior schedule and he viewed me as somebody who would be in the Wheat Kings franchise for three or four years — I was there for three — and he coached me accordingly. He had tremendous hockey knowledge. When you'd walked the walk as he had, you could talk the talk.

Dunc McCallum had played defence in the era of the Original Six. He'd played in the NHL for Pittsburgh for four seasons beginning in 1967-68, and he'd played in the minors. When you think about that era, there were, what, 30 defencemen (and only 18 centremen) in the NHL? Some franchises today have almost that many players in those positions in their system. At banquets I've addressed people have said to me, "What do you think of expansion?" I say I hope it keeps going because then I can tell my grandchildren I made it when there were only 21 teams! You should have seen how tough it was then! But the Original Six of Dunc's day — that was a whole other ball game.

We had a good year. It was a great group of guys. We had chemistry. There were guys like me who had to accept a role, and that didn't always mean playing a lot. I was a fifth defenceman who could play a little power play. We'd go on road trips and sometimes I wouldn't play; I'd just ride the bench, but I was only 17. There weren't a lot of 17-year-olds in the league. There was no underage draft at that point. I liked my role. When you play on a team where you lose five games all year, wow. They still have the thing up in their dressing room that Brian Propp wrote. It says "125 points. Beat that." That's what we had as a team that year, and it's never been touched.

Propp had 94 goals and 100 assists in 71 games for us that year, and went on to have a great career with the Philadelphia Flyers. I had 43 points (37 assists). All I had to do if I had the puck behind the net was pass it to one of those guys. They were going to take it down to the other end and score! Being my first year in the league, and getting that will-to-win attitude, it was good.

Of course, losing out in the Memorial Cup was a big disappointment. We had been touted as No. 1. It was overtime. We'd had a rough start in the Memorial Cup tournament, as we'd lost our first two games. But we won our next two, which ended up getting us into the final against the Peterborough Petes. We were supposed to play in the Montreal Forum, but that was when Don Cherry had too many men on the ice with the Boston Bruins. The Bruins lost, and that took it to the sixth game in Montreal, a Sunday in the Forum. We ended up playing the final game in the Virdun Coliseum in Quebec, the junior rink where Ray Bourque played.

The game was televised and I did play in it. I lost a tooth in it. A guy slashed at my stick, and it deflected up and hit me in the mouth. Peterborough had Billy Gardner, Bob Attwell, Stuart Smith, Tim Trimper — they had more guys than that that went on to play professionally, but being from another league you didn't know anything about them. The same thing with Three Rivers, the Quebec representative. All good players, but we didn't know anything about them, and they didn't know anything about us. We were notorious for being brawlers.

We actually had a brawl in our first game at Three Rivers. It got pretty hairy there. Their fans were involved. My Dad and Bob Astle had gone down to the game; their bus actually got there late, so they didn't know what had gone down in warm-up. We had a full-scale brawl in warm-up. So the fans were just buzzing. Three Rivers was a logging community and probably pretty rough to start with. I can remember the Three Rivers'coach, Bergeron, pulling his team off the ice when the brawl was on and leaving us with the fans. The fans were on the ice and fighting. It was pretty scary there for a while. They realized they couldn't stand up on ice the way we could on skates, so they'd end up bailing out after taking a couple of bops on the side of the head with a stick or something. I was in the middle of it all.

## Worsley gives warning

Our fans showed up late as I say, and Bob Astle was pretty boisterous. He used to be the postmaster in Deloraine. He's a tremendous hockey fan. Something happened, and of course you're not going to get a call in your favour in that rink because the ref wants to be able to get out of there in one piece when he's done. And Bob started yelling, "What the heck's going on!" and stuff, and he and Dad were sitting amongst a bunch of scouts. Dad said Gump Worsley, a famous NHL goalie who had been in many scraps himself, was among the scouts watching it. Worsley reached down and tapped Bob and said, "I think you're better off maybe being quiet," and then they explained what had happened. Worsley was concerned that the Three Rivers fans would come along and scrap with Astle. It was tough. People were running around and burning Wheat Kings banners.

The next day I'll never forget: one of the French papers had a photo of Timmy Lockridge, who was a tremendously tough guy, who held a guy he was pounding in a headlock, and the headline in French read, "Big Bad Westerners Try to Goon Their Way through Memorial Cup." And it got to be pretty tough even where we were, in the hotel. We had some biker guys hanging around. Two of our guys had a beer bottle thrown through their window. In that hotel we couldn't get served any meals. And you didn't walk out of there by your-self. So we moved to a different place. We were the Big Bad Westerners.

Ernie "Punch" McLean, who had coached the New Westminster Bruins, and had been in countless Memorial Cups in Western Canada, Ontario and Quebec, came to talk to Dunc and our team. "Here's the deal. You guys are behind the eight ball. You're going to have to put up with whatever goes on and quietly go about your business." We handled it quite well. Chartier was a guy who spoke French, so we always made sure we sat close to him so we could get our food!

The whole tournament took place in about a week. We started on Monday and the final was Sunday. We played each team two games, and it was total points or goals for and against if it came down to it. The top two teams played in the final.

Nothing surprised me that year. I was ready for it. I was 17, 6 - 2, 190 or 195 pounds. In those days I was considered not a bad size. I was by no means a tough guy or anything like that. But I tried to stick up for myself if I had to. We always had guys on the team that did that. But each year I played for the Wheat Kings, we'd have maybe 10 full-scale brawls in a season. Maybe one or two of them in the game where you actually got penalty minutes. A lot of them happened in the warm-up, when there were no refs out there or anything. It was knock 'em down and drag 'em out, and then you had to play against them. That's what happened in Three Rivers. After the fights we picked our stuff up, they resurfaced the ice and away you go! There was no brawl in the game, which we lost, 4 to 1.

## Intimidation

For the type of team we had, fighting was a part of what we were. Intimidation was big, and we definitely had guys who could intimidate. It wasn't a matter of what was said on the ice as much as what was done. When you have guys on your team that are tough, it makes you grow an inch. You're tough too. I remember we used to go into Saskatoon to play and we'd do our warm-up and do two on ones and line up from the red line back to their blue line, and just hem them in their end. They couldn't do anything about it. And yet we'd run into teams where we'd try to do that and they didn't like it and come in and clean some guys out and then away we'd go and there'd be a little brouhaha. When everybody was done you picked your gloves up and went in, they resurfaced the ice and then the game started.

Intimidation was, and still is to me, part of the game. I'm not saying that I was an intimidating figure, but it makes a difference. When you have guys who are out there to protect their better players, you think twice before you run that better player over. It's something that I think is missing in the game today. The instigator rule (by which a player is penalized for starting a fight) I think hurt. Hockey doesn't protect its superstars anymore. Hence, you could take a run at Gretzky. Years ago we saw Mario Lemieux fighting in the playoffs. He and Gretzky shouldn't need to do that. If they worked their butts off to be as skilled as they are, why should they also have to fight? When I played against Gretzky, if you ran at him Semenko was going to get you. That was an unwritten law. If you did that and Semenko dropped his gloves and you didn't and you turtled, and you got five minutes for receiving it, and then you sat in the penalty box with him for five minutes, he'd be so mad because you wouldn't fight him that he'd come out and beat you up again. He had three majors to do it in. So you were better off to get your gloves off the first time and make it look good! That becomes a factor.

Guy Lafleur said it on the radio recently: Hockey has been the same way for 100 years. Let the refs call it. Don't start making the instigator rule and the Edmonton Oilers rule (four on four). In the '50s and early '60s when you got a two-minute penalty you sat in the box for the full two minutes, no matter how many goals they scored. But the Montreal Canadiens had such a potent power play that the NHL made a rule ending the power play with the first goal.

Getting back to our team that year, intimidation was a big part of what we were. Then of course in the years to come there's a bit of trickle down when you lose all those tough guys, and the other guys don't forget! Yes, we lost guys because the year that came up was the first year of the underage draft. Brad McCrimmon, Propp, Allison and Boschman all went in the first round. We had other guys who were drafted, there were only six rounds. Mike Polonich got drafted, Lockridge, Knickle, Brad Kempthorne, Dave McDonald, Donny Gillen, they were all underage guys, 18 years old. Seventeen year olds like me were not eligible for the draft.

My second year was 1979-80. I was quite excited about it because we had lost three veteran defencemen from the year before and I was to be a go-to guy, one that was counted on for lots of playing time and expected to play well. I knew that I'd have to play a full schedule and be consistent. That was the biggest thing. At that level, the one thing that Dunc always stressed was you couldn't be great one game and bad the next. You had to be good all the time.

Over a 72-game schedule that's pretty tough. That's what he always said I should strive for. Dunc liked me as a player and a kid. He made me assistant captain that year. Kelly McCrimmon was captain. I took it quite seriously, to heart. It was a different year because I think we hovered somewhere around .500 that whole season. It was quite a few more losses than I'd ever been used to, Dunc definitely. He ended up bringing Les Jackson in, a guy who was coaching in Great Falls, Montana. They were called the Great Falls Americans and they had folded. They brought Les in to help.

## *Scouts watching*

I was eligible for the draft that year too. Every game was important, including all your away games because scouts were watching you. We were the farthest team out east, so scouts didn't often come to Brandon unless they were playoff games. So when we went into the other provinces, that's where you were watched. So you had to play well on the road too.

Again, it was quite a learning year for me. It was the first year I was on a team that experienced lots of trades. It was the more the business end of things — having friends leaving for other teams and sometimes having to play against them that night. We actually made a trade with Medicine Hat when they came into town and the guys pretty much went from one dressing room to the other when it happened.

With the underage draft, there were lots of good players who had left the league, like Laurie Boschman, who would still have been eligible to play otherwise. Before the underage draft you were drafted at age 19 or 20. Now 18-year-olds were eligible. That was in 1978-79. So you didn't have some of those teammates who were 19, in their third or fourth year. They were gone. All of a sudden there were a lot of 16-year-olds in the league, because they moved the amateur draft age down again to 17 the year that I was drafted.

The WHA had started up and they were drafting young players. It was a tough year. I had 43 points my first year and the next year, 65. I was an offensive-style defenceman. I wasn't modeling myself after anybody in particular. It was just that on the team that I was on, I got power play time and killed some penalties and was out there to move the puck and settle things down in my end and take control of the game if I could. That was my role.

I never had that knack for running over guys, although I was big. Some people in the Keystone Arena in Brandon were pretty hard on me because I was big and they figured I should be out there rolling heads. That year in the playoffs we were playing Calgary and I got in a scrap and Dunc gave me heck for getting in a scrap because he wanted me on the ice. You know? But I would rather have been in that boat rather than the other way, with him wanting me to do all that scrapping — which is a tough way to make a living.

We weren't paid much. I think my first year I got maybe $30 a month. The next year I can't remember what it was but it wasn't a lot. Thank goodness for my parents having a key to my vehicle and throwing a $50 bill up on my visor once in a while, and Dad giving me a Shell credit card to make sure I could put gas in the car. I mean I worked all summer too but you had to have a bit of spending money to do a few things.

Which brings me back to Dunc. He used to always say to us, "Your junior hockey years would be the best years of your life. Riding around on a stinking iron lung (that is, a bus) and not making a dime." My best friendships still come from junior hockey, even though I played 10 years professionally. My best friendships are from those three years of hockey. Like I said, you're riding a bus from the west coast to Brandon, you play in Vancouver on a Sunday night and you have to be back in Brandon for a Wednesday night game. That's a lot of hours on that bus with the guys.

Dunc McCallum passed away on March 31, 1983. He'd retired from hockey as a player eight years earlier, and then made his name as a coach. He coached the Brandon Wheat Kings from 1976–81, compiling a 251 – 123 – 41 record and winning the WHL championship in 1979. Today the coach of the year in the WHL receives the Dunc McCallum Memorial Trophy.

On the bus we slept, mostly. We actually had bunks put in that year. We shared a bunk. I shared with Kelly McCrimmon. Spent a lot of time sleeping and lying horizontal and going along. It was good. There were a few seats at the front, and a card table and stuff at the back.

## Super Brandon billets

We didn't have to eat much restaurant food. Kelly and I were billeted together with Dorothy and Ivan Marnoch of Brandon. Great people. In my first year my billet was Ma Muirhead. She was a 75-year-old lady that treated you like she was your grandma. I actually went up to about 210 pounds while living there. She always had deserts and lots of food made for me, which Dorothy did too. At that point I realized I'd better watch my weight.

Dorothy always packed a huge cooler full of food — huge sandwiches, rice crispy cake and stuff like that. We got treated pretty well; the guys were envious. Sometimes you end up in the junior hockey world with billets that try to make money off you. Then there are other people who don't care about the money, you get fed well. I was fortunate in both places I was. I had tremendous billets. I got fed and the laundry was done. It was good.

We'd get on the old bus and head out. My middle year to me seems like a blur. Because, when you're playing a lot and you're having a good time, time goes by. The first year I didn't play a lot but I was learning a lot. When I didn't play, I watched. And I watched Brad McCrimmon. I watched Lindy Ruff, and the good defencemen we were playing against and tried to learn from them. That's when I learned about my opponent; who are we playing against today? That became a factor in my second year, who my opponents were.

That's one thing I always liked about playing pro. You always got a stat sheet on the team you were playing against, so you could see who the goal scorer was, what goalie was hot, who was the tough guy, and everything else. Instead of going out and finding out the hard way, by fishing the puck out of your net, or getting the crap beat out of you! It helped me to prepare for who we were up against.

Like I say, that second year we lost more games. And with being a go-to guy you felt a bit of that responsibility. There were also pressures of the coming draft. All that season they had me rated quite high. Central Scouting had me at about 21st overall in the WHL. So I had the odd agent phoning me. Dunc didn't like that because it was a bit of a distraction. But with all that stuff coming at me, it made the year go by quickly.

In the playoffs it was different. We played a round-robin against teams and the top teams played each other in a seven-game series. We played Calgary in the first round and beat them in seven games. At the end of the year I tore a groin muscle with about 10 games left. I shouldn't have been playing but I played in the playoffs. Which is something they said took me down the scale because I ended up being a ninth-round pick. Because of the injury I couldn't skate very well, couldn't stride. Against Calgary they targeted me as a key player and I ended up tearing my ankle ligaments when a guy tried to run at me. I can remember trying to play with a torn ankle in my seventh game of the playoffs against Calgary.

We went to Regina and played the next round-robin series with Lethbridge or Medicine Hat too. We lost out in that series. We were out-gunned and out-classed. Regina had Doug Wickenheiser and Ron Flockhart, Garth Butcher. We had Knickle in goal again and Chartier and Gillen up front. I won Defenceman of the Year with the Wheat Kings. With me on defence were Kelly Elcombe and Greg Mann. But it took me all summer to recover from that groin injury.

## Disappointing draft day

Getting knocked out was a tough pill to swallow. And being injured. And the draft was coming. The day of the draft was one of the most disappointing days of my life, because I didn't get drafted until the ninth round. I was upset. I was at home and sat through about five or six rounds. Then I went down to the Legion to the bar. Dad was upset with me because Bob Pulford had called and they had picked me in the ninth round and I wasn't home. That was at 6 at night or whatever. I'd been up early at 8 o'clock listening on the radio because that's where any news would have come through.

I figured that if I didn't get picked by the fifth round I'd be better off not getting picked at all. Then I could have been a free agent and signed somewhere and done something that way. Now these guys had me. What had happened was they'd lowered the draft age again so the guys who were my age, like Denis Savard, Dave Babych, Doug Wickenheiser, Dale Hawerchuk all went in the first round. These were the elite 18-year-olds in Canada.

The next rounds consisted pretty much of 17-year-olds and some 18-year-olds. If you were 19 you didn't get drafted at all because you were too old. Usually 19-year-olds got signed as free agents, and away they went. That's what I was hoping for because being drafted meant I was Chicago's property. All they had to do was offer me a contract and I was with them again even after my last year. I knew that primarily the Wheat King team coming back would be full of 16- and 17-year-olds which it was, and a few 19-year-olds which I was. I just knew that it wasn't going to be good for me when it came time to do a contract at the end of my third year.

I was upset about it. But again, my Dad enlightened me. He said there were hundreds of thousands of kids in western Canada who would give their right arm to be selected in the draft. And he was right. It brought me into the proper frame of mind. So when Bob Pulford phoned again I was home and was very grateful and thankful that they had selected me in the ninth round. He said, this is Bob Pulford and we're happy to say we selected you in the ninth round. There were no cell phones in those days and they had phones at their desk. I could tell they were in the midst of wrapping things up.

Life's not fair sometimes, and you have to make the best of what you're faced with. That's basically the talk I got from my parents and they were exactly right. Deal with it and get on with it. Don't dwell on it and bring yourself down.

I was given some workout stuff from the Blackhawks through the summer and it was like a whole different world. I've got to run two miles in 12 minutes? I used to use the junior camp to get in shape for the season, and now these guys are telling me how many chin-ups I should do in 30 seconds. Wow. There was stretching too.

I still worked. That summer I worked for my Dad at the service station. His partner was Lloyd McLeod. I worked down at the front shop which is now Maxwell Motors. It was a Ford dealership and service shop, and I was supposed to be selling cars but I maybe sold three cars that whole summer. I was a gofer.

Prior to that I'd worked at the Chimo Lumber yard for Bryan Tyerman, since I was about 14. Piling lumber all day built me up. That's all we used to do was pile lumber in the back and get hired out with the Hiebert brothers or old Melvin Cummings to put roof shingles on. That was at the beginning when Tyerman was just starting to get into the pole barns. Chimo Lumber was over where the RM office is now. It was a big yard. Reg Warren worked there. He was the second in command; he's a fine curler. I worked there in the summer and after school. It was pretty good.

At the end of that summer of 1980 I was OK physically, but in preparation I had to go down to Chicago for camp. You talk about being the petrified 15-year-old kid going to Brandon. Now I'm heading to Chicago. The Big City. I turned 19 in April that year. I've got my flight, I had a one-week visa to practise with Chicago, and never in my life had I been in that situation. I was wide-eyed. I mean, Tony Esposito. Doug Wilson. Stan Mikita. Keith

Magnuson. They were Hockey Night in Canada. I have goose bumps now, as I had then. I never even imagined that I would be in the same rink as Terry Ruskowski or Tom Lysiak.

Not that I didn't think it was attainable, but they were there. All of a sudden I was too.

Age seven. At home in Deloraine, Manitoba.

With sister Donna and Chico.

Age two with Dad.

Age four with Chico.

My parents, Olive and Roland Dietrich.

Age two. "Wanna play ball?"

Me, goalie Kenny Crowe and Jimmy Teetaert, age 12.

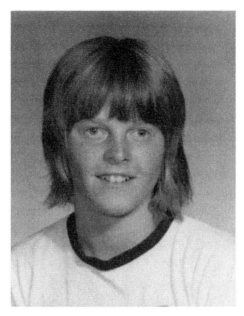

About age 12

Signing my first professional contract, age 20.

December 31, 1983, my first NHL game as a Chicago Blackhawk, against Detroit.
Tony Esposito is in goal.

With the AHL's Springfield Indians.

Reg Kerr, No. 9, played 263 games in the NHL, scoring 66 goals and adding 94 assists, mainly with Chicago. I'm No. 21

More action with the Springfield Indians early in my pro career, between 1982 and 1984.

Pokecheck

# Chapter 3
## MY FIRST NHL TRAINING CAMP

*"I turned and went over and they had this list: I'm rooming with Doug Wilson, a future Hall of Famer. I'm afraid to go up to the room! I'm 19 years old. I'm thinking I'll be staying with somebody from Medicine Hat, some other kid. And I'm rooming with Doug Wilson!"*

THE BIG ANTICIPATION for me for 1980-81 was my third year of junior — plus I had a training camp to go to in Chicago, the team that drafted me. That was big. You have something that you think you're going to get, and it looks so far away, and now it's a little closer. I'm talking about a chance to play in the NHL.

My agent, Bill Watters, had worked under Alan Eagleson. I picked him up early in the summer after I was drafted. He was the guy that phoned the most, I guess. My parents and I didn't know exactly what route to go. But they insisted that I needed an agent, and Bill Watters was well known. He had just branched out on his own a year or two before that, and he had a big entourage of players as well.

I got all that arranged and thought I was in half decent shape. I skated a little with the Wheat Kings, because NHL camp didn't start traditionally until the 15th of September. Wheat Kings camp started about September 3rd, and they had a rookie camp the same time as the veterans arrived, but we went on the ice by ourselves at the start, and then everything was combined.

I'd had a bit of a tough time going from small-town Deloraine, with 950 people, to Brandon, which I thought was a big city. Brandon had about 36,000 people. Now I'm thinking Chicago. I had no idea how big it was. Well, Chicago and area had a population of 7.9 million – 200 times as big as Brandon and 8,000 times larger than Deloraine!

I can remember getting on the plane in Winnipeg with my hockey bag and a couple of sticks, a direct flight to Chicago. I know that O'Hare is one of the busiest airports in North America, and I'm thinking when we arrive, it's not that bad. I follow the signs to the luggage carousel to get my suitcase.

I'm sitting there and the place is filling up a bit. There's the carousel from my flight and four or five others. It doesn't look that busy to me. Of course I'm in the international part of the airport. I haven't even hit the domestic yet. I don't know where to go from here. On my itinerary it said I had to head for the domestic terminal and go outside, get a taxi cab and make sure I had x amount of American dollars in my pocket for the cab ride to the Bismark Hotel, where the team was staying.

I see the signs, domestic terminal, I've got this big hockey bag, two or three sticks taped together and my suitcase. I come through to the domestic terminal and it is just people — people on people on people. I'm a 19-year-old prairie pimple-faced kid. Out of the blue, right behind me, were Darryl Sutter and Brian Young, who played in New Westminster. Brian was a big rugged defenceman who played for the Bruins when I watched the Wheat Kings as a kid. He played in Chicago's minor league system and went on to do well in Europe. Darryl Sutter, well, need I say more? He was an NHL star, one of the famous Sutter brothers from Viking, Alberta.

So they see me, a lost westerner. I didn't realize until I went to Chicago's camp there were westerners, Ontario league and Quebec league guys. The westerners were considered the rugged guys who would go in the corners. I can remember us doing a drill where they'd throw a puck in the corner and you always had to go in there against a Ted Bulley or a John Marks or some tough guy like that, and the western guy he went in there and took his licks and I remember hearing the vets going, "He must be a westerner."

These guys Sutter and Young take me under their wing and we get into a cab. It's one of these big Checker Cabs. We throw our bags in the trunk, it was big enough for everybody's suitcase, and away we go toward the Bismark Hotel. Probably a good hour we're driving in this cab into town. I'm thinking holy smokes. Primarily we're on a freeway. There were three lanes going into Chicago, three lanes going out, and then there was the middle express lane that at different times of the day was either going in or out and it was going in at that time, which must have been for rush hour at 4 or 5 o'clock, which is about what time I got in.

We're in this middle lane, and I don't really see much but cars going each way on both sides of me. Then we start to get into the city. It looks to me like downtown — huge buildings and stuff. Something about what was there didn't jump out at me but I knew there was something different about what was going on. I couldn't quite target it at that time, which I'll get to later on.

We arrive at the Bismark and the Wirtzes, who own the Blackhawks, own the hotel. It's a pretty nice ritzy looking place. Lots of rooms, lots of floors. I head towards the desk. I look back and see Sutter and Young at a table, so I think that's where I'd better go to get my room. I walk up and there's a lady behind this table and she says, "And who are you?"

"Don Dietrich," and she looks down this list.

"Oh," she says, "Wheat Kings? OK. Who are you rooming with?"

"I don't know."

"Well, take a look on the board."

I turned and went over and they had this list: I'm rooming with Doug Wilson, a future Hall of Famer. I'm afraid to go up to the room! I'm 19 years old. I'm thinking I'll be staying with somebody from Medicine Hat, some other kid. And I'm rooming with Doug Wilson!

I actually sat there for a second, thinking how am I going to go up to that room? How am I going to go up there? Doug Wilson and me? I'm going to have to sleep out in the hallway! The previous year, '79-'80, his third with the Blackhawks, Wilson put up 61 points. He went on to win the Norris Trophy as best defenceman in 1982 and played in over 1,000 games during 16 years with Chicago and San Jose. He wasn't Bobby Orr but he was close, and he was a classy guy.

I get my key and the lady can tell I'm a little flustered and intimidated but I'm sure she's seen 100 greenhorns come through the same way. So I take the elevator upstairs and I've got my bag and stuff, and now I'm thinking, "Geez, I'm sure he doesn't have a hockey bag, because he plays for the Blackhawks and his stuff will be down at the rink, and maybe he doesn't want my stinking old bag in the room."

So I knock on the door and don't hear anything. I'm knocking first; it's my room and I'm knocking. I've got a key so I open the door and peek in, and nobody is there. I look around and can see somebody has been in the room. And then I hear the toilet flush. Now I'm thinking, "I've got to disappear because he's taking a crap or whatever and I've interfered with him!"

So I go into the room and I'm just standing there. He comes around the corner and says, "Donny, how are you doing!" Wow. My first name. I mean he'd look at the list too and see what was going on. He was fantastic. Made me feel so comfortable. It was really nice.

Doug Wilson said, "C'mon, we'll go out and get something to eat." Well, I had some American money, and I was hungry. Down we go to the lobby and there's all these young guys with vets from the team. Terry Ruskowski's got Steve Larmer and other young guys there. There's probably about eight of us altogether.

We pile into a couple of taxi cabs and we go down to some rib place, and we sit round a big table much like this one here, and of course I'm 19 years old, I can have a beer at home but there I can't. You have to be 21. We're sitting there and I'm hoping they don't ask me first what I want. So the girl comes up, "Can I get you guys a drink?" Some guys have a beer. She didn't ask me first, which I was so thankful for. I got a diet Coke or something.

## Order a steak

I'm looking at this menu and I see it's stuff that I don't know — and then I see, sirloin steak. That's what I'm going to take. And I'm paranoid, because I'm looking around and trying to watch what other guys are doing and I'm trying to play the part. I'm sitting with four NHL guys and three or four future NHLers, and I'm just pumped. I'm just above everything. I'm sitting there and the girl comes up and she says, "So what'll you have?" And she's looking right at me.

I'm thinking, Why me? So I said, "I'll have this sirloin steak."

She said, "How would you like it done?"

Well, all my life it just came to me on the plate. At home, Dad cooked it on the barbecue and put it on the plate. At my billets, Ma Muirhead and Marnocks in Brandon, I came to the table and it was on the plate. Every Saturday night we had steak at home, it was on the plate.

I'm sitting there thinking, what does she want? I know Mom puts it in the oven. They don't boil steak. I'm sitting there and I'm starting to sweat and the guys are looking as if to say, "C'mon, we want to order." So I sat there and said, "Cook it."

The table erupted in laughter.

They're all sitting there laughing and Doug Wilson goes, "He'll take it medium rare." And she says, "Do you want rice pilaf or —?" And Doug Wilson says, "He'll have a steak medium rare with baked potato, sour cream, no vegetables."

And I'm thinking, "Oh, thank you." I'm just drenched in sweat, red-faced and embarrassed, and all these guys are laughing. I'm the true western guy from cow-town Manitoba. I remember playing my first year of pro, I wouldn't order veal parmesan because I didn't know what it was. I knew there were noodles with it. Guys were ordering it all the time for pre-game meal, or chicken parm.

That whole week at camp I was flying by the seat of my pants. I saw stuff that I'd never seen before. We'd go down to the rink on the school bus toward Spring Street and there are bums on the street, buildings are all boarded up, or heavy duty fencing and security around them. The closer you get to the rink the more run down it is. I remember sitting on the school bus and looking out the window and thinking, hmm, that's interesting. Then we'd go to the next set of lights and see another. They were chalk lines. Dead people. Like on Hawaii Five o. Every day there was a chalk line or something down there. Whether he died from the elements or whatever, they still had to consider homicide first. That was a big deal to me.

## Tony Esposito

The area of the rink wasn't the best. We were told that you didn't go outside the arena itself, the fenced-in area. Never did, anytime I was there. Went to camp and had the experience of skating with NHL guys. One thing that stands out for me was we all went to a bar-lounge to eat one night, and in the door came Tony Esposito. The juke box was playing the Paul Simon song, *Late in the Evening.* "The first thing I remember I was lying in my bed, I couldn't have been no more than one or two, doo doo doo!" There's Tony with the Andy Capp-style hat on. There's Tony Esposito! Every time that Paul Simon tune comes on I can see Tony Esposito standing there with this hat on. I was tremendously awestruck and respectful of the guys.

■    ■    ■

Remember I said there was something different around being in Chicago? The next morning, after the supper when everyone had the big laugh at me, right across the street was a McDonald's. I'd got up early and headed over for a sausage and Egg McMuffin. That's what I liked. And I didn't get to eat at McDonald's very much. I had a bit of money. At that point they'd given us a per diem, which was per day money — about $50 a day. I had $300 in my pocket. This is pretty good! So I'm standing in McDonald's and looking around and again I felt, something's different here. So I turned around and panned the crowd. I'm the only white guy in the whole place. I'd never seen Afro-Americans in Brandon, or anywhere up here in Manitoba. I realized, I'm a minority here.

I don't consider myself to be prejudiced or a bigot or anything like that. I just didn't see it. There were lots of people going to work. It wasn't a dangerous area of town. It was just predominantly black. I thought that was neat. It was just different.

The Chicago camp I attended was the main camp. Since then they've started rookie camps. We got to participate in the entire camp; we mixed with the NHL greats. Actually that year, I went to Stan Mikita and Keith Magnuson's retirement party, where they presented them with two rocking chairs, and everything else. They had a party in a bar — a bar that Mr. T of the A Team used to bounce in. That's where he actually worked. I remember seeing his picture on the wall. We had the whole upstairs to ourselves, which brings me to another story.

I used to be number 21; that was my favourite number. Stan Mikita was 21. We get up into this place, and we're not getting ID'd for alcohol or anything so I'm having a few beers and we're all sitting around, us young guys, and we've been there for three or four days now. We're getting a little more comfortable and I had a pretty good buzz going. I see two guys, Dave Kingman and

Heathcliff Johnson, who played for the Chicago Cubs. They were sitting up at this bar, so I wheeled up there and was standing beside them, checking out how big they were.

And they had this presentation, in which Mikita and Magnuson were given rocking chairs, as a bit of a joke. It got to be 11 or 11:30 and we had early practice. They had retired Mikita's number 21 the year before. He'd played 22 seasons in the NHL, all with Chicago, winning the scoring race four times, the Lady Byng after that, and the Hart Trophy twice as most valuable player. Stan Mikita was probably the best all-round centre of the 1960s. He was part of the famous Scooter line, with Kenny Wharram on left wing and Ab McDonald and Doug Mohns on right. At first he fought a lot, and was somebody you didn't want to cross. In one of his books *(Stop it There, Back it Up!)* Howie Meeker tells the story of how one time, after being hacked by a goalie, Mikita stopped and pointed at the guy's head with his stick. Later in the game he hit that goalie on the mask with a slapshot. Six stitches. Meeker figures the shot would have killed him if he hadn't been wearing the mask. Mikita was born in 1940 in Czechoslovakia as Stanislav Gvoth, but had moved to Ontario as a boy to avoid the political troubles of communist control. An aunt and uncle adopted him and gave him their surname, Mikita.

So anyway, Stan Mikita I see is sitting by himself. I mosey over and I'm half in the bag and I'm talking to him a little bit. And I said, "Some day I'm going to pull that sweater out of the rafters and wear it." He just kind of laughed, and hit me on the shoulder, "Yeah, right kid." But what a stupid thing to say. I felt so bad the next morning. I was a bit hungover and knowing I had to get to practice. I'd rushed up to him and hit him with it and felt so bad about it. And I still do, because he deserved respect, not some snotty nosed kid telling him he's going to pull his sweater out of the rafters. Anyway, I did it.

Another thing I remember is going to my first Chicago Cubs baseball game. This was the day before we were leaving and we had the afternoon off. Dennis Hull took a van load of us young guys to a game. We sat on the third base side, close enough that you could hear what the guys were saying in the dugout, but high enough back that you got a real good perspective of the field. We had good seats.

The balcony hung almost over us. If we looked back we could see whatever was going on. So Dennis Hull is saying, "Do you guys want a beer? You can have one." This is an afternoon game in Wrigley Field, because there are no lights there. We're there with our beer and worried that the cameras will see us and Bob Pulford is going to catch us. We shuffled them under the seat.

## Harry Caray sings

Dennis Hull comes back and says, "You know, it's getting close to the seventh inning. You watch. There'll be a guy up here hanging out of the press box, singing Take Me Out to the Ball Game." We didn't think anymore of it, and when the seventh inning came along, all of a sudden there's a, "All right everybody," — Harry Caray, famous baseball announcer, and they used to say he was half in the bag when he was announcing, he's hanging out over the balcony, with the mike and is going, "A one, a two, a three, Take me out to the ball game, take me out to the —" and we're all standing there watching this guy and we're singing away with him. Everybody was singing. That was my first experience with Cubs baseball.

Scrimmaging didn't go very well. Being 19, I was too respectful. And some guys abused their privileges too. Nothing unusual happened. There comes a time in tryouts that you realize you can compete. You can play. And that's what you're there to do. When you're not ready to, you're maybe too respectful of guys you're up against. It's not a bad thing. I don't think it is. It just shows that you're a respectful person. That's the way I was. I wasn't going to take Tom Lysiak and try to kill him in the corner. But later on, when I definitely wanted to stay there, I would do that. I knew I was destined to be coming back and finishing my last year of junior. I didn't have a contract, and I was there for a week and I was coming home.

Most guys didn't wear helmets then. Doug Wilson didn't, nor did John Marks. The year I was drafted was the first year that everybody from that year on had to wear a helmet. 1979 or earlier, you didn't have to wear a helmet. I was drafted in 1980, so I had to wear a helmet. I hadn't planned on wearing one. I ended up wearing one of those Wayne Gretzky helmets for a number of years, which was like not wearing one at all.

The other funny thing I remember about camp was that we always had new equipment, the rookies did. Yet I would look in the gloves and mine would say No. 5. Well, No. 5 was Phil Russell. So I'm breaking them in for him! Half way through camp I get these old ratty ones and I say, hey, where'd they go? And Russell's got them on. "Hey, thanks, kid." Not a big deal. I've got to break gloves in, new shoulder pads, new shin pads, pants and all that stuff. They just told me to bring my skates and sticks. Everything was supplied. I did have my hockey stuff with me but I didn't need it.

Keith Magnuson was coach that year. Cliff Koroll was his assistant. And I'm still in touch with Cliff Koroll. He was an assistant there for a lot of years.

## The Wirtz feasts

The Wirtzes were always involved. Every year that we went to camp they did a special training camp thing. They had a farm with a nine-hole golf course on it, and that's where their race horses were. They fed everybody there. Steaks, open bar, later in the week. Everybody went, scouts, coaches, American League coaches, players — there would be 150 people there.

An interesting guy they brought there that day was the man who invented all the cars for the James Bond movies. You know what the first thing he invented was? The little mechanical riding horses outside the supermarket that you put a dime in. He had brought to the party a James Bond car, a Thunderbird from one of the movies. It was one where the camera went up in the middle and could pan around. The bar came out with the martinis in the middle.

This camera was recording everybody's conversation. At that time he had invented an air-compressed car that could go 90 miles an hour even on a dirt road. He was explaining this to us, how it propelled itself down the highway. But he was in a bit of trouble with the oil companies. They were trying to buy the patent for it. They didn't want him to market it. I can remember this conversation going on and standing in the background, and then Bill Wirtz said, "Well, if we win the Stanley Cup, cars for everybody!" The guy goes, "I've got the camera on that!" I think he said he could make them for $8,000 in 1980 dollars.

One year the Wirtzes took the whole team on their yacht. They had the second biggest yacht, next to the Queen Mary. Just a fantastic setup. They did things like that at camps. They always had a big meal. I never really saw them around the rink. You'd see the old man Arthur Wirtz, the original owner. The only reason we got to see the yacht was that they were bringing it back to put elevators on it because he was having trouble getting around.

The week was a blur. The on-ice stuff I can hardly remember. I do remember Terry Ruskowski — I remember working so hard in practice and skating that Terry Ruskowski came up to me and said, "Way to work. Unbelievable." I mean, he was the captain of the Chicago Blackhawks. I remember watching Keith Brown skate. Denis Savard. These guys could fly.

And all I had in my mind was Brad McCrimmon, a first-round pick of the Boston Bruins, who could skate faster backward than I could forward, phoning me at my billet at Marnock's. He'd say, "Dieter, you can never skate too well in the NHL."

I said, "You're telling me *you've* got to improve?"

"Yeah. You can never skate too well in this league."

That's when you realize you have to work. That year I got drafted I was about 205 - 208 pounds. I ended up playing at 195. Dropping that weight made me quicker in my last year of junior.

■   ■   ■

I spent my token week there which is all you could do as an underager, and came back tremendously fired up to play. Went through a bit of a downer-type of a start. They were finding that these underage guys that were coming back from pro camps were maybe a little high on themselves, which I'm sure I was. We weren't doing maybe what we had to do; I came to that realization after four or five games. I was made captain of the team that year, which I took as a tremendous honour.

Dunc McCallum no longer coached. Les Jackson was our coach. Les was a very good people reader. He knew how to read people and was good outside the rink with PR and things like that. I know he used to get really mad. We didn't have a great team. We struggled around .500 or less, but I played tons. That year I played defence and forward. I'd play defence, get a rest, and go out and play forward for a shift. That year in the playoffs I never came off the ice at all, unless I had a penalty.

We had a very young team. There were lots of guys who remembered those days of intimidation and paid me back. Like I said, I was by no means a tough guy or anything. I had 80 points that year. We just made it into the playoffs, and played Regina in the first round. They were really strong.

My partner on defence for pretty much that whole year was Dean Kennedy, the last Winnipeg Jets captain. He was drafted by LA. At 17, a very tough kid, and a tough man when he played. He had a knack for just melting through guys. He's another teammate I developed a very good friendship with. He actually married a girl from here. I think the first time he saw her was up at the lake at Metigoshe, when he was there with me one time. She was water skiing and I remember him standing on our beach going, "Who's that? Who's that?" She had fallen. Tammy Olson, Johnny Olson's eldest daughter. Tammy Kennedy.

We had some pretty funny character guys on that team. Ron Popplestone, who lives in Brandon. He does colour commentary for the Wheat Kings games. He's quite a comical character. Dave Chartier was a gifted skater who scored quite a few goals that year and got quite a few penalty minutes. Ken Schneider was just an all-round great guy. A lot of my best friendships are from junior hockey, when we were riding on that smelly old bus not making a dime. Kelly McCrimmon and I are still very close. He's the coach, GM and owner of the Wheat Kings.

## 10 brawls

In my last year in the WHL, the 1980-81 season, I remember not winning, not liking it, and teams evening the score with brawls. The beatings we used to lay on guys were getting laid on us. The warm-ups turned the other way. All of a sudden they were coming after us. Again, we probably had 10 full-scale brawls that year, eight in the warm-up when you didn't get a penalty minute for it. You just hoped you wouldn't get hurt. That was part of the game at that time, the junior game.

We had a fellow on our team that year, Greg Mann, who ended up dying. He had some issues and a combination of medications and alcohol and tobacco that he maybe shouldn't have been doing and he ended up passing away right before the playoffs. It was pretty emotional for us. He was a good little defenceman, a good player; and he was from Brandon. We all felt bad. We kind of alienated him. But he ended up alienating himself, too, because he ended up being off the team. He had some off-ice issues.

I found it tough because I was the captain of that team. Since I've been home I've often wondered what kind of a guy I was back then. Was I a jerk? Was I cocky? And then I start hearing stories from my old teammates who appreciated the way I was and what I had done. I ran into a guy who was a teacher in Brandon, and he said, "You know something? What I remember the most about you? I don't know if you remember this or not, but you guys were at a house party one time, all you Wheat Kings. And things started getting out of hand." I'm thinking, what did I do now?

He said, "But you know what? You stood up and settled everybody down and got your teammates out of there. I was just 22 years old, just into teaching, and there were three or four of us teachers just out of university so we were not too much older than you. But I looked at that and thought, 'That guy's going somewhere.' "

That made me feel good, knowing that I was making good decisions. It had to do with upbringing and the coaching I had received. And that goes right down to minor hockey coaches.

As far as team-oriented things went, I didn't think the year was very good. In terms of personal growth I thought it was quite successful. I did a lot of growing that year, learned to handle the negotiations between management and players, be that go-between guy, be the captain, step up to bat for guys when needed and also confront opposing players — and maybe having to take a punch in the chops for doing it. Then hoping that guys were there to back you up on your own team. Later on in life these became tools that you needed to live by to survive.

I thought that, having played three years of junior and being drafted under age, things would be pretty good. But when it came time to negotiate a contract it was very tough, because I was a ninth-round pick on a last-place team. It didn't matter that I had 80 points; I was a dime-a-dozen as far as defencemen went.

## Reality of the business

There was a guy that scouted for the Blackhawks out of Winnipeg. He used to come to Brandon and he said that to me one time on the elevator, "You know, you're just a dime a dozen." I took that pretty hard, until I went and talked to my old coach, Dunc McCallum. He said "Frig him. Does he not realize you play 50 minutes of a 60-minute game?" and on and on. He said, "You just go out and play and whatever happens happens. If you get in a scrap, you get in a scrap. Just go out and play and let it happen." It was refreshing to hear that from him and he's a guy I respected. Not that I didn't respect the other guy, but he took a shot at me. But that was the reality of the business. All of a sudden it was, here's where you sit.

I was faced with a three-way contract to sign. This meant I got a certain amount for playing in the National Hockey League, which was $60,000; $12,500 to play in Moncton in the American Hockey League; and $7,500 if I got sent to Fort Wayne in the I, or International Hockey League. I didn't want to get sent down there. Or, I could have chosen to come back and play over-age, and maybe go back into the draft. But the draft was getting so young that there were lots of 16- and 17-year-olds coming into the league. I didn't think it would be a good idea for me to come back, and that's all I had in front of me. My agent sends me my contract Fed Ex and I sign it and send it back to him. I got a signing bonus of $5,000, which was good.

I signed it and was excited to be going back to Chicago's camp. This would be my second time at camp and this time I was going to make an impression. Realistically, when I looked at their depth chart I was not going to make the Blackhawks. They had Bob Murray, Greg Fox, Doug Wilson and John Marks. They had Jack O'Callahan from the American Olympic team, and different guys who were in Dallas, their farm team in the Central Hockey League. They were also putting guys in Moncton, N.B. of the AHL.

With a three-way contract, I could be heading for the I. To me, the movie Slapshot wasn't far from the I. Not an attractive proposition. That's how I viewed it. One thing going for me in my contract was that if I played 62 AHL games the third way of my contract would be wiped out. And I would go up to $19,500. That was a big issue, because in those days if you sat on the bench but didn't play a shift you didn't get credited for that game. So you at least had to get a shift.

I worked out through the summer of 1981. Scotty Olson gave me a pair of roller blades, about the 50th pair ever made. I've still got them. They're attached to a pair of skates out there. He played backup goalie for us. My last year, he played a bit in the Central Hockey League but had invented roller blades. We saw him at Brad McCrimmon's wedding. He roller bladed out from Winnipeg. He'd made his first million.

I may have gone to Chicago's camp ready. But when I walked into the dressing room I pretty much knew where I was heading. It was what they did about sweater numbers. The first-round guy wore No. 11 from a guy that just retired, and the ninth-round guy was No. 58. There weren't many No. 58s playing in those days. There may be now because so many teams have so many sweaters retired. But that brought me back to reality. You knew where you were heading. Instead of doing my token week and going back to junior, I was doing my token week and my real camp was beginning in Moncton.

I was No. 39. Dale Hunter I think wore 32 that year. He was the first guy to wear a number like that and play in the NHL. This may sound immaterial, and some people on that side of hockey may say I'm reading stuff into this, but those were the facts. We all had Blackhawk sweaters on at camp whether we were dark or white, but there were guys who were underage juniors that were going back who were like 68 and numbers like that. And there were those with lower numbers who were staying. You knew where you were coming out in the wash. Thirty-nine was close, but still no cigar!

They also had us in different dressing rooms. The Blackhawk guys were in their room, the Moncton guys were elsewhere, and the guys who would get some exhibition games were off in another place. Eventually I ended up being that guy who would get some exhibition games. My number came down from 39 to 32. I ended up being No. 32 with the Blackhawks. But that was a few years down the road.

# Chapter 4

## MONCTON, MY FIRST PRO SEASON

*"I remember Russ Adam coming up to me on the bus afterwards and saying, "Man, Dieter, that was an unbelievable scrap. You were just throwing them." And I can only remember taking them."*

I HAD MIXED feelings about going to Moncton. It's not a really big city. There's not a lot to do, some said, yet it's bigger than Brandon. I had one guy put it to me rather indelicately that if there was a rectum in the world, the enema would go right through Moncton. This was from a player who had maybe had a bad experience there. Not everybody likes their situation in hockey. If things don't go well for you on the ice, then off the ice becomes a critical issue for you too.

At the training camp in Chicago in the fall of '81 the writing was on the wall. I was there for a week and knew where I was heading. There were junior guys who were being sent back and then there were probably 15 to 20 of us who were heading to Moncton. Everyone had to see Jack Davidson, who was the assistant general manager to Bob Pulford. We also saw Pulford, who wasn't much for mincing words. You knew where you stood with him.

Before leaving home I got some fatherly advice from Dad. People with titles are just like the rest of us, he said, so don't be intimidated. Yet it was hard not to be a little in awe of Bob Pulford, who as well as being GM of the Blackhawks had been a heck of a player with the Toronto Maple Leafs. He'd won four Stanley Cups. So I went in there and Mr. Pulford, in a gruff kind of voice, said, "You've got to pass better, shoot better, skate better. You're going down."

He was right. I did have to do those things. At that point I realized that the pats on the back were coming fewer and farther between. That's part of the professional game. If you have a good game, they always want a little bit more. I remember going to camp in pretty decent shape, trying to show my best, but still being that guy who was on the outside looking in. Ninth round pick, three-way contract. I'm not saying this for anybody to feel sorry for me. Those were the facts.

I remember getting on the plane and flying to Moncton and wondering what it was going to be like, with everything everybody had said. I was also nervous and excited, because this was going to be my camp. This was where I would have to show that I wanted to stay. It was pretty nerve-wracking leading up to it.

We get there and the whole team is not in a hotel but a boarding house. There are a couple of beds in each room, there's no TV in the room or anything but one in the living room. We can access the kitchen for breakfast or whatever. Quite different from the Bismark Hotel. No vehicle. They had a couple of vans that ran guys back and forth. We were downtown where we could get to restaurants and stuff on foot.

I started out having a pretty good camp because I was more among the calibre of guys that I should be competing with. I remember having success throwing out some pretty good bodychecks and trying to make an impression on the coach, Orval Tessier. He was an emotional, boisterous French Canadian who coached the Blackhawks the next year. Our team in Moncton was called the New Brunswick Hawks, the last year it was called that. After that it was the Moncton Hawks.

We had some guys who were obviously looking for contracts. They didn't have anything, they were there on a tryout basis, were pretty much heading towards the International League and I was worried about teetering on that. Now you start looking for who shows up the next morning, who got sent down from Toronto, who we were splitting a farm team with, or from Chicago. You start doing the math again. The Leafs had sent Dave Farrish, an NHL defenceman who played in New York and Toronto, an older fellow by my standards. He was probably 28 or so. They also had a farm team in Cincinnati in the Central League. They were sending a lot of their older guys to Moncton so they could pay them in Canadian dollars. Usually how it worked was you got paid in the currency of whatever country you were playing in, unless it was specified in your contract that you were making American dollars no matter where.

We played a few exhibition games. I remember we played against Halifax in Prince Edward Island. John Brophy coached Halifax. He'd been a notorious bad boy in his day. He had a pretty good selection of fellows on that Nova Scotia team. We played in PEI in the home town of Jeff Leverman. He was an amateur Golden Gloves boxer and just a big guy. Played defence. We were actually beating them by a goal or two and I remember looking out on the ice and they had lined up five guys that were pretty tough. Four of the five of them were defencemen. I thought, this is going to be interesting.

I looked around, and we didn't have a big team. My defence partner was Dave Feamster, not a big guy by any means but certainly a gamer. There were a couple of French guys. In those days, leagues didn't trust leagues, either. The Quebec League guys didn't trust the Western League guys and so on. I mean we're basically still strangers, and fighting for ourselves, for jobs against each other. This is basically my first experience with that train of thought. I was used to junior where we had it made. We could rely on guys in certain situations. Now I 'm not sure.

They drop the puck and bango, everybody's scrapping. The guy standing beside me was this Golden Gloves guy, Leverman. So I thought, well. In junior hockey I wasn't considered a scrapper but I was big enough that I never got beat up too bad. Sometimes I won, but you always only remember the ones you lose. So I dropped my gloves and started throwing punches as hard as I could at this guy, and he was bigger and taller than I was. I was throwing right hands and I don't know if I hit him or not. The first punch he threw hit me right on the forehead. My helmet went straight up off my head. I kind of lost my balance a little bit and he smoked me one more time. I went down and he sat on top of me and tried to throw a couple of punches and I was warding them off a bit.

He said, "Don't move."

I didn't say anything. I'm thinking, I'm in a bit of trouble here. My guys on the ice were trying to get there but a bit of a brawl ensued. Then the benches emptied.

He said again, "Don't move. I'm going to get up and I'm going to go grab somebody else."

I didn't acknowledge anything so he took another poke at me, and I deflected it, and he said, "I'm telling ya, don't you effing move!"

I said, "OK."

He got up and went on his way and I got on my way and I never did run into him again. I know I'd hit him a couple of times because my right hand was sore and swelled up afterwards. And I had a pretty good black eye.

I thought, boy, I took a pretty good pounding out of that one. I remember Russ Adam coming up to me on the bus afterwards and saying, "Man, Dieter, that was an unbelievable scrap. You were just throwing them." And I can only remember taking them. And then I thought, maybe it wasn't that bad of a deal. Like I said, you tend to only remember the ones that you lose or think you lose.

I had a three-way contract. I really didn't want to go down to the International League. The money was one thing, but there was supposed to be a lot of scrapping too. Then I found out it wasn't really so. But it was the wrong direction, and I never did play a game there.

The next exhibition game we played was against Fredericton. They were a Quebec Nordiques farm team. I remember playing them in Moncton without incident. I thought I'd had a pretty decent game. I still had a black eye and my hand was still sore.

## John Wensink

The big hype at the time was an older Bruins guy by the name of John Wensink. He was sent to Fredericton. He had played in Quebec the year before and had cleared waivers, which meant that no other NHL team wanted him, so he was sent down. The season is soon to start and we've got to go back into Fredericton and apparently John Wensink's going to be there. He was about 29 at this time. Wensink played four seasons with the Bruins, in addition to his year each with Quebec and Colorado. There's a website or two that ask whether he's the toughest Bruin of all time. He's up there with Terry O'Reilly and Stan Jonathan. Wensink played for Don Cherry, and Cherry loved him. Some believe he was the best fighter and the toughest Bruin ever. He was listed at 6 feet and 200 pounds and played 21 years pro, mostly minor league, ending up in Holland. He was of Dutch ancestry.

We went into Fredericton and Wensink's mad. I'm sure he's protected a lot of guys in Quebec and they've abandoned him, and he's on the end of his career. He's not where he wants to be. The game gets under way and every time the whistle blows he beelines toward somebody, and everybody takes a wide swoop around him. You don't want to tick him off because you never know what's going to happen.

At one point I got into a little scuffle in front of the net and got pushing with a guy. He threw his gloves off so I threw mine off but the refs were already between us. Nothing really came of it. I skated over to the penalty box with a linesman and all of a sudden I feel this tug on the back of my sweater. I turn around and it's John Wensink.

I'm out in the middle of the ice and he wants to dance. My heart was just pounding. I thought to myself, well. I didn't have my gloves on or anything. The linesman who was with me kind of let me go. I thought, OK. I'm standing there and I kind of faked like I was looking away from Wensink. Then I smoked him as hard as I could.

I know I punched a foot behind his head. When I had trained with Rocky Addison the boxer in the summer, that's what he told us to do. It puts more into the punch. Well, Wensink just growled, literally, and grabbed hold of me and started throwing punches. I'm yelling "Help!" My hands are going, my face is getting peppered and I'm trying to hang on to him. I did kind of get him a little tied up. But I was done. I couldn't see, my eyes were watering. Wensink was this big head of hair and eyebrows standing out. I said that's it. I folded my knees to go down. He picked me right up.

Now I'm screaming for help. Dave Feamster jumps on Wensink and we all roll around. So we're sitting in the penalty box because we were the initial fight; everybody around us got thrown out. My face was swelling up and I'm thinking, "I'd better learn to pass and shoot and skate better because this is a tough way to make a living!"

Dave Feamster was from Detroit. The Blackhawks had selected him 96th overall in 1978, and he'd had a successful career at Colorado College, making all-star teams and setting records for most assists in a season and a career by a defenceman. But he could fight, too. He was 5-11 and 180 pounds, a real gamer. After retiring he opened five pizza franchises in Colorado and did quite well. Before that, Feamster had a fracture in his back that ended his career. What happened is that Chicago sent him down to its I league team in Wilwaukee in 1984, but he refused to report because of the injury. Chicago team doctors said Feamster was healthy and the team threatened to suspend him. Feamster went to the Mayo Clinic for a second opinion, and they found the problem. Pulford said the team never would have let him play with a broken vertebrae, and said Feamster had a hereditary back problem. Anyway, Chicago ended up buying out the remainder of his contract and letting him finish the season as an assistant coach in the IHL. Feamster moved to Pueblo, Col., and organized the city's first high school hockey team while working on his Little Caesar's Pizza enterprise.

At that point, early in the season, Orval liked my effort. I did have some skill and ability. When the cuts came through, I ended up being there. But I never ever felt that I was there the whole year, because I was a borderline player. I was the 6th D. Sometimes I sat in the stands. I did have in my contract that if I played 62 American League games the third way would be done for the rest of the contract, which was two years plus an option. In those days if you dressed for a game but didn't hit the ice you didn't get credited. The ultimate diss in hockey is to have to serve a penalty if there's a bench minor. Yet I used to volunteer to serve it because I knew if they didn't score I could get on the ice and get my shift. If they scored, I got no shift. Again, I was learning the business end of it, realizing the business end of it. Having a chance to get credit for a game meant more to me than the humiliation of serving that penalty.

Where you're in that situation — it was much like my first year of junior, my first year of pro — you're watching, you're learning, you're working hard in practice. Then all of a sudden in practice you realize now you're out there with men who have some years on them. Our captain Bill Riley was 35 or 36 years old. He and others really didn't want to be showing up at practice at all. So if you wanted to skate hard you started way back in the pack. You didn't want to embarrass the older guys. You know what I mean? Little things you pick up along the way to make yourself fit in, to be a team guy.

Initiation was always an issue then. Even in junior there was hazing. It was done. Not everybody got it. In junior I got shaved. My body. Not my head or eyebrows. Some guys got it worse than others. I didn't care for it myself. They're doing the right thing about it now, I'll say that. There's zero tolerance for it nowadays and that's the way it should be, or should have been. I'm sure that if my parents had known half the things that happened to me they'd have been furious. It went from being a rookie and having no seat on the bus to lying on the floor and sleeping, to whatever. I thought it was all part of the experience. If you're a good player and a good team guy, you usually don't have much to worry about. There's a certain cockiness that wasn't tolerated by veterans. In this day and age I think cockiness is allowed.

Getting back to where I was, I was grateful to be in Moncton. That's the attitude I had. I was going to learn as I went along. I knew there would be some down time and some up time, but I always had it put to me that my worst day in hockey still had to be a good day in life. "Life is swell in the AHL," we'd say. Where else can you make that amount of money and you're not putting in an eight-hour day?

We were in that boarding house right to the bitter end until they finally booted us out. Then I roomed with a guy by the name of Warren Skorodenski. He was a goaltender. He played in Calgary, and to this day we're really good friends. We rented a basement apartment that wasn't even finished. Skoro had found the place; he had a bit of experience from the year before. He was looking for a roommate. I thought this would be great, and it was. Three hundred and 50 bucks we split, $175 each way, that was utilities and everything included. We had a black and white TV that got maybe two channels. We didn't have a vehicle and used to bum rides or take taxi cabs wherever we had to go. He cooked, I cleaned and did dishes, he did the laundry. We didn't spend a lot of time in the place but it was what we considered home. There was a single lady upstairs and I hardly even remember seeing her.

I talked it over with my agent and was budgeted for $750 a month for everything, housing included. And you know what? I didn't have a problem with that. Lots of afternoons we'd go to the tavern and have lunch and a couple of beers and carry on with the day. We had a lot of older guys on the team like I say, so they weren't really too into where we were at. Chicago had younger guys. There was myself, Skorodenski, Feamster, Sean Simpson. Simmer was a touted up-and-comer off a big line out of junior that played in Ottawa. In 1979-80 he got 65 goals and 149 points for the 67s. Very gifted. In the Chicago organization he maybe found himself in the wrong place at the wrong time.

We started out just terrible. I think in the first 13 games we were five and eight — not starting out very well at all, and Orval Tessier would be blowing a gasket on the bench. We'd be up 3 to 1 and they'd score to make it 3-2 and he'd be saying, "You're going to lose, you guys, you're going to lose." We also had Steve Larmer, Steve Ludzik, who ended up playing in Chicago the next year. We had Louis Begin, a French guy who had just a tremendous shot. Then there was Mike Kaszycki, Bill Riley, Dave Farrish. We had Bob Janecyk and Skordenski in goal. Curt Ridley, a goalie from Winnipeg had been there, but he retired after Skoro was with us for a while. Ridley had played about 10 years of pro. He'd had some time up with the Leafs and Canucks.

## Tessier furious

I remember we were playing in Fredericton and we lost. The Fredericton Express were the lowly expansion team. They came back and beat us. They had some pretty good players. But they were experiencing the growing pains of being a first-year franchise. Orval was furious when the game was on. Sometimes the mouth would engage before the brain kicked in, you know? He knew that and he would tell you that. I can remember him just losing it. He'd throw sticks in the dressing room and berate us verbally. Some guys are sitting there wide-eyed with their mouth open, and some guys are laughing — not literally, but the older guys who had been through it. We got back on the bus and he said, "Two-a-day practices starting tomorrow. Seventy-thirty be here, and be on the ice at 8."

We got there next morning and got dressed. Orval had a little office that he dressed in. We were sitting there, and right before he came in for his meeting, our older guys stood up and said, "When he says to go out on that ice, nobody move." I was concerned. Mutiny was something I definitely hadn't experienced. I worried and I wondered, what am I going to do? They said, "When he comes back in here, every one of us is going to say something we don't like about him. Otherwise we're going to be putting up with this all year."

Their theory was, we're grown men. You can't treat us like we're junior kids. But I was just out of junior, and felt a bit like a junior kid. So I'm sitting there all paranoid and nervous and Orval comes in. He says, "OK, let's go onto the ice," and he goes through the door. Nobody gets up. Now I'm thinking, here we go. So he comes back in the room and he's just furious. I didn't play a lot. The only thing I didn't like about him was his negativity, when we were still winning. Everybody around the room had something to say, and the older guys were maybe more effective than us younger guys.

I remember him being really, really mad. He waltzed into this office, took his stuff off, and walked out. We didn't see him for four or five days. Didn't know what happened. We had a week off, a week between games, and that's why there were going to be two-a-day practices. You see, normally you practice once a day around 10:30 in the morning till 12 or 12:30 or so, on your days off. Bill Riley came out, he's the captain, and he ran practices. Riley had played for the Washington Capitals and Winnipeg Jets. He was very tough and a good scorer, a tremendous competitor. We continued practicing under him. It wasn't up to me to contact the general manager, a local guy, and find out where Tessier was. As far as I was concerned that was for the older guys. The farther away from it I was, the less trouble I was going to get into.

Word got back to the two parent teams that something was up. On the fourth or fifth day we were getting ready for practice and in the door came Orval. He had a really good discussion with us. He said he would try to improve, but he couldn't help being emotional. He wanted to win. He talked about winning, and I was mesmerized by him talking about winning. Winning was everything. He'd say things like, "Who won the 100 metres in the 1980 Olympics?" Everybody knew the answer, Ben Johnson. "Who finished second?" Nobody knew. That's the way he was. He said he'd try to change. And you know what? After this discussion, he still didn't come out to practice that day.

I remember Bill Riley running lots of practices, even throughout the year. Orval when he came out, he talked and motivated. "There's nothing better than going home at the end of the summer and when people ask you why you're home, you say: "Had to go home, there was nothing left to win." He'd ask us if we'd ever won our last game, even when we were kids. I never had. Even when we went to the Memorial Cup we lost in overtime. Never won my last game, never in baseball, football, volleyball, hockey, whatever I played, I'd never won my last game. We'd be sitting on the ice, and he'd come out and start talking. He'd talk for about half an hour, and we'd be on one knee or lying on our sides on the ice listening to him. So we got to know him a bit better, and in turn, he knew where we were coming from.

Tessier had played in the minor leagues, out in Portland in the old Western League it was called in those days. He played some games in Montreal; he was a small and quick guy. He was your typical emotional French guy. I'd heard about some of the Quebec League coaches who were pretty emotional. I mean I had instances too where Dunc McCallum would come in, dump the table and be upset. Water and drinks are flying all over the place. At that point I think they're at their wits' end. That's part of a 72- or 80-game schedule and being with each other every day. There are going to be conflicts of personalities or whatever.

## Action stations!

For some guys, when their hockey careers are done, it's hard to be away from the team. It's a hard thing to get away from "the guys." That's what they always talk about. What do you miss the most? I miss the guys. Going to the rink, going out for drinks after games, after practices. That was part of the game in those days, alcohol, being together, being in a group. The wolf pack was the thing you wanted. In this day and age with the dollars the way they are you can't do that. You can't be out and pissed up two nights before a game.

We used to do that. In Moncton, one thing Orval Tessier would say is, "In your own end, get to your action stations." That meant, get in your position defensively. We used to joke that our action stations were certain places in the Cosmo bar in Moncton where we used to stand. We'd walk in the bar and some guy would say, "OK, get to your action stations!"

There were always two or three guys you chummed with in the bar. You're making money, you're on your own, and that's basically what pro was. There were no curfew calls anymore. They didn't care if you went out and got drunk the night before the game, because if you performed that's all that mattered. That year with all those guys, we played hard and we partied hard. From that point on we became a really close-knit group. We'd go over to some of the married guys' places for supper. We were all single guys. I remember the scalloped potatoes that Kim Davis's wife used to make. Her name was Kim, too.

When we went on road trips we roomed with different guys, so we got to know everybody that was involved. I think that was Orval's doing too. We had some characters. Mel Hewitt, a notorious tough guy, somebody that you even feared in practice. But he wasn't real big. He was like a junkyard dog, 185 pounds, five foot 11, but just a bundle of dynamite. And a good guy.

One thing about going up the hockey ladder was that the jerks tended to disappear. You didn't survive if you were an idiot. The more years I played, it seemed as if these guys were weeded out: a guy who was selfish, who worried about his goal production as opposed to how the team was doing.

We ended up finishing first overall that year. I think we maybe lost five games for the rest of the year. We found a way to win. There was a stretch of about 25 games from Christmas to February where I played tons. We had guys hurt, and one D got called up to Chicago, and we still won. I was part of that, I jumped in and played. When somebody returned, I was out again. But not once did anybody on that team make me feel like I was the outside guy. I wasn't forgotten. I had a role or a place to play. Mike Kaszycki was our leading scorer and the leading scorer in the league that year, with 36 goals and 118 points. He had originally played with the New York Islanders and got traded to Toronto. I mean a heck of a player. Even if I didn't play that game, he still acknowledged that I was there. In the Cosmo, he didn't ignore me. Rather it was, "Yeah, Dieter, you're in your action station!" He didn't have to do that. But all those guys were like that. So when it came time for me to be that guy in that 25-game situation, I fit in. I was very comfortable.

My first pro goal came in the last or second-last game of the year. It was funny because I'd had numerous chances throughout the year, even open nets, and sometimes I'd just hit the post. It was in Halifax. I guess this would show what the team thought of me. I came down the left wing with the puck. I was playing defence, carried it in over the blue line and got to the top of the face-off circle and just let a howitzer of a slapshot go. Right over the glove and into the net. I just went ballistic. We're playing this Halifax team with John Brophy and all these bad guys, tough guys. Jeff Brubaker was on that team. He was a big dude.

I remember celebrating and my teammates going nuts and one of them grabbed the puck for me. I'm going down the bench high-fiving everybody. Brubaker is lined up for the face-off and he says to Steve Larmer, "Hmmmph. I didn't get that excited about scoring my first goal in this league." But I was the only guy who didn't have a goal. So I was pretty pumped about it — still have the puck. But my teammates were so happy for me. They were as excited for me as for Steve Larmer's first goal, which he probably got the first game he played.

So we ended up making the playoffs and finishing first overall. We played Adirondack Red Wings in the first round. Their home rink was in Glens Falls New York and they were a farm team for the Detroit Red Wings. They had Pete Mahovlich, and he was by far the toughest player I ever had to play against, as far as size goes. He'd put his big butt in your face, and you couldn't even push him anywhere. They had some other pretty skilled players. Dave Hanson was there.

It was the best of five, and they almost beat us. They were the fourth place team, we were first place. They beat us the first game in Moncton. I remember there was an ice show in Moncton at the time and the ice was terrible. We were skaters. The puck was bouncing all over the place and of course it favoured them. They were a gritty team who liked to bump and grind. So we were behind the eight-ball.

We had four days between games, and we were supposed to go to Adirondack, but there was something going on there so we went to Lake Placid, where the American hockey team had just won Olympic gold. We practised there for three days, and we really bonded as a team again because we were in this little village. A bunch of us, Sean Simpson and some of us younger guys who weren't playing much, we were out there on the ice after practice and pretended we won the Calder Cup. We're scoring the winning goal in the seventh overtime or whatever. We made noise like the crowd cheering. Simmer was a good guy in whatever we did, and we ended up rooming together because we were guys who were in and out of the lineup.

## Mahovlich down

So it went to five games. The turning point was we had a defenceman by the name of Miles Zaharko, a big guy about 6 - 2, 225. Pete Mahovlich went into the slot and let a slapshot go. He followed through on it and scored. But when he scored, Zaharko hit him on the side and separated his shoulder. So Mahovlich was out for the rest of the game and I mean, we could hardly contain him. So we ended up winning.

We played Halifax in the next round. We beat them in five games; it was the best of seven. The final was against Binghamton, and we beat them in five. I dressed about four playoff games out of 15. I didn't dress for the game we won the Calder cup, which is the AHL equivalent of the Stanley Cup. But, like I said, I never felt that I wasn't part of it. At some point or another I helped to get us there and that's the way I viewed it and that's the way they viewed it. I got a goal and five assists on the season. I filled a role and I've got a big ring to show that we won our last game of the year.

At the end of the season Orval had lots of praise for me. He said that I was going to be a player some day. I was 20 years old. The next year, I would be a veteran. As it turned out, Orval went to Chicago and we went to Springfield, Massachusetts where we had our own farm team.

We hung around Moncton for a week afterwards. This place where the enema was going to go, we loved. We were in an area where we'd won our last game. It was hard leaving the guys. Two of them, Miles Zaharko and Bart Yachimec, stopped at my house here in Deloraine on their way back home to Alberta. I'd flown home, and three days later I'm in the basement and my Mom answers the door. I hear this, "Does Don Dietrich live here?" That's Zeke — Zaharko. He came in and brought some Newfoundland screech with him and we sat downstairs and reminisced about the week before.

Zaharko was born in 1957 in Mannville, Alberta, and was four years older than I was. He played the 1982-83 season with the Springfield Indians and was named to the second all-star team that year, after 24 points in 54 games. Then he played in Germany, as I did.

Maybe a month after being home that summer I was with a friend from Deloraine, Ross Roy, when he said, "I've got to go somewhere."

I said, "I've been thinking about going to Moncton."

He said, "I'll go with you." Next day we booked flights, flew out of Winnipeg and went to Moncton for a week. Had a blast. But of course nobody was there; my teammates weren't there. But we still had fun.

You come to realize later on, and my Mom pointed this out to me: "You know how good your season was by how bad you miss it. If you're home two weeks and can't wait to go back there, then it's been a good year." And that's the way I felt. That group of guys I'll never forget. We used to have team parties and stuff and Russ Adam, he'd turn the Kentucky Fried Chicken tub over, get some knives and play the drums. We'd think, he's not bad. He told us he played in a band and we didn't know for sure.

As the night goes on he's getting a little full and he plays some more, and it doesn't sound bad to us because we're a little full too. When we won the Calder Cup we went to the Cosmo bar. We got there a little late a bunch of us, and as we entered they announced, "And playing the drums for the band tonight, for this song Born to be Wild, is New Brunswick Hawk centre

Russ Adam!" The lights came on and it was him! And could he ever play. He grabbed the mike and sang, "Born to be Wild!" We stood in front of him going, he can. He can!

A big thing like I said was the 62 games. Near the end of the season, with about five games to go, Orval went around the room and said, "OK. Where are we at here, fellas. We've got five games left. Has anybody got any bonuses or anything they may not attain? Because if somebody's got 39 goals and he needs 40 for the bonus then he's going to be out there for every power play or whatever." And I think the guys really respected that in him. Those were the little things he did right. His home was in Ottawa. If we were out on a road trip and we went through there, he'd have us into his home. I remember right before Christmas, we all went to his house. We were coming across the border and he knows the border guy. "I'm just taking my boys to the house." We all pile off this bus into his house; his son, wife and kids are there. Wow. How many coaches do that? But he was proud of us.

I told him I needed 62 games for a salary boost. He made sure I was in them. It went to $19,500 the next year. It was a big deal, because I thought this is something I need to do. If I'd had five games to reach 62, even if I broke my arm I think he would have made me get out there and play a shift.

# Chapter 5

## MY "OLD PAL" PARKINSON'S; AND COACH ORLAND KURTENBACH

*"Should we postpone this interview? No. I'll be fine. I think this is an important part of something you can add. I can still talk. This is what I deal with on a daily basis."*

DON AND I started talking over a tape recorder in October of 2004, once a week, for an hour at a time. Sometimes Don's wife Nadine was there to give valuable input. We did this at their kitchen table in Deloraine, Manitoba. Down the quiet residential street was the Doc Bonar Arena where Don's Chicago Blackhawks sweater No. 32 hangs from the rafters. I lived half an hour away at Lake Metigoshe on Turtle Mountain.

Deloraine is about an hour's drive north of Minot, North Dakota and an hour south of Brandon, Manitoba near the Canada-U.S. border, in wheat and cattle country. Between sessions I'd go home and transcribe the cassette tape, using the old "ghetto blaster" that Jack Johnston, a dog breeder friend of mine, gave me over coffee one day. Then I'd bring the transcript to our next chat for Don to look over.

During the first four sessions, which we usually did between 11 a.m. and noon, Don experienced minor Parkinson's tremors but nothing serious. When I arrived at the Dietrich home for our fifth interview on Oct. 24 he was not having a good morning. His Parkinson's was acting up and he was shaking a lot. Also, and this really stood out, his facial expression was blank. As he said, "This is what they call the Parkinson's poker face." Don insisted that we carry on as scheduled.

Parkinson's disease is a disorder of the central nervous system. It is a non-curable illness caused by nerve cells dying off in an area of the brain that produces dopamine. As Don's doctor, Doug Hobson of Winnipeg, Manitoba, told me, "Without dopamine the body behaves as a body running out of oil; the body slows, stiffens and frequently shakes. Everyday tasks become a challenge."

Parkinson's impairs speech and the ability to move. Symptoms are muscle rigidity, tremor, a slowing of movement and, in extreme cases, a loss of physical movement. Symptoms of Parkinson's have been known and treated since ancient times, but it wasn't until the 1950s that the changes in the brain were identified. The disease can be inherited. It is also thought to be caused by chemicals such as insecticides, or blows to the head, but this is uncertain. Over his career, Don had a number of blows to the head. Boxer Muhammad Ali is another athlete with Parkinson's.

As it progresses, Parkinson's disease (PD) can make it hard for people to walk, talk, chew and swallow. Problems with sleeping and depression can arise. It can lead to choking, pneumonia, or falls. While the average age of onset is 60, five to 10 per cent of people with PD have "early-onset" disease that begins before age 50, as in Don's case. While there is no cure for PD, a variety of medicines can help reduce symptoms dramatically. There are also electrode implants that can help.

In this interview Don spoke about PD. He also talked about the family dogs, four golden retrievers. (They also have a cat, Jinx.)

░    ░    ░

Ranger had testicular cancer and he lost his jewels a while ago. He's been gray like that around the snout since he was three years old. Lexus is the mom, and Puddy is the pup.

Genny was one of two pups that were born to Lexus, the old grandma. At first only one came out. It had a severe under bite and wouldn't take a nipple. Lexus hadn't passed any afterbirth for a day, so we ended up taking her to the vet. The vet said she needed an emergency C-section because there was a puppy still inside her, which the vet thought was dead.

So we're sitting in the vet's office with the one that was deformed. Nature has a way of taking care of that and the pup died, while the mother was having surgery. While we're sitting there, having just lost the one, all of a sudden we hear "Yip yip!" It was a live new puppy. We proclaimed her to be Genesis, the beginning of life. Because she was the only pup of the litter, and I was taking chemotherapy at the time, I would take her and put her up into my neck. When I had the anxieties of my Parkinson's disease she learned to feel what was going on and really got in tune.

If I got on that couch beside her, she would get on top of me. I've got a bad foot cramp right now, which goes with Parkinson's. Should we postpone this interview? No. I'll be fine. I think this is an important part of something you can add. I can still talk. This is what I deal with on a daily basis.

This device [he shows me an instrument like a TV remote] controls the stimulators that are in my head. I was operated on, and these stimulators were implanted in my head. They produce pulses of a certain amplitude, which is the strength of the current that goes through the electrodes. I have four electrodes, two on each side of my head. Think of what happens when you toss a stone in a pond. The pulse width is how big the waves are. The frequency is the stones hitting the water. More stones, faster pulse.

Sometimes people say, "Well, you had this surgery, is it not working?" I'm going to shut this off. I might have trouble turning it back on. See this here? [he points to the right side of his chest]. Feel what's here [it's a hard implant]. That's where my battery pack is. You just push this once [the remote] and it'll come on. Now I'll turn it off. [Don begins to shake almost uncontrollably for a few seconds and then turns the remote back on. Instantly he returns to only a minor tremor.]

I was getting a bad cramp on my right side too. Sometimes when I get upset and think the thing doesn't work, I just need to shut it off to see that I'm 100 per cent better with it on. The way I was there before is what I used to have to put up with five or six hours every day. I used to lie on the floor. For some reason, stretching my trunk area out on the floor relieved some of the tremor and some of the stiffness. I laid right there on my stomach until my medication kicked in. I used to take Sinemet every hour in liquid form. I also took Mirapex. They say it causes gambling addictions in people. I'm not a gambler.

Sometimes this happens to me in the middle of the night. I'll wake up and sit in that chair, and Genny comes right over and lies on top of me. That's without me saying anything or moving around a lot. She finds me. Whenever I have a Parkinson's episode, she's there. You know what Genny's like when you arrive — very protective. Then she's gone. You'd see old Ranger, Puddies and Lexus. Those three hang around, while Genny finds a way to disappear.

I call it my "old pal," Parkinson's, because it always jumps into my life when I don't want it to, when I'm trying to get ready to go somewhere, for example. It shows up at the most inopportune times. When I got bad cramping on my left side, my foot would turn in and my toes would curl underneath, and Genny would come and sit on my foot. It's like my phone line doesn't work, and I'd sit and concentrate so hard on getting it to go away.

Whenever I have bad tremors, I have to think carefully about every step, every move I make. For me to pick that coffee cup up I'd have to go through all the steps. And I can't talk and do it at the same time because I have to concentrate on what I'm going to do.

It's like there are three steps to getting through a doorway. One, you turn the doorknob; two, you push the door open; and three, you walk through it. When one of those steps breaks down you can't go through the door. That's what Parkinson's is like. That's why for me it's tough, having been an elite athlete in my past, when I relied on my body to make a living. All of a sudden, for whatever reason, it's failing.

I don't produce enough of a chemical called dopamine. Dopamine keeps the phone line going, the communication line between my brain and my muscles. When I don't have the right amount, these stimulators are in a spot where the electrodes help the brain.

Two out of 10 people who get these implants have a complex situation and have some trouble. Three out of 10 get a setting at the start and never worry about them again. Six out of 10 need adjustments for six to 12 months. And then there are two out of 10 that they're always dickering around with; I seem to be one of those. Yet I still have very good results from it.

When I was waiting for you to come, I got in a bit of trouble. I couldn't get out of the chair over there. I'm going to turn it down a bit. You're going to see a major improvement in me because now I've fooled my brain into thinking I've done it a favour. [After he adjusts his remote, Don's face takes on expression again.] That's what I have to do sometimes. There might be a day when you come here and I'll even be worse. But I figured that's something you need to see or need to know.

Later we'll get into the story of when the Parkinson's first came on. For now, let's get back to hockey. My second pro season was interesting.

■　■　■

Like I said, I couldn't have asked for a better place to start my pro career than Moncton. But in my second year, Chicago took over its own farm team, rather than share with the Leafs. So we went to Springfield, Massachusetts, to play for the Indians.

The team was owned by Peter Cooney, whose father owned it before him. The AHL head office was in Springfield. Eddie Shore, a famous hockey man, used to own a team there. This was a hockey town.

## Coach Kurtenbach

We had an assortment of players: young guys, older guys signed to American League contracts who made their living that way, to help bring young guys along. Orland Kurtenbach was the coach. He was the first captain of the Vancouver Canucks — a tough old buzzard and a great guy. Like me, he was raised in a small prairie town, Cudworth, Saskatchewan. He played 14 years of pro hockey, and most of his first seven seasons were in the minors. When he moved up to the NHL Kurtenbach was a solid two-way player, and he was among its best fighters. Some of his best years were with the Rangers in the 1960s.

I was in my second year, thinking I'm going to get an opportunity to play and prove myself. We went to camp and lo and behold there was a first-round kid who was my age who had played in Chicago the year before, Jerome Dupont, and a couple of second-round kids who were a year younger than I was who were right out of the WHL, Len Dawes and Darrell Anholt. They were ahead of me. Just the way it worked.

I played the whole year and went from being a guy on the outside looking in to trying to get into the inside. I went from a top four defenceman to being five or six if things didn't go well. It didn't seem to matter what the other guys did, they were always in that top four. I'm thinking, that's not fair. I'm not playing as much as I thought I should.

My agent said, "Look, you're making $19,500 US. If you fall out of bed for the next two years you're going to make x amount of dollars. Where else can you do that? You're making money at something that you love." If they cut me lose they'd have to buy me out. I'd never had it posed to me like that. So now I'm starting to pick up more of the business end of things. He said you can control what you do: play well, be prepared to play on given nights, and give it your best.

We didn't have a very good team that year. We struggled well below .500, which means we didn't win even half our games. The ultimate thing was to get called up. We had some older guys such as Miles Zaharko. He'd had his kick at Chicago and now they were bringing the young guys along. So I found myself in that role of fourth, fifth or sixth defenceman.

But I liked Orland Kurtenbach. He was good. In practice we'd go out and play keep-away, and he would play, and I mean you could just see the intensity and he was about 58 years old. He's going all out with us and he's got no equipment on. This guy's a bona fide NHLer, and I'm thinking, what intensity. He's 58 years old and playing keep-away! He used to just hack the crap out of us and he had good moves with the puck. We'd play it after every practice. There'd be three or four of us. That's how intense he was.

## Desperation a motivator

He had that same intensity on the bench. He wanted your best. At the time I didn't realize it but one thing that separates the elite guys from the others below is desperation. They play with desperation — the fear of losing. Part of that is intensity. That's what gives those elite guys the edge.

I'm also dealing with the fact that I'm paired up with one of these players that might get called up to Chicago instead of me. I want him to do well — but not too well. You know what I mean? So around Christmas time I really don't feel that things are going as well as I thought they should. We got to go home for Christmas, and I came back here to Deloraine, for the first time since junior.

We talked things over, and my folks said, do you like it? They basically hit me with, your worst day in hockey still has to be a good day in life. So now I'm getting the message that I've got to be happy because I'm making money, and yes, I do have a passion for the game. Even though it's a bad day in hockey, it's still a better day than carrying a lunch pail and going to work for eight hours, is what my Dad was basically telling me. He was agreeing with my agent.

So I was having a little trouble motivating myself, and all of a sudden I've got the demands of an 80-game schedule and I'm 21 years old, playing against older men who are physically stronger and bigger than I am. I came to the realization that before games, I wasn't getting motivated enough. I had to deal with this on my own because, like I said, the other guys didn't wish me to play any better; they wanted to get called up.

## Changed my attitude

I hovered around minus eight, got a few points but being minus on any team isn't great. So I thought, maybe I can clear that up. Every guy wants to be a plus player, which means being on the ice for more goals for than against. I thought, why do I play this game? I'm really trying to come to grips with what's going on. I thought, how much fun did I have when I was a kid? So before each game I used to sit and remember when I was 12 years old, when we were winning, and how much fun I had. And that's how I motivated myself to play.

I checked the stat sheets to see who my enemies were: who the passers were because they had a lot of assists, the goal scorers, the tough guys with penalty minutes. If I had to take my nervous bowel movement before a game, I was on the toilet reading these sheets. Honestly. I did that throughout my career, check to see who I was up against on those given nights. As time went on you got to know guys, and you knew who they were automatically.

I also got more concerned about each shift that I was on the ice. When I lined up across from somebody, they weren't going to beat me. They weren't going to put the puck in my net. I actually started to play pretty well. By no means was I a tough, punishing defenceman, but I could move the puck quickly. And the little things Dunc McCallum had taught me, I concentrated on. I didn't work on the things I wasn't good at, I worked on the things I was good at, and tried to fine tune them. It's easier to work on the things that you're good at. To fit into the team well, I needed to be an offensive defenceman and a plus player.

As the year went on, we ended up being out of the playoffs, maybe 15 games before the season was done. But I ended up being plus-nine at the end of the year. So I had made quite an adjustment and had a lot of success with it. Orland Kurtenbach was very pleased with the way I had brought my game along. After games he would say, "You're doing great, keep up the work." He said, "Chicago is probably going to take a couple of guys up when our season is done. I'm not saying you'll be one of them, but you've really improved."

By the end of the year I led the team in plus-minus. I was plus nine, and there were maybe three of us who were plus on that team. I got six goals and 26 assists, which is how I needed to play.

When it came time to take guys up, they took Dupont, their first-rounder, and Zaharko. So I was a little disappointed. I lived in a townhouse with Darrell Anholt, a big strapping defenceman from Alberta, a second- or third-rounder, just a huge kid, a great guy, a great teddy bear type guy. But if he lost it on the ice, he was 6-2, 235, a human demolition derby. And Dan Frawley, he was a 10th-round pick the year I was drafted. He ended up playing in Pittsburgh for a number of years, and Chicago before that. He was a big right winger with a knack for scoring.

The three of us and Rod Willard, who I'd played with in Moncton the year before, we decided to heck with it, we'll drive down to Florida. So we went down to Florida for a week and partied, right at the end of spring break, the second week of April. We got all tanned up and came back home to Springfield, partied there a bit because the year was done, packed our things up and flew back to Deloraine.

So now I've finished my second year of my three-year contract, two years and an option. I really haven't proved a lot, though I thought I'd done quite a bit. I get a phone call from Bill Watters who I still hadn't met personally. He says, Chicago's offering you a termination contract. That meant I would become a free agent after my next year without compensation. Compensation means if you sign a contract with another team, your team can offer you the same thing and you have to go back. Or, if they don't, then your new team has to compensate your old team with a draft pick.

I'm thinking this will be OK for me. Obviously Chicago is deep on defence and I'm not going to get an opportunity so I might as well sign it. I know I'm going to camp, I know where I'm heading, back to Springfield again. I signed.

Through the summer I played baseball locally which I loved. I golfed a bit and spent the odd weekend at our cabin on Lake Metigoshe. Summers weren't very long because I went and helped at the Wheat Kings hockey school in mid-August and got skating again.

So I went back to camp with a termination contract, which meant they didn't really have any plans for me but one more year in their minor league system. At camp I'm still No. 39, but this Blackhawks camp went better than the first one. Maybe I had a bit more strength and maturity. Camp went well.

All of a sudden Doug Wilson gets hurt. Bob Murray gets hurt. All these defencemen are getting hurt at Chicago's camp. There's a bunch of guys down and out. We had our intra-squad game, and at Chicago Stadium there were maybe 9,000 people there. I made some pretty good plays offensively, got some loud cheers and some razzle dazzle and lo and behold I get asked to play an exhibition game against the Detroit Red Wings. Things were looking up.

# Chapter 6

## PLAYING AGAINST GRETZKY, AND THE OLYMPIC TEAM CALLS

*"That was the big joke in those days: You could always tell who was in the option year of their contract because they had good years. Maybe so. That being said, I think that's what makes the professional athlete what they are — the ability to rise to the occasion."*

AS WE PREPARED for our sixth conversation the four golden retrievers galloped into the house and greeted me. Genny was the friendliest she'd ever been while Ranger, Puddy and Lexus gave me their usual woofy hello. Don and Nadine adore their dogs. Don proceeded to tell me about Ranger and another honoured pet, Max, whose large portrait adorned a wall.

■　　■　　■

Ranger came from the States. He has show dog in him. When he's wet, he's just soaked, whereas the water tends to run off the other dogs, which are the hunting breed. He's show; hence he sheds terribly. When Ranger is up to the lake he's just one big burr when he comes out of the bush.

See that portrait on the wall? That was Max; he died when we got here. He's one of the best dogs that Nadine and I ever had. We never had to tie him up. He never left the yard. He went to Europe with us. He used to go in restaurants in Switzerland and Germany all by himself and sit in the back in the kitchen. The people all just loved him. When the Swiss army was doing maneuvers one time they came to our house and wanted to set up in our garage. So they've got radio equipment all set up in there, and Max was always outside, so I went to get him. The guy says, "Oh no, leave him here, he's good." So he's out with these army guys all night. They loved him, they thought he was great.

■   ■   ■

This is a big year as far as things that turn around for me. I was given an opportunity and for the first time in my pro career I'm maybe in the right place at the right time. I signed the termination contract for 1983-84 and looked at it in a positive way. It was another opportunity to prove that I belonged. I'm now 23.

The game against the Red Wings was in Peoria, Illinois, two hours up the road by bus. My number went from 39 to 36 for this game. To me it meant I'm coming down the ladder. And I had a pretty good game. Detroit in those days had Danny Gare, Steve Izerman and other stars. There were a few NHL guys but mostly American League players in the game. The reason I got to play is that a number of guys were hurt.

We played four games in four nights. The Players Association had a rule that at training camps you couldn't play all four games, so they systematically put guys into the puzzle so they could play them all. I was only going to play three out of four because of the rule.

Guys were saying I played quite well. The token week goes by; I'm still there. I'm thinking, this is all right. Now all my buddies have headed to Springfield, the guys I played with the year before, and I'm among the 30 to 35 guys they're keeping around for exhibition games.

We ended up having another exhibition game in Detroit, where they had a brand new stadium. I mean the Chicago stadium had its own mystique. It was one of the original six rinks. They had that big pipe organ going. In Detroit they had just drafted Izerman and they had quite a potent lineup. I think we lost 4-3, but I had played pretty well again.

I didn't do anything offensively, but I wanted to look after my own end and make sure I didn't get scored against. I actually found playing defence in the NHL a little easier than in the AHL. This was because everybody knew their job. In the AHL you have young guys that come in who maybe don't understand what they have to do because they've never had to. If they were 65-goal scorers in junior hockey maybe they weren't worried about their own end.

We came back to Chicago and again, veteran guys like Keith Brown were commenting that I was playing pretty well, keep it up. There were 30 or 35 of us and it seemed like we're all pulling for each other, as opposed to that minor league approach where, I hope you play well as my partner, but not too well, because I want to play better than you.

## Play Edmonton

Then we had an exhibition game against Edmonton. You talk about pumped. The Oilers are just coming on at that time, and a lot of those guys are my age, like Wayne Gretzky, Mark Messier, Glenn Anderson, Paul Coffey, Charlie Huddy. They're just starting to put their nucleus together that went on to win four Stanley Cups in a row. The powerhouse at that time was the Islanders. They had three Stanley Cups in a row.

They dressed Gretzky and some pretty good players. I remember the stadium being packed and it's our first home game, so we've got every available Blackhawk in the lineup. There are still some defencemen that are injured, hence I'm in the lineup again.

I'm thinking this is awesome. I'm playing against the best player in the world, Wayne Gretzky. I think we won 6-5. I remember sitting on the bench and being a bundle of nerves. On our first shift a bunch of guys went out and Jack O'Callahan passed the puck to Rich Preston who passed it to somebody else and it was a highlight reel goal. Well, they sounded that big horn. I didn't know it was coming. My helmet just about popped off my head. The hair on my arm is standing up now just talking about it. I was so pumped.

I was fifth or sixth D and again played pretty well. Orval Tessier was coaching then. He was in his second year with the Blackhawks. The year before he'd taken them to the conference final. They had Denis Savard, Al Secord, Tom Lysiak, Steve Larmer, Steve Ludzik, Doug Wilson and Bob Murray on defence, Tony Esposito and Murray Bannerman in goal. I'm right in there. You talk about being a fortunate guy. I'm living my dream. There aren't many people in the world who can say that.

We had Behn Wilson and Curt Fraser, two tough guys. The Norris Division was at that time a tough division to play in. If we went and got a tough guy, the other four teams went and got one.

The writing was still on the wall for me. I was No. 36. When those guys came back, I knew where I was heading. I lasted for a couple more practices and got called in by Bob Pulford and Jack Davidson — again, thinking of what my Dad had told me. They were very happy with the way I had performed, but I was going to Springfield to play for the Indians.

So I went down there excited. We had a young team there. Philadelphia was also sending players there like Dave Brown, Ross Fitzpatrick, and a Japanese Canadian guy who was 5-5 and just a bundle of fury. He played very well. A lot of the guys had played in the WHL and I knew them.

I got there late. Most of the guys had already paired up for accommodations. Darrell Anholt had got married in the summer and he was living with his wife and their dog. They had an extra bedroom so they let me bunk in with them, which was great for me because I was still budgeting myself. I didn't have enough money to be paying $700 or $800 a month to rent an apartment, with furniture on top of that. They had got a house for $600 and we split it. It worked out well. What we used to do was go down to a used-car dealer and pick up a $1200 junker and drive it, then sell it back to the guy at the end of the year. He'd buy it back for $500 or $800 and if they were bad enough we just left them junked in the parking lot.

The coach, Doug Sauter, remembered me from Brandon Wheat Kings days. He was a young guy, 27 or 28 at that time, and he remembered how I'd played and that's how he used me. So I was on power plays, penalty kill, regular shift and was playing a lot. I had 35 points — 14 goals and 21 assists — when I got called back up by the Blackhawks. Ten of the goals came on the power play. I was having success, and showing that I'd likely be an American League all-star. Again, I had a termination contract. So I had to play well. It was the only way I was going to get a contract for next year.

That was the big joke in those days: You could always tell who was in the option year of their contract because they had good years. Maybe so. That being said, I think that's what makes the professional athlete what they are — the ability to rise to the occasion. No matter what it was, if I was playing baseball, bases loaded, bottom of the ninth and tied up, I wanted to be the guy batting. Or the guy they hit the ball to and make that last out. Or be in that situation in hockey.

Springfield was five to eight games over .500. We were a young team with an average age of probably 22. It was mid-December and I get a call from some of my buddies here in Deloraine. Four of them — Brian McMechan, Dean Laval, Danny Maxwell, and Kevin Sorensen — were coming down to Springfield to visit me on January 2nd. I'm looking at the schedule and this is great. We've got four or five days off, then we play right around Springfield. We play three or four home games there, and then to Newhaven Connecticut which is 45 minutes down the road. They can go there. This is going to be great.

## Called up for New Year's Eve

So I'm playing well, and life is swell in the AHL. And my buddies are coming. I get a phone call December 30th. Chicago wants me in Detroit for a New Year's Eve game – my first regular season NHL game. And I've got guys coming on the 2nd. I phoned Dean Laval and he said, "Hey, you've got to go." So they still flew to Springfield, then rented a car and headed to Florida.

Doug Sauter says to me, "You're going, I don't know how long for but good luck and away you go." He was a big reason why I got the opportunity that I did. He liked me, and the way I played, and played me accordingly and I'm getting a shot.

In the meantime, in that mid-December period, I get wind that Dave King, who coaches the national team which is going to the Sarajevo Olympics in Yugoslavia, is interested in the way I play. And there may be a Canadian amateur rule that will allow American League guys to play. His team has been together since the fall, with college guys and junior guys and so on.

So I head to Detroit and get there a little late. I hadn't put a suit on or anything, and the guys were already out on the ice for the game-day morning skate. I like to have a pre-game skate so I went out there after practice with my jeans on and Tony Esposito was still hanging around. He wasn't going to dress that night so he was still in net.

Esposito comes up to me and says, "They are probably going to room you with me." I was of the understanding that Tony, who had 20-some years in the league, got his own room. Apparently there was some bickering going on. They wanted him to retire and he wasn't ready to, and hence there were three goalies there, including Bob Janecyk and Murray Bannerman. He says, "Just go up and throw your stuff in the room."

## My first regular season NHL game

Doug Wilson's one thing, but this is Tony, who as far as I was concerned was Mr. Blackhawk. I'm in The Show! This will be my first regular season game in the NHL.

We had a pre-game meal and got settled in. I usually had a snooze the day of a game but I couldn't sleep, I'm just wired. New Year's Eve. We're playing Detroit. Al Secord's hurt, Doug Wilson's hurt. Behn Wilson's hurt. I'm paired up with Jerome Dupont, a first-round pick the same year I was and a year younger than me. Good guy.

Guess what number I am. Thirty-two! That's the number I stayed with in Chicago. It's the number hanging in the rink over there (Doc Bonar Arena in Deloraine). That's pretty good; I always liked that number. When I got to the rink, there was 32 Dietrich, hanging in the stall. This ain't no No. 36 or 39. This is 32. Dale Hunter wore 32. So did some other pretty good NHL guys.

I remember warming up and the place is buzzing. Detroit has Brad Park on defence on gimpy knees. Couldn't move, but just so heady it was unbelievable. I couldn't believe how well he played. He was an older guy then. He'd starred with the Rangers and Bruins and had been a runner-up to Bobby Orr for the Norris Trophy.

I played pretty well. I was fifth or sixth D, and we always had to play against the third or fourth line guys, and I think we lost that game 4-3. We went out after the game and had a few beers. We had the next two days off.

The next day we were heading to Minnesota. We get up the next morning and have a team meal and head to the airport. I'm with the guys. I mean I don't even have to touch my equipment bag. In the NHL that is the equipment manager's job. In the American League we came back from games at 3 in the morning and we unpacked our bags. Here, we don't see anything. We go to the airport, a guy walks up and hands us our plane ticket, tells us when to be at the gate.

We get into Minnesota and we get on a bus and go straight to a hotel.

84

We have no practice scheduled that day. Next day at practice our stuff is in our stall. In the meantime, my Dad had got wind that we were playing in Minnesota. So he and friends from Deloraine — Delmar Main, Blaine Smith, Ron Amey, Dennis Olischefski the jeweler — get on a plane for Minnesota to watch me play.

I've played my first NHL game and thought I played pretty well. I'm pumped. Now I've got some home-town people coming in. Just before we go to practice, there's definite word that the national team wants me to play. Their ruling is in Canadian amateur hockey that you have to play 10 or more NHL games to be considered a professional. I've played one, so I'm all right.

After practice, Jack Davidson the assistant GM calls me in and says, "What do you think about playing on the national team?"

I said, "Well, conceivably how long am I here for?" I knew that I was there because some guys were hurt. "They're probably going to be back before I play five of six games. If you're going to send me back, please do so before the 10 games, so I at least have that option."

He said they would think about it. In the meantime I'm on the phone trying to get hold of my agent, Bill Watters, to tell him what was going on. But we played the game in Minnesota that night and this was a Norris Division rivalry. They've got all their big guys dressed and we're missing all ours. No Behn Wilson, no Curt Fraser, no Al Secord, no Doug Wilson. I wasn't the only young guy that was called up, either. They took some forwards too. They had a lot of guys hurting, and they'd been losing. This was going to be a tough game.

## Dad and Delmar

I remember going out in warm up, looking up in the stands and I see Delmar and Dad there. They'd made it. I knew they were there because they stayed in the same hotel we did, and I went down and met them for a coffee. I was allowed to give them a couple of tickets. I'd been inside that stadium before because Dad used to take us down for baseball games, and the Metrodome and stadium were in the same area.

I used to watch and I respected guys for how they prepared themselves. At that level it was even more evident. Guys did certain things to prepare, so you stayed out of their way. Tony Esposito didn't dress that game but in games that he played he was miserable. You couldn't talk to him, you couldn't have music on. But he was a Hall of Famer.

I was particularly impressed with Darryl Sutter. He stands out in my mind because he was a guy who really came from nowhere — he was a late-round pick who played in the AHL — and now he's captaining the Blackhawks. He was a captain who didn't forget anybody in his ship. He always seemed to have the right thing to say.

Also, Orval Tessier was having trouble with his team. The previous year they lost out in the playoffs and he made some remarks to key players, questioning their desire to play. It was costing him this year. You don't question the heart or ability of certain guys. He really wanted to win. But he had questioned Denis Savard's heart. And I mean there's nobody that has a bigger heart. Now whether he was trying to motivate him or not, I don't know.

So the coach was back-pedaling, and he was changing the way he was because he had so many injuries, and when you change the way you coach, now there are inconsistencies. When there are inconsistencies, guys doubt what you're doing. So it was kind of a bad situation, but for me it was great. I'm there. I'm living my dream.

I remember picking the puck up in my end and skating along the boards and Al McAdam was fore checking on me. I thought, I can dust this old guy. Man, he wiped me right out. He was a hard-nosed type of player and strong. He just pasted me. I thought I'd just go right through him. He didn't seem to be that big of a guy, but he certainly was. I think Minnesota tethered us a bit, 6-2.

After the game I saw Lou Vairo, head coach of the U.S. team. He's standing off to the side. He's arguing with somebody down there. I don't really know what it's about.

I meet Dad and the guys afterwards, and of course Dad is strutting with his chest out, he's pretty proud, and I had played pretty well. I did what I was supposed to do. I didn't do anything more. In hindsight, realize I should have. I played a certain way in the AHL; I was offensive. In the NHL I played safe — which I probably shouldn't have. But I played safe because we were hurting for guys, goals against were an issue, and everything else. I did an interview in Winnipeg later on that year about why I didn't play my offensive game, and I was getting upset with the guy, but he was right.

We went back to Chicago and played against the Winnipeg Jets and we won. We played Toronto in Chicago and we won again. Now all of a sudden I'm hovering over five or six games.

We played Edmonton. At that time Gretzky had a point-scoring streak going. We put old Tony Esposito in the net. They used to play him about every three weeks, but they put him in against Edmonton and the better teams.

I had just an unbelievable game. I've got it on tape. I made a nice pass, I got an assist, I hit the post. I had three or four good shots on goal, I was flying. They scored an empty-netter and beat us 5-3. And guess who scored it. Wayne Gretzky, and he hadn't had a point yet. Looked up at the clock, there were three seconds left. We had pulled our goalie trying to tie it up. We could have kept him in and snuffed his record, but it couldn't be about personal things like that.

## *Gretzky incredible*

You want to talk about desperation or intensity? Troy Murray had checked Gretzky that game for us immaculately, and Esposito stopped him many times, on breakaways and stuff. He hit a couple of posts. We were under a bit of pressure and Troy fired the puck down the ice. Gretzky knocked it out of the air on his backhand. He headed towards the net. Troy Murray, who was probably 205 pounds, a checking centreman, skated and caught him and was literally draped on his back. Gretzky would not go down.

There's a guy who would be 170 pounds soaking wet. He skated that puck into the slot and put it in for an empty-net goal with Murray all over his back. I can remember sitting on the bench and Tony Esposito was sitting beside me and he goes, "Unbelievable." I was sitting there amazed. That's the thing that separates the top guys from the rest — that intensity. There was no way he was going to be denied that goal.

He put it in and there were two seconds left. Their bench emptied. They had a fabulous team. I was on the ice against Gretzky many times in that game. I poke checked him a couple of times.

So, I hovered at six games. Remember, the cut-off point is 10. Now I'm getting calls from my agent saying, "These guys want you to go." This is mid-January. The Olympics are starting soon. So Jack Davidson the assistant manager and Bob Pulford the GM call me into the office and say, "It's six games, Don, and we've got some guys back. We're going to let you go with the Olympic team plus we're going to keep you on the payroll."

Wow. They did not have to do that. The Olympic guys were getting a pittance, and I'd been budgeting so I had enough to get me through the next couple of months with them. But they were going to keep me on my American League salary, which was unreal.

Back in Springfield I grabbed a change of clothes, bought a couple of suits and some shoes and stuff. I'm heading to Milwaukee, where they're going to play an exhibition game against the U.S. national team. Dave King wants to see how I play, whether I'll fit in or not. For me, this is a test.

The rink in Milwaukee seats maybe 10,000 people and it's filled to capacity. King is talking to me before the game and he's a real x's and o's guy. "You be here when this guy's here and blah blah blah." I'm thinking, I don't know if I can do this. Jean Parent, who was coach of the Moncton University team when I played in Moncton came up to me later and said, "I've seen you play. You just go out and play." That was reassuring.

The Americans had a good team. They had won gold in Lake Placid in 1980, so there was big hype for the '84 team. They'd been together for four years. Well, they hammered us pretty good, about 8-1. And the thing I remember most about that game was, you're in Milwaukee, Beer City. One side of the stands yelled "Less filling!" while the other side shouted "Tastes great!" like the beer commercial.

As I say, we got hosed 8 to 1. I thought, what am I doing here? I was on the ice for two or three goals against, which I never was in Chicago. Afterwards Dave King said, "You're going to be OK. Why don't you go back, pack all your stuff up, come to Calgary. We'll spend a couple of days there practising and then we'll head over to Germany for an exhibition series." The Olympics was slated to start mid-February.

So I get on a plane the next day, fly to Springfield, gather my stuff — I've got no sticks. I've got none of my own patterned sticks that I've been using for three years, because they are all in Chicago. I'm upset now. I used to have this great big blade, a Sherwood 50-30. Featherlights. I needed my sticks. My sticks were everything.

I packed up and took off, got on some little puddle-jumping plane that took me from Hartford to Montreal. Then a long flight to Calgary, where they had us in dorms. They'd just built the new rink, the Saddledome, and the national team was practising out of there.

The next day after practice the guys said, "We're leaving tomorrow." I said, "I don't have a passport."

"You don't?" They also told me about the international adapter for your razor, which I knew nothing about.

After practice I went up to George Kingston, an assistant coach, a good guy. He was the go-between. He was the good cop. Dave King was the bad cop. Kingston coached the University of Alberta.

Kingston takes me under his wing and runs me to a couple of places. They have to fit me for national team suits, then he takes me to a government building for a photograph. An hour later I've got a passport. It's unbelievable.

Next day we have another practice and we're leaving at 10 o'clock that night for Frankfurt. Which is fine, we can sleep on the flight. I don't have any of my clothes yet, the national team suits. I don't have sticks. I'm using somebody else's pattern and struggling with that. Nothing seems to be working out.

But the guys are great. I'm basically going in there and taking somebody's spot. Somebody that's been there for a long time. So I'm a little uneasy about that as well. And we've got good players there: James Patrick, Doug Lidster, Bruce Driver, Carey Wilson — young guys in university or college who had committed to the program since August. And I'm going to bump somebody. But they all treated me very well. Just walking into that dressing room was a bit uneasy. But guys on the up and up knew I was coming.

We arrived in what was then West Germany and practised in Fussen for three or four days. It was up in the mountains and it was tough to breathe. Our first exhibition game was in Rosenheim. This is my first taste of Europe, my passport's fine and I'm traveling with a bunch of guys. It's going well.

Every place we stop, the bus driver — who is an ugly man — has women all over him, all the time. We have a German translator in the bus who speaks good English, and I went outside during one stop and said to the guy, "What's with our driver? He's been trucking us around a few days and everywhere we stop he's got women flocking around him."

He said, "He's a national hero."

"Well," I said, "who is he?"

"In 1969 the Germans won the bonze medal in hockey, and he just stood on his head. Played great in goal."

Our first game was in Rosenheim. We'd been there about five days and got over the jet lag. I remember we had a morning skate in Rosenheim, and all these little kids are waiting for us. We're the Canadian national team, and they're asking, "Where's Gretzky?"

"Well, Gretzky isn't here."

And they'd take off, looking for him.

In the process of everything, there was a bit of press. Lou Vairo had raised a stink about me playing. The U.S. national team had been training out of Minnesota, and he was wondering how the Canadian national team could play a guy that he watched three weeks earlier playing for the Chicago Blackhawks.

So it started a controversy. Nothing really came my way other than if I was to read a paper such as *The Hockey News*, which had blurbs about it.

## Coach King upset

We played the Germans that night and we got hammered. Big ice surface and we weren't used to it. Now I'm starting to wonder. Are we going to be OK? Can I play this game? Dave King's pretty hard on us. He's really serious; we're skating a lot. But he's trying to get players who normally peak in April to peak in February.

He was pretty upset that they beat us. We had to play them again in Mannheim next game. They hammered us again. I'm thinking, this isn't very good. We're struggling against the Germans, by no means a hockey power. They had one guy by the name of Eric Kuhnadek. He was 6-6 or 6-7 and he could play. He had opportunities to play in North America but he was the king in Germany. Hockey was a big sport there. Why come over to North America and get the crap beat out of you? And they had some other good players, some Canadian guys with a German background on that team as well. It was an eye-opener for me. The international game was tough.

I thought, how are we ever going to play the Russians? They had Fetisov, Krutov, Makarov, Larionov, Kasatonov — these guys were young then and could fly.

So we ended up going back to Fussen and we had a few days off there before we headed to Sarajevo. Dave King basically said, if you guys are going to blow some steam off, this is your last chance. Well, Fussen has maybe 400 people. We look around for where we can have a couple of beers and there's this beer house with a big table in the middle and a bunch of us sit down.

We have a couple of beers and all of a sudden this lady brings us over a round of beer. We don't know who's ordered it. She stands up and rings this bell by our table. All of a sudden the local people start singing this song in German. They're all swaying away, and German beer is pretty potent compared to the Bud Lite of the States. It comes in these big mugs. So we're sitting there and swaying along with them, thinking this isn't too bad. They must have given us a free beer.

There's Pat Flatley who played with the Islanders later on, Dave Tippet, a lot of good players. Flatley stands up and hits that bell and all of a sudden everybody starts singing again — there's not a lot of people yet, just a few — and swaying again and laughing. We're having a fun time. All of a sudden this lady comes over with a big mitt full of mugs again.

A couple of hours later, Flatley has hit that bell two or three times. We start looking around and the place is just packed. Standing room only. He hits that thing and everyone starts singing again. Well, what it was is if you hit that bell you're buying the house a round! But we didn't know that!

The lady comes back with this big bill. We ended up throwing in about 50 Marks each. There were 20 or more of us there. We didn't know the culture, and it probably spread through the whole town that these crazy Canadians are buying everybody beer, so they're just crawling out of the woodwork. I'm here! If they want us to sing a song, we'll sing!

But playing on that national team and wearing that sweater was big for me. I was representing my country. That was one of my biggest accomplishments and most memorable moments. But it was also my biggest disappointment.

# Chapter 7

## LOST IN YUGOSLAVIA

*"'Are you Don Dietrich?'*
*I said yes.*
*He said, 'I'm so and so from the Canadian consulate.*
*We've been looking for you for two days.'*
*I just hugged the guy."*

AS DON AND I settled into our seats for our next conversation, I heard a click, clack, click, clack from the kitchen. Something with claws was approaching. Don saw my puzzled look and said, "Just so you know, the lizard's on the loose. Tristan always lets it out. He's usually looking for dog food, he eats tons of dog food." The lizard was an iguana named Iggy. I laughed as this long green reptile clattered its way slowly along the kitchen floor toward us and onto the carpet to its cage (with sun lamp). Ranger the dog sat beside me, staring at it casually. Don's mother-in-law entered the picture and remarked that yes it had a name, but the darned thing wouldn't come if you called it. Don got up, saw that it was safely in its cage and closed the door.

▩   ▩   ▩

We were now finished our exhibition series. We cleared customs at Frankfurt's airport and were heading for Yugoslavia for the 1984 Winter Olympics. We'll get there about 10 days ahead of our scheduled first game.

At Sarajevo we got off the plane and our stuff was all put on a bus and we were heading to the Olympic Village. Of course we had to go through security and it was tight. The first thing that came to my mind was the '72 Olympics in Munich, when PLO terrorists killed 11 Israeli athletes in their dorms. Small wonder we needed all this security. We needed certain tags, and always had to go through metal detectors.

The Canadian men's hockey team was in an apartment complex with the Japanese national team. They were keeping the big bad hockey players away from the rest of the Canadian team. We had the top three floors of this building, and in each apartment there were four bedrooms and no kitchenette. Single beds in each room, and that's where we got set up.

## Labatt house

We had 45-minute practices scheduled at two ice facilities there. We're doing the Olympic thing. There were a couple of guys who had been with the team for a while, and they found themselves out because I was in. Warren Anderson, I think his name was. He and another guy were staying in the Labatt house. What Labatt's Beer had done was rent a house from a famous race car driver. So they were there and we were in the village.

The security was so sensitive that I had a stick of Juicy Fruit gum in my pocket and it kept setting the alarm off. The guard kept saying, "Empty your pockets. You've got something in your pocket." It was the foil wrapper on the gum.

I can remember looking out at night and seeing lights come on. There was a big hillside where our apartment was. The next morning I looked over the place in daylight and there were guys out in foxholes with machine guns. That's how tight security was.

The cafeteria was huge, with an enormous variety of food. There was a phone centre with English-speaking operators who could help you phone home. There was a whole wall of phones. I remember going to the bank and getting dinars, say $300's worth, and get maybe 300,000 dinar. You come out of there with a great stack of bills, and I just wanted to throw them in the air!

One day we watched the Russians practise after us. It was unreal. I sat there with my jaw open. Their practices were a lot different than ours, and they were so highly skilled. They were in a routine. Those guys had been together for years, and it was like they knew what each other was doing in their sleep.

One day we decided to head out to this old village in the old part of Sarajevo, and our translator was a woman who had played on the Yugoslav basketball team. She was about six-feet-six and spoke really good English. We went into this village, and some of us prior to that had gone there to watch some bobsledding. And the one-man luge. They're sitting on this thing and have spikes in their gloves and they get going hard and then lie back. They're going about 90 km/hour.

There was this one guy, a black fellow who came out on his sled. He sat there inching it slowly towards the edge and sat up the whole time and went down. What we later found out later was that he was the only athlete from Uganda, and he was carrying their flag. He didn't care how fast he went, he just wanted to finish it; he did his practice. But it was funny to see him sitting up all the way down the hill.

We came down the hill in a trolley and then went up into this old village. That's what our whole team did. This woman was our translator, and man, there were people all over the place. We'd been given a bag of pins because we'd been told that people would want to trade for Canadian pins. We had our Canadian ski jackets on and they wanted our pins. I had in my pocket 20 or 30 and went through them all. So I made trades with athletes from other countries and have since given their pins to my sister, who has a huge collection on her wall at home.

Merchants had their stuff out on a cobblestone sidewalk. Smoke came out of the stacks. Old to me is 70 years; this place was maybe 600 years old. We go up to this one store and I'm looking around it. They've got some nice plates with the image of the Olympic mascot, a little wolf they called Vuchko. This wolf symbolized the desire of humans to befriend animals. According to the International Olympic Committee, Vuchko helped change the image in Yugoslavia of wolves as frightening and blood-thirsty. I thought these plates would make nice gifts, and they were cheap. I grabbed about four of them.

I go up to the counter and this guy walks up. I said, "I'll take these." He just looked at me and started yelling something. I didn't know what to do; I panicked. Maybe I wasn't supposed to take them off the shelf.

I walked out and ran into our translator, this woman. I told her I was going to buy these plates from this guy, when he started yelling at me. She started laughing. I said, "What's so funny?"

"He wants to argue."

I said, "What? He wants to argue with me?"

"Yes. You take it up and tell him what you'll pay for it. He'll bicker with you."

I went back in. My plates were sitting there. They had 500 on them. I said OK, 200. The girl was with me, she said 200.

The guy went ballistic. "Ooooohhhhh!" and marching around. He starts heading out the front part of his shop. He's saying something but I don't know what. He comes back with, "450."

I said, "OK, 250." He went back near the street and carried on some more. What he was doing was creating a crowd. So now, I'm going to pay less than the price on the sticker and he's going to drum up some business. So I walked out with these plates and saved about 200 dinar. It was a neat experience. And that's how we shopped.

The Olympic Village had everything: a dance place, a huge arcade, cafeteria, you name it, it was there for the comfort of the athletes. I'm running into different people, some Austrian-Canadian guys that I knew such as Kelly

Greenbank, guys older than I was on the Austrian national team. Sarajevo was an incredible experience, even though I was tripped up by the politics of hockey.

## Alan Eagleson phones

I'm in the village, doing my thing, going to the practices every day, and it gets to be closer to our first game. We're to play the U.S. I phoned home and said things are looking good. There hadn't been any complaints that I was aware of. I'm here under a rule sanctioned not only by the Canadian Olympic Association, but also by the International Ice Hockey Federation.

That night, before our first game, Alan Eagleson phones me. He's president of the NHL Players' Association, and he tells me to come down. So I go downstairs, myself and Mark Morrison. This is the young guy who had played in Victoria. He played two games with the New York Rangers as an underage.

Eagleson told us the International Olympic Committee had just passed a rule. And in that rule it states that if you play one NHL regular season game you're considered a professional. I had played six, Morrison, two. And seven other guys from other countries couldn't play — which meant if you played in the WHA at that time, and played five or six years and made more money than I'd ever see in my life, you weren't considered a professional.

That really upset Eagleson. The protest was filed by the Finns but was backed by the U.S. Now I can remember the arguments that Vairo was having. I remember the stories in the press about him complaining. He wanted a definite ruling. I think it was Sanchez who was president of the IOC. Eagleson is standing there telling us, "The SOB, he comes out with this gawd-damned robe on, and the only thing he thinks ice is for is his drink; he knows nothing about hockey and he passes this rule!"

Anyway, I can't play. The next day I've got to be out of the village. The other two guys are coming in to replace us and we're going to the Labatt House, Morrison and I. We all played jokes on each other. I short-sheeted the beds and put peanuts shells in there. They short-sheeted our beds and put beer bottles in ours.

We've got to play the U.S. team that night and now there's some real controversy going on. We have a morning skate, which I'm not a part of anymore. Afterwards there's a press conference. I've been prepared by the press guy for the national team that there's going to be quite a few reporters there. It's a big deal for Hockey Canada. After the skate we have an interview. The press guy takes us through this curtain.

Well, there were microphones that would fill a kitchen table sitting before Morrison and me. The room is packed, and I'm stunned. The whole world is involved in this. There was a guy who wrote for the Blackhawks, and he came up and sat beside me. He bent down and coached me a bit. "Just relax and answer the questions to the best of your knowledge. You'll be fine."

We were asked a variety of questions. At that time I didn't really care to let anybody know that I was making $19,500 a year. There were other guys who were making a lot more money than I was in the World Hockey Association who were still allowed to play. But they'd made their decision and that's how it had to stay.

It added quite a bit of fuel to the fire for our game that night against the U.S. We hadn't had much success, remember. In our previous two games the U.S. beat us and the Germans hosed us. The U.S. was getting a lot of press because they'd won at Lake Placid in 1980 and now a major TV network was behind them. There were high expectations for them. There was a lot of pressure for those guys to play well.

We ended up beating them 4-2. I watched it from the stands. Again there was a press conference afterwards. Morrison and I were again invited to it, which I didn't think was fair because the guys who had played should have been the focus; it was their game, their victory.

Morrison and I went back to the Labatt House and found ourselves on the outside looking in. I'm hanging around this house because I don't have a ride. I'm used to somebody telling me, here's what time the bus is leaving and away you go. Now I'm feeling a lot more alone.

In that house there were some NHL general managers. Serge Savard was one of them. Murray Costello was president of the CAHA. And I remember a couple of guys from Hockey Canada asking me, what should we do with our national program? Should we pay guys on a yearly basis leading up to the Olympics? Would I have been interested in that? I told him I would have been. I'm 23 years old and they're asking me big-decision type questions. I'm trying to answer as best I can. When I walk out I see Scotty Bowman. He's staying in the same house I am.

It turns out Chicago has been calling the national team; they want me back. I'm supposed to fly out the next day. I'm given a train ticket to go from Sarajevo to Belgrade that night. The train leaves at 11 that night. I'm supposed to arrive at Belgrade in the morning and get to the airport. My flight the next day was at 1 p.m. That's how quickly it happened.

I'm sitting in my room and it's getting to be about five o'clock and I'm wondering if I should go to eat. I had the door of my bedroom open. All of a sudden Eagleson bursts in. "Get your stuff on. We're heading to the Canada Cup banquet." All I had was Team Canada sweater and a pair of blue jeans and some sneakers. I said I have all my stuff packed, I'm supposed to be heading to the train station.

He said, "No, you're coming with me. We're going to this dinner."

So I get into the car with these guys — Eagleson, his press guy, and Murray Costello — and this was the first meeting about the first Canada Cup. On the way Eagleson is annoyed and says, "And I didn't invite the Finns or the effing U.S. I hope they show up. I'll kick their asses out," and all this stuff. He was upset over the whole situation. "We'll take you there, Donny," which is what he was calling me. We were heading to a hotel in Sarajevo.

## Kirk Douglas and Lorne Greene

In the hall I'm sitting there and everybody's in suit and tie and dresses and such and I'm under dressed. I look over and Kirk Douglas walks in. You know, the old movie star with the cleft chin. He's been over there doing blue jeans commercials. Other famous people are coming in, and I'm thinking, what am I doing here? I'm totally over my head.

People are having drinks, and I grab a beer and slide way to the very back. I'm taking it all in at a table by myself. Eagleson's press guy comes up and says, "Are you OK?"

I said "Yes, just a little intimidated. There's Lorne Greene over there, and Kirk Douglas and other celebrities. There are a lot of famous hockey people here. I'm just fine here."

All of a sudden I look over and Eagleson is talking to Lorne Greene. I hear "Don! Don!" I'm thinking, what's Eagleson doing? "Don!" he says, "come over here."

So I put my beer down and waltz over there and he says, "Don, I'd like you to meet Lorne Greene." He says, "Lorne, this is Don Dietrich, he just got ruled ineligible in the Olympics because of the Finns and the U.S. I'd like to get a picture of you with him. His mom and dad watch Bonanza all the time!"

So I've got a picture. It ended up in the *Deloraine Times*. Dad put it in. I'm standing there with my arm around Alan Eagleson and Lorne Greene!

We sat down and had a meal. It got to be time for me to head back to the Labatt House, pick up my stuff and head to the train station. Murray Costello takes me to the train station. We're sitting there waiting and I'm thinking, I'm traveling by myself. I've never traveled by myself. When I flew to Chicago I ran into Young and Sutter. I always seemed to be with a team and a guy that gave me my ticket, told me when to be at the gate and how to get there.

Well, it can't be too bad. My train gets in at 6:30 a.m. It comes time for me to board. I've got a sleeper. I throw all my hockey stuff on the bed. Some guy was above me in the top bunk. I was reading *Scarface* at the time so I had it unpacked and left it there.

## 'Be prepared to beg'

I came back out and Murray is standing just outside the train. He says we'll talk when you get back to Canada and good luck. And just as the train is starting to pull out, he says, "By the way, Don. In international travel, you've got to be prepared to beg."

"What?" The door's closing and I'm thinking, "Murray, what do you mean? I don't get it." But he's gone. Now I'm paranoid. I'm afraid I'll oversleep and miss my stop. I set my alarm clock for five. I read until two or three.

The train is stopping a lot. My alarm goes off and I wake up. The guy above me is still snoring. I'm in my little enclosure, the curtain closed, my light on and I'm reading my book. I'm supposed to get off at 6:20 or so in the morning, then grab a cab to the Belgrade airport and fly out of Yugoslavia.

It's getting to be 6:05. We've got to be getting close. I go out and walk through the car. Don't see anybody. And we're way the heck out in the boonies. I don't see anything but snow. I go back in and 6:20 comes the train hasn't stopped, we're still moving. All of a sudden the train stops. I look out and people are looking out the window. It's seven in the morning. I go, "Belgrade?" They just start laughing. I duck back into my berth and this guy's up. He looks like he's had a bender from the night before. He doesn't speak any English.

I hide in my berth for a bit and the train takes off. I'm thinking I just missed my stop. What's going on? So I throw on my ski jacket with CANADA across the back and am walking up and down the train. "English? English? Anybody speak English?" I remember Costello saying you've got to be prepared to beg.

I don't want to get off at the wrong place. Now I'm thinking, I'm in a communist country. I'm traveling by myself. I don't have a team to back me up. So I went down to this car with a bunch of people sitting there. Finally this lady in her mid-30s with two small kids, she said she knew English. But she didn't speak it very well. And I was talking too fast. "I've got to get off at Belgrade." She goes to a map and points to it. We're about half-way up to Hungary, it seems. Belgrade's down below. I haven't got a clue what's going on. She's saying something to me, and I don't get it.

I keep saying "Belgrade?" It's a one-word conversation. There's no food or water or anything. Whatever you've got, that's it. We go on through the day and I come back to her every once in a while. She's getting frustrated because she can't explain to me. But she understands I'm going to Belgrade, which everybody was. So she's going down the train looking for someone who maybe speaks better English. Nobody does.

We end up being on this train for 22 straight hours. I've got no idea where we are, other than following her on this little map. We went up, and were now coming back down towards Belgrade.

We get into the next day. There were people drinking something that tasted like gasoline. I was thirsty and they handed me this glass and I took a swig and blaaahh. When the train would stop, every once in a while there was a train going the other way. I went off and was eating some snow, and these Italian guys poke their head out the window and a couple of them spoke English.

"You got anything to drink? We'll trade you; we've got some bread."

So I went back and told this lady. We can trade. They gave me this big bottle of this Sleepovitch or whatever, and I took it over and the guys handed me a big loaf of bread. I took it back into the car and everybody's cheering because I brought some food. They're all half in the bag from drinking this stuff, the people in this part of the car.

We went through *another* full day on the train. So I've been a night, all day, through the night and a day again. I think it ends up being 34 hours I'm on this train. It goes 10 minutes and it stops. It goes and it stops for half an hour. We're slowly working our way back down to Belgrade.

So I've missed my flight. I have no way of knowing where I am, what's going on. I'm in a communist country and I can only think of Midnight Express. In that movie a guy gets caught with drugs and he's put in jail in Turkey. He gets buried in the system. I'm thinking, I'm never going to get out of here. And I've got no team to back me up. You think the worst.

Finally we get close to Belgrade and the station. I thank the lady with the kids and grab all my stuff. My three sticks still bundled up, big bag, big carry-on. So I get off at this train station, and it is just commotion. It's about eight o'clock at night and it's dark. People are running.

I haven't got a clue where I'm supposed to go. How it was supposed to work is, I would get in early and take a cab to the airport and be there five hours ahead of my plane leaving. Now, I don't know where to go. I don't even know if my plane ticket is still valid.

I'm walking through this train station and look up and see this Olympic emblem with the bands. That's something. I go into this place. And I get headed off right at the door by two guys with machine guns. They're standing there and tell me to turn around. I said I need help. I'm lost. I showed them the CANADA. The guy's kind of cross-checking me out the door with his machine gun. I'm going, "SOS. Help!"

All of a sudden I see this old lady. She sticks her head out from the back. She yells something out and they stop. She walks out to the front and says, "You are English?"

I said I was Canadian but I speak English.

She said, "What do you need?"

"I missed my plane. I was on a train from Sarajevo to Belgrade. I'm 34 hours behind."

She said, "This is the Olympic office but we're closing up. You hang on a bit and I'll take you down to a hotel and help you out."

I wait for her; these guys totally back off. We go out the back.

"You have your plane ticket?"

"Yes."

Apparently you can still catch a flight the next day. But you need your ticket to get a voucher to stay in a hotel. I must have walked an hour or more with this lady. We're downtown. There are no vehicles running. There had been a big snowstorm — snowbanks all over the place.

She takes me to a hotel and I get into a room. I've got a food voucher. I don't know what to order, and the waiter's trying to help me out. He doesn't speak any English. In the meantime I tried to phone home. Every time I got an operator the operator didn't speak English. So I've got no way of phoning home, and I'm sure they're wondering where I've been for 34 hours.

I said to the guy, "I want a steak." I ended up getting a steak with noodles. For a drink, Coca-Cola. Everybody knows what that is. First food I've had in a long time.

I went up to my room and tried to phone again, couldn't get through. Went down to the lobby and the hotel desk. The guy spoke a little English. I said I'm trying to phone home, can't get an operator. He said, well. Shrugged his shoulders. I arranged for a wake-up call for seven a.m.

In the meantime this lady had showed me where I could go to an Air Yugoslavia terminal downtown to get my tickets, get on a bus and head to the airport.

I got up at seven, showered, brushed my teeth and said to heck with it. I'm heading down to the airport right now. I get out and start walking along and it's probably about five or six city blocks to this terminal. This guy pulls up in a taxi and says, "You want a ride somewhere? I'm actually going out to the airport but I've got to stop at this terminal over there. We're not supposed to be driving around in taxis right now."

"Why?"

"The roads have all been closed. All our snow removal equipment has been moved from Belgrade to Sarajevo. So only certain lanes are open, and they're for buses only."

I go down to the terminal with him and see these buses pull up. They're just crowded with people. And then they take off. I'm watching and thinking, OK. It gets to be about 9:30 or 10 o'clock and I've got my tickets squared away. I know my flight's still leaving at one o'clock. My bags are inside the terminal. The lady says I don't have to board the bus until about 11.

I look out there and there's an old gentleman out there and he's got an attache case with BRITAIN on the side. So I go out and talk to him and he says, "Yes, I can't get on the bus. I'd put my bags underneath but I can't get on."

"Why?"

"Because people are paying people to reserve them spots on the bus."

I said, "What?"

"It's just been chaos, here. The Olympics are on so they're catering to the Olympics. Anybody who's going to the Olympics gets to ride. I'm just trying to get home."

I said, "What time did you put your stuff on the bus?"

He said, "Seven o'clock. My flight was leaving at 9:30 and it's 9:30 right now."

So I'm panicking. I grab my bags and get out there, thinking I've got to get to the airport. Three buses pull up and there's a rush. People get on and away they go. Man. This guy put his stuff underneath. I'm going to put my stuff underneath, but will I ever see it again? Then I've got to try to get on the bus.

## People rushed for buses

So I waited. The next three came and people rushed for them all. There were hundreds of people there. I watch. Two buses come early and people crowd to them while they park. The third one hasn't arrived. So I run over and stand where the bus doors open to put the luggage on underneath. People start to crowd around and the bus pulls in, stops right in front of me. I lift the thing up, throw my bags in underneath. I look down the side, and there's nothing but people, and they haven't got the doors open yet.

I made sure I had my passport out, had my dinar and my voucher. I went down the side of that bus and knocked everything over and out of the way. I knocked old ladies over. I just grabbed people and I'm throwing them. Old ladies. Old men. Into the snow bank. Just went right down the side of the bus.

I'm in a communist country here. I've got to get home. I'm in a bit of a panic. I've never been in a communist country before. I don't know what the heck's going to happen to me. All I can think of is Midnight Express.

I get on the bus, hand the driver my voucher, he looks at me — and I go sit in the back. People come on and they're pretty annoyed. I'm going, "Hey, tourist. Canada. Sorry." They all get on and we head to the airport. There's just one lane open all the way to the airport. Nobody coming at us. We get to the airport and I'm thinking, it's got to be bad there.

We pull up to the airport and there are no people around. Again I'm not in the international terminal but the domestic one; I don't realize it at the time. Grab my stuff from beneath the bus, walk into the terminal no problem. The gate says to head to the international.

We get there, the automatic doors open up, and there are people on people in there. People are sleeping, people are up. The monitors that show departure times are flipping through like gambling machines. Times are being moved back, and I don't know what to do.

By this time it's a quarter after 10. I see these booths with JAT on them where you take your tickets. I stand in line now, for about half an hour. I get to the front of the line, push my tickets in, and the guy pushes them back to me. He points to the side.

I said, "I've got to get in that line?" He doesn't even nod or anything. I look and there are about 20 people in it, so I stand in that line. I stand there for the longest time, and it's getting close to 12 o'clock, an hour before I'm supposed to board. I've got no boarding pass. I get to the front of that line and push my stuff underneath. He pushes it back and points to across the way.

I said, "I've got to stand over there?" He just pushes them back to me. So now I'm panicking. I've got nothing. I've got to get out of here. I'm by myself. Nobody knows who I am.

I went across the way, stood in line again. Now it's a quarter after 12. I'm getting worried. For international flights you've got to be there an hour and a half ahead of time to get your stuff on, make sure it all makes it. My flight leaves at one. I get to the front of the line, push my stuff in, and the guy pushes it back to me. He points right beside him. I said, "Can't you just give the guy my ticket?"

He gestures as if he doesn't understand. I stuck my head right in there and said, "Look, you SOB. I know you speak English, I know you all do." And with that, I felt this tap on my shoulder. I've got my hockey bag and sticks sitting there beside me, Canadian ski jacket on. It's a guy with an official police suit.

"That's it," I think, "I'm going to jail. I think I'm done."

## 'Are you Don Dietrich?'

He's got a guy beside him with a nice three-piece suit on. He goes, "Are you Don Dietrich?"

I said yes.

He said, "I'm so and so from the Canadian Consulate. We've been looking for you for two days." I just hugged the guy.

He repeated, "Yes, we've been looking for you for two days." Then more guys with suits came along. One said, "Give me your ticket. We're going to take care of everything for you."

So I went and stood off to the side. I said, "Man, this has just been hectic. I was afraid I was never going to get out of here."

He said, "There was a train derailed in front of your train. Everybody on it died. We were worried that you were on that train." That's why my ride took so long, we had to bypass it. We went all the way up to Hungary and back down to Belgrade, instead of straight across. And we had to pull over and let the local trains go through.

I thought, holy man. I'm just so happy.

He said, "Your flight doesn't leave until five o'clock. It's been pushed back. Here are some food vouchers, you can grab something to eat," and they pointed me in the direction I had to go. I was very grateful and thankful.

They'd been looking for me because Chicago wondered where the heck I was, as did my Mom and Dad and my agent. Lots of people were wondering, where is Don Dietrich? My agent said, "Oh, he's probably gone skiing." I wished that had been all it was.

And I wasn't out of there yet. I decided to clear customs and security, take my food voucher and sit down and get something to eat by my gate. That's the way it was going to be.

Now I've got to clear through customs. I slide my passport over to the guy, and I'm thinking I got this thing in an hour. I hope it's OK. He looks down at it and looks up at me. Does it again. Waves a guy over. The two of them are looking at the passport and looking up at me. This goes on. Then they say something to each other. Finally he stamps her, and sends me on my way. I'm just having a heart attack.

I've cleared that, go to my gate, and all kinds of Canadians are around. They had stayed at the Intercontinental Hotel, which was English. If I'd gone there I wouldn't have had a bit of trouble. There were CTV people in TV and radio that were being brought back from the Olympics. These are top executives.

So I'm sitting there watching the monitor and our flight keeps getting knocked back even more. It's getting to be a seven o'clock departure now. These executive guys take their company credit card and go over to buy tickets to England, where they'll catch a flight to Canada, instead of the direct flight.

I don't understand why our flight keeps getting knocked back. These guys slowly leave. They leave me there with this girl, who is apparently their secretary or assistant. She's in charge of all the equipment they're bringing back. She's not too impressed. And I've got my VISA card with its $500 limit, which isn't going to get me a ticket anywhere.

We watch the monitor together and it's like watching the slot machines. So I've been sitting in there all day. Finally it says our flight leaves at 10 p.m. In the meantime I found out they were using our plane to take people from Belgrade to Sarajevo, because the Olympics came first with the Yugoslavian airlines. These other guys, they're buying $2,000 tickets on British Air and they're probably home on the Concorde or whatever.

Finally we board. We get up there and the lights go out in the whole terminal. It's still storming out a bit. Now what? I'm not out of there yet, I'm having a fit, and all I can think of is Midnight Express. The lights come back on, we get on this airplane and it's full of Yugoslavian people heading to Canada. Everybody's smoking; the plane's just full of smoke.

## Girl not comfortable

I'm sitting there and the girl is two seats behind me. She's not real comfortable with her situation. At that point I figure I'm on a plane, a small plane, a 727 that we're traveling across the ocean on. I'm in an aisle seat and have two guys sitting beside me. It's storming out and when the plane finally takes off everybody claps. So they must have been in the same boat I was, waiting.

I was so tired. I leaned back in my seat and looked over. Lights were flashing. It looked to me like the wing was on fire. But it was just snow on the light. I reached over across the two guys and slammed the window blind shut. They looked at me, and I conked out.

We were supposed to fly to Toronto. Toronto wasn't open, so we were rerouted to Montreal. We landed in Montreal after eight or 10 hours and we're out on the runway. They send buses to get us. We get on a bus and are herded to customs. I'm thinking, I'm not heading to any hotel they're sending me to. I'm here, I'm heading the Sheraton, and that's where I'm going to stay.

I told the girl that's what I was doing and she was lost. "I'm staying with you," she said.

I said, "Nothing personal, but I've got things I've got to do." Went through, cleared customs no problem. Down I went to the luggage carousel. I'm sitting there waiting for my luggage and I thought, it's 11 o'clock at night. I'm going to phone home now. I'll make a collect call.

They have that recording thing where you say your name. "You have a collect call from"— I say, 'Don.' Then I don't hear anything at the other end. I said, "Mom!" Just silence. I said, "Hello!" All of a sudden my Dad gets on. "Who the hell is this?"

I said, "It's me, Don. Your son."

"Don?"

"Yeah." There's silence again. I'm thinking, what the heck's going on?

Dad says, "You're OK?"

I said, "Yeah."

Mom picks up the other line and she's crying. "Oh, I'm so happy to hear from you. We didn't know if you were on that train that crashed. Nobody could seem to find you. Dad has been phoning the Canadian consulate over there and Hockey Canada. Hockey Canada's been looking for you and everything."

I said, "I know. You wouldn't believe the story I've got to tell you."

I stayed in the hotel and booked a flight back to Springfield. It sure felt good to be home.

# Chapter 8

## UP TO THE SHOW

*"The biggest thing I remember about Guy Lafleur was his first shift when I was on the bench. No helmet, not a hair out of place, and he was just flying up and down that wing. And not a bead of sweat coming off him. It looked like he was made up in Hollywood."*

BACK IN SPRINGFIELD I was tired. The trip home had been exhausting, and I'd probably lost 10 pounds in Europe, so I was down to 185. I was kept busy. A local reporter wanted an interview about my experience with the Olympic team, as did our team's media guy. And the team was leaving the day I got in for a game in Hershey, Pennsylvania. I just had time to wash some clothes and hop on the bus.

We got in late that night and had a meal, and then I conked out. We had a pre-game skate the next morning. There'd been a few changes on the team. We've got a guy by the name of Pelle Lindburgh, who died later in a car accident. He crashed a Porsche. He was a Swedish goaltender for the Flyers who they had sent down for a couple of weeks of conditioning because he'd had an injury.

So we had the morning skate, and of course I'm really dragging my butt. I'm tired from the jet lag and the time change. I never really slept well the last four or five days I was there. I came out afterwards and there were a lot of reporters around me again, talking about the IOC decision banning me from the Olympic team.

It was a big story about an American League guy — bigger than I had realized. In fact the story went around the world. My friend Dale McKinnon, a teacher and Royals player here in Deloraine, had been teaching over in New Zealand. He read about me and the IOC decision preventing me from playing in a paper there. So I'm in the limelight now.

## Canadian swing

Back in Springfield, I got a phone call. The Blackhawks want me back there right away. I packed my suit bag again and sticks and flew back to the Blackhawks, where we had four days off in preparation for a Canadian swing. We'd start in Montreal and also play in Toronto, Winnipeg, Calgary, Edmonton, Vancouver and LA. It's a pretty big road trip.

I'm still a bit wasted, but I'm going. Chicago is really hurting for players. Al Secord was still out with a stomach muscle tear. I was going back because Jack O'Callahan was out. Doug Wilson had injuries too. I got paired up again with Bob Murray, who was not a big guy but he played 16-17 years in the NHL. A very mobile and knowledgeable defenceman, a really good player. I'm pretty excited to be playing with Murph.

And we're going to Montreal! All I can think of is, this is it. The shrine of hockey, the Forum in Montreal. We went for a morning skate there — but it looked old and dumpy. It was not what I had envisioned. But it still had that mystique. It was the Forum. Our game was that night and it was a Hockey Night in Canada game, but only in Eastern Canada.

In the dressing room, all the equipment representatives were there — Cooper, CCM, Bauer — making sure your equipment's good. Making sure everything's visible on your equipment. And if the brand name wasn't clear, they painted it. For example, if the white CCM was worn off, they painted it. New laces in your Bauer skates, all for the cameras.

We went out and had a half-hour skate. The Canadiens had been out before us and some of them checked us out — Larry Robinson, Guy Lafleur, Chris Chelios and others stood by their bench, watching us practise. Chelios I'd played against; he was on the U.S. Olympic team and was back at that time because they'd been eliminated.

I remember the boards. They were pieces of two-by-sixes. In those days they didn't have any advertising on the boards. When you got hit on them you stuck to them; they were just like Velcro. You didn't slide along them that well. These were upright two-by-sixes all the way around the rink. This is 1984. I'm thinking gee, that's kind of crappy. And they've got big guys, Bob Gainey and others. I'd better get well rested for the game tonight.

We go back for our pre-game meal and I remember Denis Savard yelling, "Shoe shine!" I see guys looking beneath the table so I push back — and I've got ketchup all over my dress shoes. He'd crawled under the table and hit about three or four of us with this condiment. That was my first experience with Savard's practical jokes. In Montreal I roomed with Denis Savard. I told him my story about getting lost and he was glued to it, really enjoyed it.

## *Savard a prankster*

Savard was quite a prankster and a care-free fun-loving guy. I learned quite a few pranks from him that I played later on in my career. Anyway, that night we went to the Forum. It's just a different atmosphere. As Danny Gallivan used to say, it was electric. People outside the rink were selling programs, inside it was abuzz, and the TV lights were on so it's lit right up.

I'm getting there two hours ahead of game time and people are already buzzing. I'm walking through the hallways and seeing pictures of all these great old Montreal Canadiens legends and I'm starting to get butterflies. I mean I was nervous before every game, but tonight I'm in the Forum and playing the Canadiens. This was a dream.

After warm-up I'm sitting on the bench. In those days there was no Plexiglas at the bench, so the fans are right there behind you. Orval is pumped up because he's from Cornwall near Montreal and wants his team to play well. Bob Murray and I are going out on the third shift of the game. That usually means I'll be up against Chris Nyland or somebody like that. Maybe Lafleur. I'm trying to think of the right wingers I might face.

The Canadiens are flying pretty well, and we don't have our full lineup. Tom Lysiak was suspended for 20 games because he had bumped into a linesman. That was one of the first big suspensions ever handed down.

In the back of my mind I hear an annoying sound. There's a stoppage in play and I hear this noise again. I'm up next. I turn around and there's a little French guy coming down the stairs with hot dogs yelling, "Hot dogs, le chien chau, woof woof!" I turn around and I'm laughing and can't stop.

Orval comes down and hits me on the back and says, "Are you ready to play or what!" I remember Sheldon Lanchbery from town here had a satellite dish, and a lot of local guys are over at his place watching it on the dish. So I knew that the buddies I played baseball with would be watching this game.

I said, "Yeah, I'm ready to go," and then I'm out on the ice. Montreal dumps the puck in. I go back and I pick the puck up. I look over my shoulder and Denis Savard jumps off our bench. He's heading right across the red line. We made eye contact. I go behind the net to the other side of it and slap passed it as hard as I could up the middle toward Savard. Big Larry Robinson walked right into it. He took a slap shot — it hit the post and went around the boards and out.

Back at the bench, Orval was ripping mad at me. "I thought you were ready to play!" and all this stuff. Not a good first shift for my Hockey Night in Canada debut.

## Lafleur memorable

The biggest thing I remember about Guy Lafleur was his first shift, when I was on the bench. No helmet, not a hair out of place, and he was just flying up and down that wing. And not a bead of sweat coming off him. It looked like he was made up in Hollywood. He was almost untouchable. I don't recall if I got a shift against him that game, but I remember watching him. He was the first guy in NHL history to score at least 50 goals and 100 points in six straight seasons.

Denis Savard played fantastic hockey. He was one of the most exciting players to watch in the National Hockey League in the mid-1980s. He was spinning and flying around. I remember he used this short little stick and it had a knob on it like a whole roll of tape. Between periods he used to stand it upside down on that knob. Six times in his career he had at least 100 points and for seven straight seasons he scored at least 30 goals.

When he first got to Chicago he hardly spoke any English. He had to make an effort to learn English. He invited me over to his place one time. He's downstairs getting changed and he yells up to me, "Dieter, throw me down the stairs my shoes." I played with a guy in Springfield one time who couldn't speak any English at all.

We lost to the Canadiens. We didn't win many games on that whole trip. We went to Toronto. Maple Leaf Gardens was pretty neat. Downtown. The Leafs were going through a transition. Borje Salming was older, as was Sittler. They had Tom Fergus, Billy Derlago. I played a regular shift and killed penalties. I got sometimes the last 20 seconds of a power play. When you're paired with Murr, you're going to play.

I had some shots on goal, and got five points the whole time I was up with Chicago. I was kind of focused on our next game in Winnipeg. I played defensively, tried to take care of my own end. I played too cautiously, is what it was. But I didn't know it at the time. I figured I was doing fine.

## Why are you holding back?

We played the Jets. I remember it was storming in Winnipeg. My Mom and Dad had driven in, my sister was sick. They stayed in the same hotel as we did, the Viscount Gort. There was a radio man who used to do a post-game show at Chi-Chi's. It might have been Bob Irving of CJOB, or Les Lazaruk. He wanted me to come to Chi-Chi's to eat and do an interview. He was really on me about why I was holding back. I'd put up these offensive numbers in the AHL and wasn't playing that way now. In hindsight, he was right.

But I thought I was doing what I had to do. And everyone was happy with the way I was playing, or seemed to be. To me it wasn't really that big a deal at the time. I didn't think much of it until later on when I was done playing.

The guy was probably right.

I saw my parents and my sister briefly, and then we went out to Calgary. They beat us quite handily. Now we've got to play Edmonton. I hadn't played the Islanders yet, but the Islanders were the team to beat that year. Edmonton was what everyone was talking about. I'd played them in an exhibition game, but now we're in Edmonton. Holy smokes.

Bob Murray and I are playing pretty well together; we seem to be doing all right. So we start the game in Edmonton. I remember Savard playing jokes on guys constantly, keeping everything loose. Murray Bannerman was going to start in goal. Muzz was a good goalie, but that Edmonton team came at you. I think they started Gretzky, Willie Lindstrom and Jari Kurri, with Paul Coffey and Kevin Lowe on defence. That's in the days when Gretzky stayed out there till he got tired. The next guys coming up would just go out and play with him. If he got on a roll and could keep going, he could take a three- or four-minute shift.

We're out there, and we don't touch the puck. They're in our end and moving it around and Bannerman's kicking saves out. We'd clear the puck outside the blue line and they'd do a neutral ice transition and come back.

Off the bench come Messier and Anderson and now they're playing with Gretzky. They're buzzing all over us again, and we're not touching the puck. Again we clear the zone a bit and they come out with two other guys with him. They're back in our end and running around and finally Bob Murray says to heck with this. Gretzky's standing in front of the net. He jumps on Gretzky's back. Up goes the ref's hand for a penalty. Now we have to touch the puck, at least to get a stoppage.

We still don't touch the puck. They pull their goalie in favour of an extra attacker. They've got six guys out there and we have five. Finally Murray Bannerman touches the puck because they're shooting at him.

## Gretzky fights

I'll never forget this because when Wayne Gretzky retired they talked about all the fights that he had. And I used to tell my kids, I know he had a scrap when we played Edmonton. But he never got five minutes for it. Here's what happened.

Gretzky's upset because Bob Murray's on his back and he's probably had six or seven clear shots that he didn't score on. So after the whistle blows, Gretzky drops his gloves and goes after Bob Murray. They just kind of rolled around and went down on the ice. They did this because Dave Semenko was out there.

I used to box with Semenko in the summer when I was still playing junior hockey. We trained over in Boissevain with Rocky Addison in his basement. Rocky was training a fighter by the name of Jimmy Chicoine who was going to be a heavyweight. So it was Semenko and three of us other guys. The three of us Chicoine could pretty well beat up at will. But Semenko could box him. The four of us would go three rounds with this guy, giving him a pretty good workout. But Semenko could really fight. They'd just throw blows at each other. We'd look on in awe.

So we're out on the ice, and Semenko's over there. I thought, this'll look pretty good, I know Semenko. So I grab Semenko, and he just wheeled up and looked at me and said, "Dieter, you let go of me or I'll tear off your head and piss down your neck!" I went, holy cow. There was a bunch of us in a skirmish there so I grabbed Harvey Pozar, an old Czech guy.

Semenko came up to me after the game and said, "Look, that's my bread and butter. If you want to challenge me you'll pay for it." It was stated matter of factly, and that was the end of it. He shook my hand, turned around and took off. That was a point well taken. He didn't have to come and tell me that. Again, that was an eye-opener for the realities of guys in certain situations and what they have to do.

We got through that, and I think Edmonton beat us handily 6-2 or something like that. Went out to Vancouver and played the Canucks. This was a close game and I think we beat them. And I was pretty pumped up because Orland Kurtenbach was there. He lived in Vancouver, he'd coached me before and he feels he had something to do with my being there. He's happy to see someone that he's brought along for a year and I want to play well for him, too.

Vancouver didn't have a really speedy team but they were kind of gritty. There were about four and a half minutes left in the second period. I was on the bench. Behn Wilson was carrying the puck. Behn was tough. Very tough. Scary. He might tear your head off with his stick as well as body check you.

He goes behind the net and comes around and meets Stan Smyl, the Steamer. He was about 5-8 and 215, a tremendous open ice hitter. He just steam-rolled Behn behind the net. And down Behn went. Behn got up and grabbed hold of him and started beating Smyl up. Tiger Williams is out there. Tiger jumps in and Behn throws Smyl down and grabs Tiger Williams and starts beating the crap out of him.

The linesmen jump in and everybody's paired off. I'm thinking, we could have a brawl here. I've never been in one in the NHL before. The linesmen get them separated. Behn goes by Vancouver's bench and he challenges the bench. Nothing happens. Ron Delorme, the "Chief" they called him, was probably the only tough guy they had after Smyl and Tiger.

Behn goes into the dressing room and we finish the period and I think we're tied 2-2 after two periods. Now we've got to go in with Behn. He was just marble-eyed when he went off. We've had experiences with Behn in practice and training camp and know enough to stay away from him. At some point in the year he put Denis Savard out for two weeks. Savard beat him on a 1-on-1 and Behn just tomahawked him over the back. Behn was from Ontario. Off the ice, an intelligent good guy; on the ice, she's war.

Guys are coming into the dressing room and peeking around the corner like the cat looking for the dog. The table's upset, the Gatorade and water's all over the floor. Stuff's thrown all over the room. We go in and it's quiet. Skip Thayer our trainer is in the back room. He comes out and is looking at us. "What?"

"Where's Behn?"

"Oh, he's gone to the hospital. When Smyl hit him behind the net, he broke his collarbone." All that fighting with a broken collarbone. Behn Wilson beat up Stan Smyl and Tiger Williams with a broken collarbone. He'd just lost it. That's what he used to do, lose it. That type of guy is scary, the kind of guy you have to run over in the parking lot to stop.

Later I talked to Jimmy Teetaert, who I played road hockey with as a kid. He was my back catcher for years. He was out visiting in Vancouver and he said, "How come you don't play offensively like you used to?"

I said, "Geez, I'm just trying to survive out there. Doing my job."

Again, in hindsight, he was probably right. If I'd done that a little bit more I might have stayed there. I wasn't a crunching defenceman, so I ended up being maybe a bit like the dime-a-dozen defencemen that scout told me about earlier.

Anyway, we headed to L.A. Bob Pulford is not happy. We've won one game the entire trip. We got three days off in LA. We think we're going to party and go to the beaches and everything else. Well, we've got curfews.

## 'Curfew — or $200'

And on the LA trip I'm back rooming with Tony Esposito. Like I said Tony was on the outs a little bit. So the first night we're in there we have a meeting after practice and Pully comes in. "Eleven o'clock curfew tonight. If you're not in, 200 bucks."

Tony Esposito gets up, walks over, pulls his wallet out and hands him $200. And he's my roommate! I'm not going to laugh.

I'm sitting there in my room all night and she's dead quiet. Nobody around. All of a sudden I wake up. It's about four in the morning. Tony comes in the room. He's trying to be quiet. You can tell he's half in the bag. He's probably been out with a buddy of his from the LA Kings.

He picks up the phone and calls the front desk. "Yeah, I'm Tony Esposito." I'm lying there faking as if I'm sleeping, and Tony's got the little light on over his bed. "I've been playing in the NHL for a long time, and I'd really like to have a beer right now. Do you think somebody could send me up some Budweiser or something like that?"

I looked over a couple of times and he had the TV on and the beer sitting on his lap. He was half asleep.

Next morning at practice, Pully's upset. He announces another curfew and I got switched. Now I'm rooming with Jerome Dupont. If there were hard feelings, maybe he thought Tony was saying something but he never did. I remember Tony sitting in the room. He hadn't been in there, and nobody had checked our room for curfew, and Tony said, "Dieter, aren't I a great room-mate? You'd hardly even know I was there."

We played LA. Dean Kennedy, who married Tammy Olson, was there. I spent an afternoon at his place in LA. They beat us 4-3, and LA wasn't a really good team at that time. So we hovered around fourth spot, which is where we ended up for playoffs.

That trip was memorable because it was my first road trip with Chicago. I remember flying back from LA to Chicago. We had gone out after the LA game for a few beers. I got on the plane a little bit hung over. I'd been out with Kennedy and a bunch of Chicago guys that night. On the plane I'm sleeping right away.

The stewardess tells me to raise my seat for landing. I'm still kind of dozing. We got off the plane and walk through the corridor that connects the plane to the terminal. In the terminal people are looking at me. What the heck? So I go around the corner and look in a window. My tie's cut. And I've got a great mound of shaving cream on top of my head. Know who did that? Savard.

## Islanders a powerhouse

In March, we go into Long Island to play the Islanders. We're maybe three weeks from playoffs. The Islanders are in pursuit of their fourth Stanley Cup. They've got Denis Potvin, Pat Flatley, who I'd played with on the Olympic team, Brent Sutter, Bryan Trottier, Mike Bossy, Clark Gillies, Bob Nystrom, Ken Morrow, Billy Smith in goal, Bob Bourne, Bob "Butch" Goring — countless guys coming at you. Pat LaFontaine was a rookie that year too.

We were out there on our first shift and Clark Gillies came down my wing. I took a bit of a run at him and there was a big crash into the boards. He was a big man. Back at the bench, Bob Murray my defence partner goes, "What the hell did you do that for?"

"What?" Whatever advice or criticism Murph offered me I always accepted. I thought we'd had a pretty good shift.

He said, "What did you do that for, wake that big SOB up." The other guys on the bench are agreeing with him. "Let the giant sleep." He was about 6-3, 235. In those days that was big.

They were just like robots. They systematically broke you down. They came at you with consistency all the time. Everything was the same. They just came at you.

At home that spring, all the old guys are down in Dad's shop, saying the Edmonton Oilers this and the Edmonton Oilers that. I said, "I'll bet you

NO GUARANTEES  |  *Don Dietrich*

the Oilers lose four straight to the Islanders." Dad said, "I'll back you up on that." I'd played against them. And sure enough, they did. The Islanders beat Edmonton four straight that year to win the Stanley Cup final.

The Islanders knew the price it took to win as a unit. Everybody was in that unit. Not to say the Oilers weren't, but they were on their way to getting there, and that was probably the biggest lesson that they learned, that final playoff series.

We played Minnesota in the first round of the playoffs and lost out in a best of five. I never played a game. They kept me around when they could have sent me down. But they wanted me to be there and Dupont and I watched a lot of games from the stands.

I was paid pro-rated on my NHL salary. So I was making some pretty good money. I still had to pay for my place in Springfield, but they put me up in the Bismark Hotel in Chicago. I got $300 a month from the Canadian Olympic program, my AHL salary, and then my NHL salary.

I thought I had arrived. I'd played 17 games. They wanted me there for the playoffs. People on the inside said they were pleased with the way I played. In my mind I had arrived. I just didn't have a contract.

# Chapter 9

## THE MAINE MARINERS — AND NADINE

*"Some days I came to the rink hung over. I hit the bottle a bit and drank quite a bit of beer. Tommy McVie had this weight routine that he was notorious for. I struggled with that. He used to get right in my face, and I didn't want to breathe my beer breath on him so I turned away."*

THREE WEEKS PASSED between our eighth and ninth interviews, as both of us were drawn away from Manitoba for family reasons. I went out to Vancouver Island to spend Remembrance Day with Dad, Clayton Bird, a war veteran. For their part, Don and Nadine drove to Moose Jaw, Saskatchewan to watch their son Jacob, 18, play hockey. He had asked for a trade and was sent by the Moose Jaw Warriors to the Lethbridge Hurricanes.

He was traded on a Monday night and played for his new team against his old team, the Warriors, the next night in Moose Jaw. Don said he played a regular shift and the power play, even killed penalties. "That to me was the coach showing him respect." A story in the Deloraine Times & Star of November 2005 quotes the general manager of the Hurricanes as saying, "[Jacob] adds some size along with a tenacious work ethic we believe will be appreciated in Lethbridge." Sounds a lot like his father, doesn't he?

■　　■　　■

I flew back to Deloraine for the summer with this termination contract, which meant I was now a free agent without compensation. Chicago didn't own me anymore. I had some interest from Pittsburgh, where Eddie Johnston, the former Bruins goalie, was GM. I wanted a one-way contract. Pretty risky and high demand for somebody who had just played 17 NHL games. But I figured I had shown what I could do.

However, I wasn't going to get that from Pittsburgh. My agent, Bill Watters, kept telling me, "They're going to offer you $32,000 on a two-way contract and an NHL amount." At that time I looked only at the bottom end. I said no, I think I warranted a one-way contract. He was getting a little upset with me, maybe rightly so, but that's how I felt at the time.

So the summer's going on and the June draft is coming up. I get a phone call at home and it's Bob Pulford. "We'd like to offer you a contract."

"OK, I want a one-way contract."

"Not going to happen. I've been talking to your agent, and I think I might have something for you."

"What are you thinking?"

"How about we make you a deal two years plus an option. Worse-case scenario is every year you're going to make $50,000. Start you out with an NHL salary of $125,000, minor league salary of 25 but a guaranteed 50, no matter where you play. That gives a team an excuse to call you up."

Now I'm sitting there thinking, OK. And?

"Here's the deal," he says. "In the draft this year New Jersey picks second and we pick third. We do not want New Jersey to take Ed Olczyk who is a Chicago-born player. So we're going to make a deal, and New Jersey wants you as part of this deal. You and Rich Preston for Bob McMillan and a fifth round draft choice. And Jersey agrees not to take Olczyk (I found out later they were going to pick Kirk Muller anyway). But you don't have a contract with us."

I'm thinking I could just phone New Jersey myself and say I'm available. But Pully's bared himself, played all his cards. If I go to the minors, I make $50,000 which in 1984 was pretty good money. So I agree. But not to two years. This is just after Gretzky called New Jersey a Mickey Mouse operation. I'm going from a sixth place team to a last place team. I'm going to get a chance and I don't want to be stuck in a contract. So it's one year and an option.

## $5,000 signing bonus

I signed the deal. It was Fed-Xed out and Fed-Xed back. When I had it sitting there I asked Pully for a signing bonus. A second-year signing bonus is unheard of. But he gave me a $5,000 bonus. And I still had the terms of my last contract in there. For example, if I played 10 NHL games I got an extra $5,000. Every 10-game segment I'd get another $5,000 on top of my $125,000.

At the draft this deal happened. So I'm in a transaction for first-rounders at the draft. I get a call from Max McNabb, New Jersey's GM. Again, he's an older guy, welcomes me to the team. I went through the summer, and I'm preparing to go to the Devils.

Then McNabb phones me in the first week of August. "Why don't you come down to New Jersey, skate with the guys who are living here, we'll put you up in a hotel. Play in some celebrity softball tournaments with the team and be here for when camp starts on Sept. 15."

I headed off in mid-August. I flew out of Minot this time, drove down through the Peace Garden port. They had my H1 visa sitting there for me. Down there I'm skating with the guys at the practice facility and staying at the Holiday Inn.

Camp opens. I'd been down for three weeks. My stall is in the dressing room. I'm pumped; I'm No. 27. After a couple of days of camp we go back to the hotel and there's this big entourage of people following this guy around. He's got a busted nose. His name is Uli Hiemer. He's German, my age, 23. They'd just signed him to a big bucks contract. He's a defenceman who Colorado had taken 48th over-all in the 1981 entry draft. New Jersey acquired his rights and he shows up.

The next day I go to training camp all my stuff is out of the stall. I'm in the weight room and I'm No. 61. Where do you think I'm heading? They even sent me my hotel room bill leading up to camp. My agent took care of it and made sure they paid it.

Now I'm in a whole different boat. They've got me playing rookie exhibition games. Now I'm in a room where the guys from Maine are dressing.

I was bitter. I was really bitter. They had eight defencemen there with this Hiemer. Four of these guys were over 35 years of age: Phil Russell, Bob Lorimer, Bob Haufmeir, and another guy. They were all on one-way contracts. The Devils would have had to buy them out to get them off the team.

Economically I'm the guy that has to go. And I know that now. In Maine, Tommy McVie is the coach. They called him Sarge. I heard some horror stories about him and some good stories. But I was the type of guy who would go in and say his hellos and that was it. I didn't bounce around coaches like the little dog on the Bugs Bunny cartoon, "Hey Spike, hey Spike."

## 'Keep working hard'

But I was sour. I played for Tommy for some 20-some games and every day I'd come out and he'd say, "Dieter you keep working hard and you'll get back there, you're going to get back there. You're playing well." I was plus, I killed penalties and was on the power play. He would say that to me out on the ice in practice maybe once a week. "Keep working." I'd just nod my head, didn't really say much.

Some days I came to the rink hung over. I hit the bottle a bit and drank quite a bit of beer. Tommy had this weight routine that he was notorious for. I struggled with that. He used to get right in my face, and I didn't want to breathe my beer breath on him so I turned away. The odd time he'd throw a $50 bill at me and say, "Why don't you drink a beer with a label on it?" as a joke. We'd laugh.

One day we went out to practice and he came up beside me on the ice. He said, "Dieter, do you know why you're not in the NHL?"

I just looked at him and shrugged.

He said, "Because you're not effing tough enough."

It may have been a true statement. Maybe not. My response to that was, "If New Jersey wanted a tough guy, why didn't they trade for Behn Wilson instead of me?"

And with that Tommy lost it. I sat the next game in the stands, and came back as a fourth line centre. I'd played forward in junior, but I was an offensive-type defenceman playing centre. He was upset that I would challenge him in that way, and he wasn't too happy with me. But I wasn't too happy with my situation. I'd never spoken out about myself until that point.

I was pretty mad about what he'd said. If there was truth in his statement, there was also truth in mine. That whole season was hell — putting up with that, and other things he said or did. I'd played for coaches where I'd seen guys who were picked on, but it was never me. Now it was me. So no matter what I did it was never right.

We had a meeting one day, and he walked out and put half a glass of water on the table. "Dieter, what is that?"

"It's a half-full glass of water."

"I say it's half empty, that's why we don't get along."

That's what I had to deal with. I understood that in hockey every coach had a scapegoat. I expressed dislike to my agent but I'm in the minor leagues and I'm not going to get traded. I'm reminded by my agent that if I just fall out of bed for the next two years I make $100,000.

Now my passion for the game is really being tested. No. 1, I'm not liking my situation. No. 2, I find myself playing only three or four shifts a game. And for the first time in my life I'm not getting along with my coach.

We went on like that, with me playing a little forward, a little defence. I dealt with things as best I could. In the playoffs I scored an overtime winning goal. We were playing in Halifax, one of our main rivals, and Tommy came onto the ice. When he got to me I didn't know if he was going to hit me or hug me!

## 'Want to fight me?'

He would come to the back of the bus and take beer away from us, and then say to me, "You want to fight me?" As I look back on it, in all fairness I was a bit challenging, because I always held it in my head that I could play for Chicago, the sixth best NHL team, and yet I couldn't make the New Jersey Devils. That's hockey. I was having a tough time with that.

Now I'm in a position where I have a coach who liked me, and was trying to help me, and I just shot down what he said. I probably should have done what

I'd always done — nod my head and carried on. McVie had liked me to start with. And I'm sure if we talked to him today he'd say he feels bad about things he said, as I do now. But at that time it wasn't right. That's the way I viewed it, and I stick with that.

I had a two-year contract. I came back the next year, 1985-86, went to New Jersey's camp, and they had a new coach. Doug Carpenter had taken over. I remember I was in the lobby of the hotel at training camp and Tommy was there with a bunch of the brass. He called me over and said, "Dieter, I just want you to clear something up for us. We're talking about hemorrhoids and we need an asshole." He thought it was funny.

Then I thought, boy, this is going to be a long year. I know where I'm headed. I asked to be traded, I wanted to be moved, but nothing would happen. This guy hated me for whatever reason, and I hated him. I did. He was somebody that was standing in the way of where I was going. Maybe if I'd have been tougher, I might have been there. But at 24 years old, I'm not about to change the way I played. At the pro level, it's up to you to do the things you do well, and bring that to the team. It's up to the coach to either piece you in or, if he doesn't like you, move you on to somewhere else.

That whole year I played a lot of forward. I vowed that whole season that I would just come to the rink, do my business, and go home and forget about it.

I got through that year and there was about a month left in the season. New Jersey had a lot of injuries on defence. At Maine I was the seventh D, or fourth line centre, or I'd work up to second line centre. Played a little power play on the point.

Every game for six games, New Jersey brought up one defenceman and sent him back. So all the six D went up, played a game and came back. But they still had guys hurt. They were playing in Philadelphia. Who gets called up? Me.

## A month in NHL

Tommy says, "Just pack enough clothes for one game. You'll be back." So I go up to New Jersey and played in Philly — played really well. And I stayed. I stayed for the whole month. While up there, I had press people come up to me and say, "I remember you were here. What happened? Did you blow your knee out or something?"

I said, "No, I'm fourth line centre in Maine."

"What the hell's going on?" So some things were said and written about that. But I stayed there to the end of the season, the whole year. We were going to play our last regular season game in New Jersey, and Maine was playing their last game against Moncton, who they were playing in the first round of the playoffs. I was sent back that day to Maine, which I knew was happening.

In one of the Maine newspapers they had a story about the fact I'd won a Calder Cup, and that they needed my experience in the playoffs. They had a quote from Tommy saying, "Yes, he's definitely an NHL skater, passer and shooter." That's all he would say — or that's all they used of what he said — about me coming back.

I got to the rink in Maine at about 4:30, from the airport. My sweater was hanging in my stall. I take my clothes off and I'm standing there in my underwear, no shirt on, and Tommy comes around the corner. "Dieter! I see you haven't been doing the weight program!"

You know, I had just proved that I could play in the NHL. At that point, there had been some interest in me going over to Europe. I was in the last year of my contract, which remember was one year and an option, thankfully not two and one. So all this stuff's going through my mind. I looked at him and said, "Yeah, it's hard to keep weight on when you're playing 35 minutes a game."

He just turned and walked out.

So I dress for the game. I don't play. We're playing Moncton. I wanted to play, to help. And I don't play a shift.

There's maybe five minutes left in the game. We're ahead 3-2. He puts me out on the ice. I'm cold as heck. Moncton dumps the puck in our end. I pick up the puck and go around the net. I don't see anybody, so I just fire it off the glass and it goes down for icing.

I come in for the change, and all of a sudden he comes down the bench and says, "Jesus Christ, Dietrich, I didn't put you out there to ice the gawd-damned puck. You're supposed to be an NHL passer, shooter, skater. What the hell are you doing out there?"

I looked down the bench and I mean I'd put up with this for the better part of two years. My teammates all have their heads down. I never expected any of them to ever stand up for me, although some of them did want to. I told them not to. I remember looking down the bench at those guys and I turned around and said, "Tommy, why don't you go fuck yourself."

## Starts swearing

He just lost it. He starts swearing. The whistle blew and he puts me out on the ice. I pick up the puck in our end and beat the guy that's chasing me and skate up. The guy ahead of me is Kevin Maxwell, a slick centreman. I pass him the puck. Maxy goes to dump the puck in and Dale DeGray knocks it out of the air, and it comes back on an almost two on zero breakaway for them. I stop, rush back, slide and break up the play. I ended up falling on the puck in the corner and the whistle blew. I go back to the bench and he's waiting there for me, yelling. So I turned and went back for the face-off. Told the other defenceman to get off the ice so I didn't have to go in and face him!

I stayed out there. I got tired, so I went to go in and change. He ran over, pushed the trainer out of the way, and kept the door closed. We've got a 3-2 game, which really means nothing, because whether we win or lose we're playing Moncton in the first round. Now this has turned into a joke. So I just stayed out there, with about 25 seconds left. Time-out's called, I go to the bench and he pulls me off. We win the game.

I changed quickly and went into McVie's office. He cut me down and put me in my place. Then he gave me the fatherly talk about how much I could help the team, because I could play forward or defence, and how valuable I was.

We have a couple of days before the playoffs start. One day I'm paired with a regular D, and the next I'm playing wing on the second line, going along and having a great time, thinking this is going to be pretty good for old Don Dietrich, finally.

The first game of the playoffs arrives, I go down to the rink — my sweater's not even hanging in the stall. I knew that was the beginning of the end. I phoned the agent who was talking about Europe and said I'll go. Wherever you can get me signed, I'll go.

■   ■   ■

Though I sit here and complain that those years in Maine were bad hockey-wise, they were fantastic for me personally because that's where I met my wife.

I actually met Nadine the first year that I was in Maine. My wife is a former Penthouse pet. I heard that this girl lived in the area and I thought that maybe if I was lucky I would see her somewhere.

Back in September of '84 I went to a pub and was watching the World Series on TV, and this girl is sitting right beside me. I'm watching the ball game and she says a couple of things to me. I'm thinking, she's just stunning. She talked to me and I found out she was meeting one of her friends there.

*[Nadine joins in.] I was going to buy him a drink. My part of the story is, he was different from anybody else I'd met. He was funny, and I don't usually watch baseball. We got talking, and once I found out he was a hockey player I almost walked away. I didn't have very good luck with hockey players. I had just finished a relationship with a hockey player, and it wasn't a good one.*

At that point I didn't know who she was. Then she got up to leave. She was going to another bar. She asked me about The Max, a nightclub where you pay a cover charge and bring your own beer in. As the night went on I closed down the pub I was in and thought, I'll head over to this Max and see what's up. She was over there and we got talking a bit. I could see that she was having a bit of a row with this other guy who was on our team. I didn't butt in. She said she had to leave, so I walked her out to the car and we sat in the car for a bit. At that point I could see that there were diapers on the floor. I found out they were Tristan's, who at that point wasn't a year old.

She asked me if I had a girlfriend at home and I said no, and she said, "Yeah, that's what every hockey player says."

*He said he had a problem, and I said what's that? It was either he was married or he was gay, one or the other. Then he said no, I'm just looking for a one-night stand.*

And with that she ushered me out of the car. I waved good-bye.

*He had my number, though.*

Yes, I did have her number. I went through the whole year with it. I'd bump into her here and there, and at that point I was told who she was, and according to her she would go places looking for me.

*He was just different. His personality, everything.*

These bartenders would say, "Nadine's looking for you." And I kept thinking what would a good-looking girl like that see in an ugly old guy like me? Why? I could not figure that out. I mean, she was so beautiful. Why me?

*Before we go any further, the night I first met him I went home and told my mother I had just met the guy who was going to marry me. I just knew it. Then we didn't date for six months!*

Until probably March of '85. I never called her. Sometimes we ended up in the same bar, but I basically never went near her because I couldn't figure out what she could see in me. As one guy told me near the end of my career, when I was in New Haven, "Is that your wife?"
I said, "Yes."
"Where are her glasses?"
I said, "She doesn't wear glasses."
He said, "Oh, that's how somebody as ugly as you could be married to somebody as good looking as her!" At different times she would be with her friend Brenda, and she'd say, I'm going here and there. I'd say, Yes, I'll call you. She'd say, I've heard that before.
Finally it was March. I ran into them at the same pub, the Old Port, where I'd met her the very first time. We talked a bit. Her friend Brenda

was standing there and I said, "I'll call you." Brenda jumped right in front of Nadine and said, "Yeah, right. You've been saying that crap all year!"

I said, "OK. 642-3190.

*That was my number.*

I knew it by heart. I just wouldn't call it. I didn't think I was worthy of Nadine. So I phoned her the next day. We arranged to meet, and you stood me up.

*Well, no. Because I'd been in Penthouse, a radio station wanted to train me as a disc jockey. So I was there doing that. I knew I had to be somewhere, but — this was a new opportunity. I couldn't just say, sorry I have to be somewhere. But I didn't really like it anyway. I don't like talking.*

She stood me up! (laughing).

*He kept calling my mother, and that's where I was, at the station.*

I was quite upset. I thought maybe she was paying me back. We talked on the phone after that and made an arrangement to see each other again.

*Our first date is why I fell in love with him.*

We went to Toys R Us.

*Our first date. And he danced with me in the aisles.*

I loved Toys R Us.

*And I did too because I had Tristan.*

I'm a video arcade nut. I loved Toys R Us. It's still a great place. They played music and stuff.

*I was a little embarrassed to dance in the aisles but that was him. That's what made him unique and different from anybody else I'd met. I'd always met either bar owners or restaurateurs and they were all jerks. Don was down to earth.*

Penthouse was unique. She was presented with an opportunity. I hadn't seen the magazine with her in it. When I finally went out to the farm where they lived, and met Tristan, I saw someone who was a mother. That impressed me.

*Anyone I had ever met and brought home to Tristan, he'd had nothing to do with them. Don pulled up in the driveway. Tristan was a year at that point. We were sitting on the deck, Tristan and I. He had a Bigfoot truck that kids could get in. Well, he couldn't touch the ground on this. But with Don in the driveway Tristan went up and grabbed his hand and made him push him in this Bigfoot truck.*

So I didn't even see her for the first 10 or 15 minutes that I was there.

*And Tristan had this thing about hiding his bottles. I'd find them a week or two later and they stunk. But he would take Don and show him where these were. Never would he tell me. He just knew from Day 1. Don's always been his Dad. Anyone can be a father. But it takes someone special to be a Dad. We always told Tristan, he picked Don to be his Dad. He knew the father and Mom that he wanted, it just took him a little while to get the Dad.*

I saw a heck of a mother to her young son.

*Not this snobby Penthouse pet.*

It totally changed my opinion of her. I found out that she did her photo shoot four weeks after Tristan was born. She needed the money.

*It was extremely good money, and something I'd always wanted to do. I was modeling before that. I'm not ashamed of it; I always wanted to do it. It came at the right time because I was raising a little boy by myself. You took the shot, and then all you did was go around and sign autographs. Two hundred dollars a day, even if you were just there an hour. It'll be more than that now.*

Nadine laid it on the line that there was somebody else involved in this relationship. Was I prepared to continue on?

*I said, does it bother you that I have a child? He goes, would it make a difference? Tristan was mine forever. I wouldn't give him up.*

My No. 1 priority was hockey. I ended up driving back home to Deloraine. I bought a Jeep that winter, the first vehicle that I'd bought for myself. I found that I missed her quite badly. This was the summer of '85. I'd finished my first season. She had to go over to China for Penthouse and do her thing and she stopped in here after and saw me and we had a good week together. Then she went back. I went back to Maine a bit early. She was working in a bar. I surprised her showing up at the bar, and that was the first night that I told her that I loved her.

*He hadn't told me that yet.*

I couldn't tell her that — and I couldn't tell her that on the phone. We made arrangements to live together that winter. Which kept my sanity. It was really bad, and when you come home to a little guy who doesn't understand that your coach is a jerk, you forget about it. Tristan and I spent a lot of time together.

*The first time he called him Daddy, he ran and hid in the closet, because he didn't know if that was OK. Don went in and told him you can call me Daddy if you want.*

*We got married when he was three. We had dated for a year and a half. We married on June 14, 1986. Tristan was adopted two days later. The judge couldn't have been happier to do it. We had to have letters from his biological father. The judge didn't allow him to have visitation rights, because he wrote a letter saying he wanted Tristan only if I became unable to look after him. He had a bar and restaurant and I was only his ornament. He left me because I was pregnant and wasn't going to be that ornament on his arm anymore.*

*That's the day we walked out of there, the three of us hand in hand. In everything we've been through, we can say our kids are our sanity. That's what keeps us intact. Our kids. We have three boys — Tristan, Jacob and Nick.*

And we're proud of each one. They're all good guys.

# Chapter 10

## SUCCESS — AND INJURY — IN EUROPE

*"I scored four goals and we beat them 5-4, in Schwenningen.*
*Our stadium held 8,500 people, and it was full. They chanted my name. 'Die-trich! clap*
*clap! Die-trich! clap clap!' Every time I'd pick the puck up they'd chant my name."*

THROUGH MOST OF that 1985-86 season I'd been in contact with a player agent named Rollie Thompson who at that time was the czar of agents that got guys over to Europe. Rollie was adamant that I would be a good defenceman over in Europe. He was specifically looking at Germany for me because I was playing forward at the time in the American Hockey League and had decent skills offensively that he thought could fit well in the European game. It didn't hurt that I had a German name. He had a team in mind, Schwenningen (pronounced ShWENNi-gen).

On the Maine Mariners we had a goaltender named Karl Friesen. He was older than I and had played in Germany and had German citizenship, though he'd been born in Winnipeg. He had nothing but good things to say about Germany, and of course he was thought of as kind of a national hero there, as he played on the national team.

At that time each German team was allowed two foreigners only. You had to be a complete hockey player. I mean you had to offensively be able to put some numbers up and you had to play well defensively. Karl thought I could do that.

### I turn down New Jersey

New Jersey offered me another year. The contract was $32,500 in the AHL, but I had had enough. I always gave myself a time frame. I thought that in five years, if I hadn't made it to the NHL, then I would look into doing something else. I thought I could have played in the NHL, but for whatever reasons, it wasn't going that way.

Europe seemed like a pretty good deal. One of the things Rollie Thompson stressed was that you're never away from home a night. Though you do practice twice a day you play half the games of an AHL season, so less wear and tear on the body. They had a 36-game schedule. I'd been playing 80 games in the AHL and NHL.

The team paid you in after-tax dollars. They paid your taxes for you. The one catch that they had was that it would be easier and better for them tax-wise if I was married. Nadine and I had discussed marriage, and we decided to do it. We were married on June 14, 1986, as Nadine said.

All I had was a one-year contract. If you failed as a foreigner, you were done. You had a lot of pressure on you as a foreigner. There were 10 teams in the Bundis League or first league in Germany. If you finished ninth or 10th, you had to go down and play against the top teams trying to get up from the second division. We hovered around seventh or eighth, all the time. We stayed out of that round, but the team we were on was of a lesser calibre than others, so there was a lot of pressure on me and the other foreigner, Tony Currie, a proven NHLer.

Nadine and I thought it would be a good fit. After we married we came back to Deloraine that summer and had a bit of a social party that the local people put on for us. I went to return to the States, crossing at Goodlands. But I no longer had my year-round H1 visa because I had no AHL contract. We were planning to fly from the U.S. I couldn't get into the U.S.

We had to drive back to Deloraine, and my Dad got on the phone. He knew some senior customs guys and we ended up sending the border port a contract (it was in German), showing them when I would be out of the U.S. I finally got to go down, and we flew from Boston to Germany.

The team started dry land training in July. This was something I'd never experienced. We arrived in Germany in the morning. We'd bought German language tapes, and I had a calculator-type thing that gave you the German word if you punched in an English one. We'd be living down by the Black Forest, near the Swiss and French borders, close to Lahr. A beautiful area.

We landed in Stuttgart, which is about 100 kilometres from Schwenningen. At the airport meeting us were two guys, each with a vehicle. One was the general manager, who spoke English. The other was Manfred Gruel, the CEO of our major sponsor, a beer company. An older guy. Spoke absolutely no English at all. Guess whose car we get in.

## Action on the Autobahn

You've heard stories about the Autobahn. Well, Manfred Gruel had a 500 Series BMW, a hot car. We're just flying. He doesn't speak any English, nor I any German. Nadine is riding in the back. I'm pushing the floor trying to hit the breaks. There are three lanes to the Autobahn. There's the right lane where guys go about 110. There's a middle lane where they go 150 or 160 km/hour. The left lane is, get out of my way: Porches, Lamborginis.

All of a sudden Manfred gets into this left lane to pass a car. He's flicking his lights because the fellow ahead isn't moving. He's only feet from this guy's bumper. He's looking at me and saying something; I'm looking at my little machine trying to figure out how to say "Slow down." Finally I look back at Nadine and said, "Do you know how fast this guy's going?"

She said, "No."

"He's going 200 kms an hour."

"How fast is that?" she said, being from the States.

"That's like 120 miles per hour."

"No way."

He blew us 120 kms back to Schwenningen in 40 minutes. The other guy was driving ahead of us.

For accommodations, we ended up going to an older couple's house. They lived upstairs, and we would have the basement. Again they spoke no English at all. We're starting to wonder, have we done the right thing by coming here? It was a bit of a culture shock. We went into this place and the GM showed us around. They'd put some things in the fridge but we had to go shopping.

The owner of the home comes in and talks to me like you and I are, in German, trying to show me around the house. I'm at a loss. At this point, Nadine went into what was supposed to be our bedroom in this little place. The fellow left, and I came around the corner: she was in tears.

We looked at this bed. I don't know what you'd call it. It's like a duvet, a really thick thing. We didn't know if we were supposed to unbutton it and get in it, or get under it, or lie on it. So we were sitting there and had a little bit of a breakdown.

We decided to go shopping. We went to leave, and this old guy's standing by the door. I locked the door to our suite; he was standing there with a key to a car. The team had given us a vehicle, a BMW, low end of the line. I said we're going shopping.

Shopping was a chore in itself. Over there you have to buy bags or bring your own. We didn't know that. We didn't know what half the things were on the shelf. So it was quite a culture shock to start with. Now we had to do everyday living, not like when I was over there for the Olympics and the meals were provided and everything was regimented.

It was quite an easy transition for me because our coach was from Boston. He had played in Germany in the 1970s and married a German lady and stayed over to coach. Billy Flynn was his name. We also had half a dozen German-Canadian guys. These were guys Junior A, or played in the Western Hockey League, and had German citizenship. So when I went into the dressing room, the coach was English; he spoke German but we'd get the translation afterwards. The bolder

German guys tried to speak English but they really appreciated it if you tried to speak German.

I had to go down in the morning for dry land training. The first thing we do is go for a 35-minute run. And the coach is leading it. So it's not like the captain is, it's the coach. And he's in fantastic shape. He led us in aerobics too. We went on this 35-minute run, and they had all these fantastic walking trails. I'm probably middle to the back of the pack. We began each day with a run, every day, seven days a week. Aerobics was every day, weights every other day.

After the run we're going to play soccer for an hour. We pretty much just have the team. There are no tryouts. There are some German guys there, but they're going to play on the local junior team. Ten guys each side, one guy in goal. I can see the older German guys are saying, I'm playing goal. You guys go and run for the next hour. Me, I'd never played soccer. Oh, a bit in elementary school, but not to the calibre of these guys. Soccer to them was like hockey to us. And they're good. And we had some Czech guys and Russian guys who were good as well.

## 'You're playing goal!'

They knew the rules. I didn't. I was out there hitting guys, body checking, grabbing. So the next day they blew the whistle for half time and this guy comes up and says, "You're playing goal." So every day I played goal, because they didn't want me out there. Eventually after three years of dry land I learned the game. But it was funny: "You're playing goal."

Anyway, I had never got myself in such good shape in my life, as I did after three weeks of dry land with this club. I was just tuned. When I hit the ice I had no sore muscles or anything. I felt like I'd been on the ice already. That's what that kind of conditioning did. We also had a mandatory massage once a week. I didn't mind it; it really turned me into a cooked piece of spaghetti. I felt blah the next day, but as far as conditioning goes it was great.

It got to be about August 20th and we went down to Austria to play an exhibition game. We lost 4-3. I had played not too bad, the first game with new guys. We basically were a team of maybe eight players. The other 12 were kind of suspect. And when we went on the road, some guys didn't show up. They didn't like playing out of their own building. They weren't real brave.

On the other hand, of those 12, about 10 of them worked. It was like playing senior hockey here. They worked all day or were in the army; they missed the morning skate but they came at night. Hockey wasn't a passion with them, it was a hobby.

When you talk about culture, one thing I don't think that anyone can be prepared for is the freedom of nudity in a country like that. We were in our second or third night of aerobics in this gym. They had three or four masseuses and one of them says to me, "I want you to go into the sauna."

I hated saunas. Hard to breathe. I had a necklace on, and it would always kind of burn me. But, my agent said, when in Rome.... So I go into this sauna. I know some guys are in there. I look for a place to sit. The German guys watched every move that I made. There's a spot at the top, it's hard to see and kind of damp in there. I go up and throw my towel down and I'm sitting at the very top. I've pulled my chain away so it doesn't burn me.

I listen to these German guys. They're sitting below me and I could tell they're talking about me. I'm starting to get a little ticked off. What am I doing? What's the big deal? So I'm sitting there, and I turn my head and there beside me was a girl with her legs spread eagle, lying on a towel.

I was thinking, wow. I looked around and half the people with us were naked women. I'm sitting there, and the first thing I'm thinking is, don't get a boner. But as soon as you think that, you know what happens. So I grabbed the towel and threw it around me and go running down and the German guys are clapping and cheering. That was the big joke. They wanted to see how I was going to respond to this.

One time we took a new foreigner, Mike Siltala, down to Switzerland and drove back. There was a man-made lake and Nadine and Mike's girlfriend were changing in the car. We went down to look to see if it was a nude beach, and it was. We get back to the car and Nadine says, "Well, what is it?" At that moment a guy jumps out of a car beside us, rips off all his clothes and runs down to the beach, his thing bobbing in the breeze. I said, "Does that answer your question?"

Anyway, that story about me in the sauna was the big joke there for a while. I never went in the sauna again.

Things like that we had a tough time with at the start. It was a lot easier for me because I had English-speaking people around me. It was very hard on Nadine. We ended up moving out of that initial house we were in and into an apartment that was beside the other foreigner, Tony Currie. Tristan and the other kids always seemed to be scrapping at our first house. The lady upstairs would take the neighbor's kid into the house and leave Tristan outside.

It was a tough situation the whole year. The good thing was, half the games and you were home every night. The money was good. I started out making the equivalent of $35,000US tax-free, plus I had a car and my apartment paid for.

And, with me being home each night, Jacob came along. Nadine had to fly home by a certain time because he was going to be born in the summer. Airlines don't let you fly if you're within eight weeks of your due date. They didn't in those days anyway. She came home in February. We were finishing up our season. We lost out in the first round of the playoffs.

I had an opportunity to go to Kloten, Switzerland, and play for a Swiss team, just for the playoffs. I thought, well, it looked like a good opportunity. Our GM took us down and worked out a super contract. They had about four foreigners there already who were hurt, and instead of bringing other guys over from North America they took us. We got $1,000 US a game. We had bonuses. We ended up beating Davos in five games. Davos was a powerhouse at that time. The owner used to come in and hand us 100 Swiss frank bills after games. It was pretty neat. Kloten was owned by a guy with a big sporting goods store. He was in with Rollie Thompson, and that's how Rollie got over there.

Then, in the fifth game, we were going into the third period. We were ahead 5-2. I was on the ice and we had a Russian coach who spoke very little German, no English. His son played with the Islanders at that time. It was funny. I used to get upset on the bench and be swearing a bit. One time I scored a goal and he comes down the bench going, "Don, Don, eff me, eff me!"

## Injured

Anyway, we were out there in the fifth game, at the start of a period. I got caught on a play and went back and slid and broke the play up. But the ice was still wet and I never lost any speed. I crashed into the boards with both my elbows and both my knees.

Both my knees hurt. I went to get up and my left leg wouldn't hold me. I can always remember my Dad saying, no matter how hurt you are you can get off the ice. Don't let them know you're hurt. Well, I couldn't get up. I knew something was bad. My left knee was on fire.

They blew the whistle. They were going to bring a stretcher out and I didn't want one. I got up and went and sat on the bench. I didn't feel too bad after I sat there for a little bit. I could move my leg. The whistle blew and I took a step on the ice and went right down. Gee, this isn't good.

They took me in and took my shin pad off. I had no kneecap. It was kind of spread out. They put a towel and an ice pack over it and rushed me to the Winterthur Hospital outside of Zurich. Took an X-ray. This guy came in, a very elderly doctor. Everything looked ancient to me over there.

He said, "You shattered your kneecap."

I said, "Well I'm flying home. I'll have surgery on it at home."

"You can't," he says. "By the time you get home your kneecap will be spread. The ligaments at the bottom and the top will pull it apart. You've got to have surgery tomorrow morning."

I said, "Is my career done?"

He looked at me as if to say, "What kind of a question is that?" He said to me, "We've got surgery tomorrow."

So I'm dumbfounded now. I don't know what to think. They take me in the next morning. Their procedures are a little different. I'm given a needle that just about knocks me out. And I'm in quite a bit of pain. And I haven't phoned anybody back home.

I've been playing in Switzerland for the better part of a month, and nobody knows that I've been rushed to the hospital. I haven't seen Tony Currie, and I'm going right into surgery. I just remember being in the recovery room, and this oriental lady kept putting her face over top of me: "Are you OK?"

I remember this tremendous pain. Her face would come over. "Do you need something for the pain?" I would say yes. I could feel a needle in my stomach. It never worked.

So then she said, "I'm going to give you something for your pain. I've got to put it up your anus." And I didn't understand what she said. I'm drifting in and out of consciousness and I recall her plopping something up my backside. I never woke up until the next day.

## A room with Bruno

I'm in a room and sharing it with a guy who'd had open-heart surgery. He's Italian, speaks no German. His name is Bruno. I have a little German and English, and I'm in a lot of pain. They'd brought a phone into my room and I talked to Nadine and Mom and Dad. I don't even remember talking to any of them.

For about three days I was right out of it, not even coherent. I remember getting up and they had a tent-like thing and my leg was stuck in it and I wasn't allowed to move. For 10 days I had to lie perfectly still.

Finally I talked to Nadine again and she said, "Do you not remember talking to me?" She was worried that I had forgotten, had some brain damage or something. She was back in the States, pregnant with Jacob. She's thousands of miles away, thinking I've forgotten that I'm married to her.

The first person I run into that day is a physiotherapist. She comes in and tells me, "OK, You've got to tense the thigh muscles in that leg." And I am just in tears. I mean they've got drainage hoses in my knee, I've got a big scar from here to there. In the meantime she spoke pretty good English. I was concerned and said, "You know, I wanted to go back home to have surgery."

She said, "Don, you're in Switzerland. You're at Winterthur Hospital. If there's ever a country and a hospital that could put Humpty Dumpty together again, it's right here. You've had the best possible surgeon in the world."

To me, everything seemed ancient. Everything seemed ass-backwards to me, but that was just the way it was done. What they had done was put wires around the bone, stapled them, and then drilled a screw into it to tighten it all together.

It had shattered in four pieces, and I had some cartilage damage underneath it as well. For 10 days I wasn't allowed to get out of bed.

I don't know if you've ever tried to have a bowel movement in your own bed. I couldn't do it. And of course I've got a guy right next to me, and every time I get the urge the nurse shoves a bedpan underneath me and I can't go.

It was five days and they were getting upset because I hadn't had a BM. I'm eating and stuff. Bruno, the old Italian guy, would get up once in a while and come over and he'd be smiling and saying stuff. Finally I was busting one day. I had a bowel movement coming, and I wouldn't have minded some privacy.

I said, "Bruno! I've got to go to the bathroom."

He gets up and is talking away and I said, "Bruno! I've got to pooh! I've got to take a crap!"

He doesn't understand that I want him to leave. He thinks I'm talking to him. He's handing me magazines and stuff. I go, "Bruno! And I point down and say, 'Explosion!'"

He goes, "Oh! Ya Ya! Explosion!" and he goes to the door and sticks his head out, "Explosion!"

I just ripped a big one. Finally could do it. Nothing worse than having a nurse come in and clean up after you. But anyway, that was part of the indignity of being stuck in a bed.

So after 10 days they put a cast on me and I could get up and move around. Well, when you haven't moved for 10 days, have you ever sat up and tried to get up? It took me two days. I could not stand up. I'd get sick, or dizzy.

I finally got up, and the team I was playing with lost out in the next round of the playoffs, and they had a flight to get me back home.

■    ■    ■

Looking back, I had a good first season with Schwenningen. Actually I won an award that foreigners don't usually win: Defenceman of the Year, in the German league. I have the trophy upstairs. It's named after a German defenceman, and it was always given to German guys. And I won it that year, 1986-87, as a foreigner.

I was quite proud of that accomplishment. It was funny because in the first exhibition game I ever played in Germany we were up against Dusseldorf, one of the top two teams. I scored four goals. I'd never scored more than two in a game. I scored four goals and we beat them 5-4, in Schwenningen. Look at my arms; I'm getting goose bumps just talking about it.

Our stadium held 8,500 people, and it was full. They chanted my name. "Die-trich! clap clap clap! Die-trich! clap clap clap!" Every time I'd pick the puck up they'd chant my name. For three years. It was unbelievable. Everything I did, I did right in that game.

So I went from a mediocre exhibition game in Austria to my first game in front of my own people. Four goals: two slap shots, one deke, one from the slot.

I was back on defence. It felt good to be back there. And I played about 45 minutes of the game. I hardly came off the ice ever, the whole year. I was having fun. That was the biggest thing. Hockey was fun again.

## *Rated 1 or 2*

There was a hockey magazine that came out, and the press always judged you on how you played. You either had a 1, 2, 3, 4 or 5 beside your name. I always had a 1 or a 2. And I did for three years.

There were up and down periods that first season too, when it was all said and done, and then of course I shattered my kneecap in the playoffs with the Swiss team. I had a contract to go back again for a second year with Schwennigen. When you get hurt, they don't show much loyalty. Six months later I had to have the pins and wires out which happened in Germany.

It was usually an 18-month recovery for a normal person. I played my first game back on October 30, 1987. March 17th I broke my kneecap. My recovery was seven and a half months.

After getting the wires out I went to a personal trainer for three straight weeks in September and worked eight hours a day with the man. His name was Klaus. And he hardly spoke any English. I hated him. But he was the best thing that could have happened — just a different training regimen. There were guys there who played handball, soccer — they had torn their knees up. Ligaments, tendons, everything. And they worked with this guy.

The second year I went back, after I'd won Defenceman of the Year and shattered my kneecap, they'd loaded up with German-Canadian defenceman, and I played forward. And played forward for two more years. Never won an award, but still would get my 1s or 2s. The finished eighth that first year. We were below .500.

Because I'd had that big first game — been in the right place at the right time — it made my reputation. I had scored four goals as a defenceman against Dusseldorf.

Playing in Europe had clear advantages for family life. I spent more time with Tristan and Nadine. You're not always on the road. We were home. We played Friday nights and Sunday afternoons usually, so we had Monday off. Sunday afternoons at 5 o'clock we'd hop in the car and look for castles. So we toured Leichenstein and another one, Neuschwanstein, which is the castle they use at the start of the Disney. It was made by a guy who was thought to be insane. We would see suits of armor inside these castles, and the guys' average height was not much more than 5 feet.

So we would tour, and find all these. Then if somebody came over to visit, such as Nadine's Mom or my sister, we'd tour it all again. That first year, hockey wise, was fantastic. I was playing and contributing and that's what I wanted. For the family it was good, as we adjusted to the different culture.

The summer we spent in Maine. The big thing about the summer was Jacob's birth. I was there and saw the whole thing. And he was just screaming. Strong.

Family I realized was important. It allowed me to put hockey behind me. I realized I loved Nadine far more than hockey. That's when the reality came to me that I hoped to live to age 80. Ten years of pro hockey — although a big part of who I am and what I am — is a small portion of my life. I have to live 60 or 70 years without hockey. And I still have to respect people, be a good citizen, and so on. Having Tristan in my life and Nadine was my first reality of that experience. Before that it was all hockey.

I shattered my kneecap. I'm having another child. I hadn't graduated from high school yet. It's 1987. I graduated that summer. And I'm 26 years old, coming to the realization that there are other things besides hockey.

Dad used to say, I raised you kids to be good citizens and stay out of jail. There's a lot of truth in that. Nadine, Tristan and Jacob came along at a vital time in my life.

A scoring play for Schwenningen.

Die-trich! Clap, clap, Die-trich! Clap, clap. After a good game in Germany, I acknowledge the fans.

Tony Currie, a heck of a hockey player, was a good friend on the Schwenningen team.

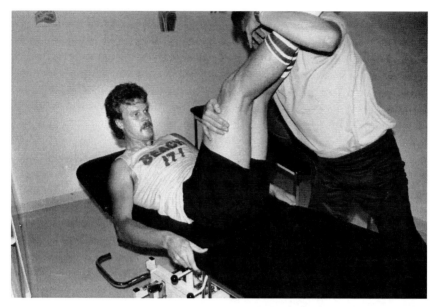

Therapy with Klaus, after a shattered kneecap in 1987. He helped me recover quickly.

With the New Jersey Devils, 1985-86.

Over in Europe.

Nadine as Miss Maine.

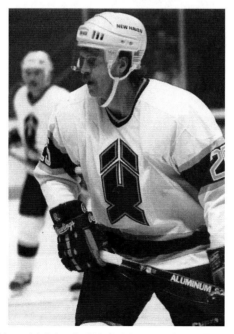

With the New Haven Nighthawks. What did a beautiful gal like Nadine see in me?

PENTHOUSE PET    NADINE GREENLAW

Tristan in his High Rider truck.

Our home in Maine.

Nick as a baby.

Jacob with me, and showing off his
great smile.

## In distinguished company

Lorne Greene, a famous Canadian actor who played Ben Cartwright on Bonanza, myself and Alan Eagleson, former hockey czar, at the Sarajevo Olympics.
From the Deloraine Times & Star, May 16, 1984.

Nick, Tristan and Jacob enjoyed playing on the pond in Maine.
This was at the end of my pro career.

Beloved family dogs Lexus, Puddy, Ranger (white face) and Genny, with my wife Nadine.

This photo was taken in Deloraine, Manitoba

This cartoon by Dave Elston pretty well sums up how many Canadians felt about the IOC ruling that prevented me from playing for the 1984 Canadian Olympic hockey team. Thanks to Dave Elston for permission to reprint it.

# Chapter 11

## ANOTHER GOOD YEAR IN SCHWENNINGEN

*"Tony Currie and I were not the most well-liked foreigners.*
*We were pretty competitive."*

ENTERING MY SECOND year in Europe, 1987-88, I had a contract with Schwenningen. Because of my injury they might have bailed on me, and maybe would have with anybody else. But because I had won Defenceman of the Year, and knowing I might miss half the season, they loaded their team with German-Canadian defencemen and kept me on.

In the meantime I had rehabbed through the summer with the doctor I saw in Maine. He pretty much told me that if I continued to play, I would likely be faced with a knee replacement by the time I was 45. I was 26, with Tristan there and Jacob just arrived. I earned my adult equivalency of a high school diploma that summer as well. I'm realizing that I have a career-threatening type of injury; but everybody seemed to think that if I rehabbed properly I'd be OK.

We had moved to a different apartment complex, a two-bedroom place in a different area. No English-speaking people around us. It was funny because we got invited across the way to suppers with a German couple. They were great. We'd just sit there and nod our heads at each other; but they were trying, and so were we.

### Knee hardware

[Don pulls out a plastic bag with pieces of wire and a narrow screw about two inches long.] That's what was in my knee. This was the wiring that was around it and clips that were stapled to it and that screw held the kneecap altogether. When I was riding a bike for rehab, those wires would heat up. My knee would look red and festered. It was a bit like taking one step forward and two back. I just never really felt that good.

They took out the wires in the Schwenningen hospital early in August. The minute I woke up from the surgery my knee felt better, even though I had a 10-inch gash on it again. They in turn took me to a guy who trained professional athletes recovering from knee injuries, Klaus, who I've already mentioned. He worked me hard, all hands-on physical therapy. He also trained the rest of my body. He told me that for a professional athlete, my conditioning was terrible. He probably wasn't far off. He felt I should have been more of a multi-athlete: play soccer, racquetball, whatever.

I was to train with this guy for 21 days, and then see where I was at. All of a sudden I'm in early September. We're playing, and there's only the one foreigner. We're struggling with putting the puck in the net, but defensively we're not bad. We had an excellent goalie.

The local press is wondering, when am I coming back? I was now on the ice. It might take six to eight weeks of skating before I can return. One night after practice we went into the restaurant near the rink, as we often did for a bite to eat or to have a couple of beers. That's where the players went. Some of the fans who came to watch practice would be in there too.

And this newspaper guy was sitting there and he spoke what I thought was pretty good English. He asked me, when are you coming back? I said, I'm not sure, but I'll come back when Don Dietrich's ready to come back, not when Schwenningen tells me to come back. But I said, it'll probably be sooner than they think.

The next day in the paper is a big story: foreigner says he won't play, even if the doctor says it's OK. So I got hauled down to the lawyer's office for the team, and they had a big flap about it. I explained to them what I had said. The newspaper guy was there and he was quite upset. He figured I was lying. His interpretation of it was, no matter what, I would play when Don Dietrich was ready to play. Which is what I was stating, but I also said it would probably be sooner than anybody thought. Maybe he lost that in the translation. Now Tony Currie and I aren't allowed to talk to the press unless we have an interpreter there.

I came back and played my first game on October 30th, which was five weeks after taking this training. The team doctors said you'll play when you're ready; only you can say that. I had been told that for the average person it would be 18 months of recovery. I was back playing after only seven and a half months.

But when I came back, I didn't play defence. I played forward. I ended up being the second-line centre who played against all the foreigners. My best quality was skating. But I'd lost about half a step from this knee injury. So I had to think a different game, and it took me a while. You learn to do your angles better, cut guys off, like a boxer in a ring when you're trying to keep somebody in a corner. You can steer them to where you want them to go, whether they know it or not.

## A point a game

For 1987-88 I played 22 games and had five goals and 18 assists, not too bad, a point a game. So I ended up doing pretty well that year. We also had an all-star game. They selected a foreigner all-star team which played the German national team, which was preparing for the '88 Olympics. We played in Dusseldorf, a major city. I was pretty excited about this because I'd never played in an all-star game. I was also excited because now I'm on a team of foreigners, and every guy out there can play.

Not that I'd had any trouble with my agent, but I'd had to sign a three-year contract to play there. This would be an opportunity to find out what kind of money the other foreigners were making in comparison to me. Tony Currie agreed that this would be a good idea.

The thing is, Tony and I were not the most well-liked foreigners. We were pretty competitive. There was an unwritten rule that you can take me out, but not too hard, when playing against foreigners on other teams. Well, we played hard. So when we went to this game, the buzz was, here are these two guys from Schwenningen. When we talked to them the first time about salaries, they brushed us off.

You see, practically every foreigner from Canada was there with this one agent. He always said, "Don't tell so and so what you're making." Even on our team, "Don't tell Tony what you're making." But we talked, and he was making more than I — which was OK. He had way better skills, he had soft hands, he was a proven NHLer. I could live with that. But if I found out that so and so on Kloten on defence was making $100,000US tax free, and I'm making $32,000, I needed to know.

That's the way I felt about things at that time. Plus I'm playing the money end of the game now, with a family at home. So at the pre-game gala, our efforts to find out what other guys were making never went anywhere. The next day at the pre-game meal the guys started to open up a bit. There was Dave Silk, who played on the 1980 Olympic team. He played in Mannheim. He liked the idea of knowing what guys made. We finally got some guys to open up. We were smart enough as players to know that Schwenningen could not pay as much as Cologne or Dusseldorf. Still, I learned that I wasn't quite where I wanted to be on the pay scale.

This is the only problem I ever had with agents: when your career is dead and gone, they still have to walk into that team office and make a living. So do they really want to risk upsetting owners by pushing too hard for you, their client? That was my theory at the time. An agent would take about three per cent to negotiate your contract, or 10 per cent to manage your funds for you. So now I've got some knowledge. I know what so and so makes, if it comes to negotiating a new contract.

We beat the German team in the all-star game. It was fun. I was all fired up after the first period. I felt I'd made a couple of bad passes, and I'm sitting there saying, "Oh, sorry, you guys." And they're all sitting there saying, "Hey, relax." I was fired up because of playing with all these good guys. I played defence. We had some Czech guys and a couple of Russians, and so on. It was a pretty neat experience, and the league did it up well. We spent three days there. After that we had the Olympic break.

In the playoffs we played Rossenheim, with this Karl Friesen in net. They were an elite team. We finished seventh or eighth. When we took them to five games, it was the first time in Schwenningen that there had been a second home game in the playoffs. We took them to the limit, a fifth game.

We lost the first game in their rink, but we came home and beat them in a shootout. It went nine or 10 rounds of the shootout, which was pretty unreal. It was a third-line guy who scored the winning goal, which meant we would be getting a second home game, which was big money in gate receipts for the team. We lost back in Rossenheim, returned to our home rink and won by two or three goals.

## National TV

Now we've got one of the best German teams on the ropes. It's down to one game. Anything can happen, and we've got the goaltender who literally won games for us, Matthias Hoppe. This fifth game in Rossenheim was on German national TV, which was a big deal.

I played forward, but I'd go back and play defence on the power play. One time we had a five-on-three power play. I was on defence. There was a face-off just outside their blue line, and they got the puck back to their defenceman. I remember the puck was wobbling and standing on end, and this guy took a slap shot. It came at my head and I'm wearing this flimsy Wayne Gretzky helmet. The puck hit me in the side of the head. I don't remember anything. What I do remember is waking up in the hospital. Klaus, our assistant equipment manager, was sitting there looking at me.

What had happened was, I got knocked out but was still on my feet. I never went down. Apparently the puck hit me, glanced up and went down to the other end. I turned and went back and picked it up. I took it out of my end and skated all the way into Rossenheim's end, then came all the way back to my end and behind the net — like I did in that game against the mothers when I was a teen.

I don't remember it. I came out of our end — remember we're on a five-on-three advantage — and I wouldn't pass the puck. I was going back and forth. Tony Currie realized I was probably out on my feet. He literally steered me over to the bench, and the coach and the players grabbed me and pulled me off. I only know this because I saw it on tape afterwards. The reports on the

TV were, what's this guy doing? And then I'm not in the game anymore. We lost the game and we were done.

What happens is, your coconut gets rattled but you're not horizontal. You're knocked out, but still skating. I didn't really think much of it, and we came home. There's the team doctor, who is our family doctor, and Nadine. They said I was rushed to the hospital and had a head injury. That's when I remember waking up and seeing Klaus. The doctor said, "You've got a concussion." I certainly had a headache.

## Paddock calls from Hershey

After a bit, an opportunity arose to play for John Paddock in Hershey, Pennsylvania of the AHL. He wanted me there. I said I'd had this head injury. This was the spring of '88. I had since negotiated a contract to return to Germany, but Tony Currie didn't. He wouldn't be back.

Tony, a right winger, played in Italy to cap off his career. Then he retired to the Maritimes. He played 13 years pro, and scored a goal on his first shot in his first NHL game. He played 22 games for the St. Louis Blues in his first season, 1977-78. In 1980-81 he had his finest NHL season, notching 55 points in 61 games, helping the Blues to a second place overall finish. In the playoffs he played probably the best hockey of his career, recording 16 points and a franchise record 12 assists in 11 games. The knock against Tony was his defensive play, though I question that. Defensive-minded coaches like Roger Neilson of the Vancouver Canucks maybe didn't make the best use of Tony's offensive talents. He retired from hockey in 1990. He finished his NHL career with 92 goals and 119 assists for 211 points in 290 games, along with 73 penalty minutes.

Anyway, I thought I'd play as much hockey as I could. Paddock and Andy Murray approached me and said, get on a plane and get over here. Andy was over in Switzerland coaching, and I'd talked to him. He was heading back to help Paddock too. In those days, there was no such thing as post-concussion syndrome. A concussion meant maybe two weeks of playing badly, and that was it. I thought I was fine, so I flew back to Hershey.

I played my first game in Adirondack, and man was I lost. I couldn't do anything right, and guys were just running the heck out of me. I couldn't get out of the way. I got thinking that after two years in Europe I can't play in this league anymore. Then I got whiplash from a hit and missed a couple of games. I kept trying to come back and couldn't do it.

What I was dealing with was post-concussion syndrome. I finally went to Andy Murray and coach Paddock and said, I can't do this. They could see I was struggling. "Yeah, you're definitely not the player you were." But nobody ever checked my head to see how I was doing.

You see, with PCS you're still dealing with the symptoms of a concussion: hampered ability to move, to think clearly, think quickly. I had no headaches then, which is why I thought I was fine. That's the only time in my career that I was knocked out. I'd had my head rattled before. And I'd seen guys out on their feet, from a fight or a hit. Lots of times. After a fight he'd seem clouded, like he was in a daze. Something wasn't right. (I'd also seen guys go horizontal and snore on the ice.)

They agreed and I agreed this wasn't going to work out. So I went back to Maine. Mike Milbury, who is now the GM of the New York Islanders, was the coach and GM of the Maine Mariners. I'd been home for about a week. He said, "Don, we're short a D. Why don't you come out and skate with us? We'll see how it goes."

It's been a couple of weeks now, and I'm over the jet lag. I do well in practice, better than I did against the guys in Hershey. I'm thinking, either these guys are worse players, or maybe I can play. Dave Silk was there, from Mannheim.

Milbury hauls me in and says, "We want to keep you."

"OK, But I want you to guarantee my German contract for next year, if I get hurt."

"No. No way. We can't do that."

I wasn't asking for a lot to play. They had about five games left in the season. I thought if I could get $5,000 plus whatever we made in the playoffs, like anybody else. I had a family to support.

I don't blame him for not doing it. He was upset with me, though. But I was in a good position: I didn't need to play. I had a contract for next year. But I wanted to play.

I decided not to take a chance on an injury. We went to Disneyland in Florida. There was a story in the paper about me not playing for the Maine Mariners. A reporter phoned, and I said I wasn't going to get into that, I'm going to Florida. That's how my season ended in 1988. Hershey won the Calder Cup that year, quite handily. I might have got another ring out of it.

The next year, I was headed back to Germany, without Tony Currie, who as I say signed with a team in Italy. I was in the third and final year of my contract with Schwenningen.

# Chapter 12

## THE BERLIN WALL AND SWITZERLAND

*"One thing about playing in Europe is that you were considered the big bad Canadian. You were supposed to be able to take a punch in the face or whatever. I think referees would turn their head if something was happening to you."*

IN EARLY 2005, Don's son Jacob was finding his feet with his new WHL team, the Lethbridge Hurricanes. A big centre, Jacob was seeing more ice time than he had in Moose Jaw. Jacob knew that even though Moose Jaw was a first-place team, the success that he wanted likely wouldn't happen for him there. He was low on the depth chart and not playing much. Being traded was best for him, because he wanted to contribute.

Jacob often talked to his Dad, who served as a sounding board. Before practice one day the Hurricanes' brass called Jacob in. They told him what they expected of him and what he needed to do. So, Don said, it's up to you. "That makes me rest easier because at least they're being up front with him. It's not always stuff that you want to hear. Like I told him, they do care, and they're just trying to make you a better player."

And how was Don's "pal," his Parkinson's? He smiles. "He still manages to bite me in the butt once in a while. I'm going into Winnipeg next week [a seven-hour round trip] for a tune-up. I'll have the batteries checked and see if there's anything they need to fine tune. It's exhausting, because they turn things off and on, and I get a little shock. He's there, my old pal!"

The shattered kneecap made me realize that I wasn't invincible. I did recover from it, but mentally it was tough. I have other things in my life now. I initially wanted to play hockey professionally for 10 years. I'm working on seven, and it's getting tough. I'm only 27 years old. The stats say the average professional career is three to five years, if you're lucky. Now I'm starting to see why. So this knee injury was a reality check.

In the fall of 1988 I'm entering my third year in Schwenningen, without my friend Tony Currie. He was a few years older. All of a sudden I've got a new foreigner, Mike Siltala. He's from Ontario and a bit younger than me, a very gifted AHL player, a natural goal scorer. I got to know him quite well. I'd played against him when he was a rookie in the AHL. He was with the Rangers' system, which would be Binghamton.

He was a pretty decent guy, and I showed him around a bit. One thing we liked to do was go down to Zurich. We'd load up in a car with our wives, maybe six of us in a car, and we'd go down and watch an English movie. By Christmas time you'd get the ones that were released in the late summer. Plus we could go to a McDonald's or Burger King, which we couldn't experience in our area of West Germany.

One time we were driving down in the fall, and we saw this flash of lightning or something. There was a reduced speed zone, and I hadn't slowed down. I was talking away. I was going 120 in a 100 km zone. Seeing that flash, I thought, is there a storm out here? What's going on? We went a bit farther along. They used to reduce the speed around towns, or in valleys where there was lots of wind. We pulled up and there were police officers pulling some cars over and moving others along. I got pulled over.

There's a German-Canadian guy in the back, and he says, "You're going to get a speeding ticket." So I played the dumb foreigner card. The officer said, "You too fast." All of a sudden he comes back with a photograph showing me plain as day. Underneath it was "121 kilometres." He actually let me off. Ignorance doesn't make you innocent, and he was kind to me.

One time we had to do a fashion show, the first year I was there, something to promote the team. There was a change room in the back of this curling rink. Then they had an outdoor rink, curling rink and then the stadium we played in. The outdoor rink was where the stage was set up for the fashion show. I remember sitting there, and I'm bent over tying my shoes.

This girl comes in, a pretty good looking girl; she flies in and takes her clothes off, and bends down right in front of me. I look up, and inches from my face were ... well! I remember thinking, people can see in. I hope my wife isn't looking. I looked down to the window and there was my coach, Billy Flynn, the Boston guy. He yells over, "What a country, eh Dieter?"

That year hockey-wise was tough. We had put in a good season the year before. That gave the team a little notoriety. All of a sudden we were starting to get some pretty good German-Canadian guys on that team. We got some better calibre German players, too. The guys who were working, who played as a hobby — they were kind of out of the way. So the expectations went higher.

## Coach Nedomansky

I had a good season, 35 points in 35 games, including 12 goals. But I'd planned on getting close to 50 points. It was a tough year in that I played forward in some games and defence in others.

The great thing about it was I had Vaclav Nedomansky as coach right from the start. He was quite a player and quite a man. His biography on the Detroit Red Wings' web site notes that in 1974, Nedomansky was playing with Czechoslovakia's national team and was considered by some to be the best player outside of the NHL. While vacationing in Switzerland that summer with his wife and child, he escaped to the West with teammate Richard Farda to sign with the WHA's Toronto Toros. "I couldn't get out legally, so I had to do it this way," said Nedomansky.

He was a star in Europe, with both Slovan Bratislava of the Czech League, for whom he scored 369 goals in 419 games and the Czech national team, registering 78 goals in 93 games for his country. He played in two Olympics, winning silver and bronze medals and led Czechoslovakia to the 1972 World Championship.

The Red Wings' piece goes on to say: *"The political battles between Czechoslovakia and the Soviet Union, stemming from the latter's 1968 invasion of the former, often carried over into athletic competition, as former Wing Mark Howe discovered while watching the Soviet-Czech game at the 1972 Olympics.*

*"To this day, I've never seen a game more brutal than that one," Howe remembered. "The Czech goalie must have broken five sticks over Russian players.*

*"The Russians were ahead in the third period and the Czechs were on the power play, with a face-off in the Russian end. They won the draw and the puck went to Nedomansky, but he just turned and wired a shot into the Russian bench."*

*That level of intensity made Nedomansky a success in North America, where he wasn't afraid to mix it up. "Defencemen around the league have just been given a king-sized headache," New York Rangers GM John Ferguson said when Nedomansky signed as a free agent with the Wings in 1977.*

*"Big Ned is an outstanding acquisition," noted Wings legend Gordie Howe, who played against Nedomansky in the WHA. "He does what Phil Esposito does in the slot – takes up space, gets the puck and snaps shots on goal.*

*"He should score 30 goals for Detroit."*

*Howe was right. In 1978-79, his first full season as a Wing, the 6-foot-2, 205-pound center scored 38 times, becoming the first player in franchise history to register hat tricks in consecutive games. Nedomansky produced 35 more goals in 1979-80.*

*His production fell off to 12 goals in each of the next two seasons and Nedomansky, 38 at the time, was let go, joining the Rangers in 1982-83, his last NHL season. After retiring, Nedomansky coached in Austria and Germany and worked as an NHL scout.*

This is the man who was now our coach. Nedomansky taught me that I had some skills that needed work, and I worked on them — skills such as passing to zones, feathering passes (not every one had to be a rocket), things like that. But now I had the guys to play with, too.

I always made an effort to learn the language, and was pretty well liked. I can remember one time, sitting at a table. For home games we always had a meal put on for us. I had been learning a bit of German through my calculator thing and they brought me my plate of food but I didn't have a knife. I figured OK, I'll ask the waitress when she comes along. She pours me some water, and I said in German, "Excuse me."

As soon as I said that all the German-speaking guys looked over, as if: what's he going to say next? So I said, I need a knife. Well, I knew it all except "knife." Couldn't remember how to say knife. Everyone's sitting there looking at me, waiting. So I try to say it in German, pronouncing it the way it's spelled in English – "kaniffee." The German-Canadian guys roared with laughter. They were just killing themselves. But at least I tried. That's what they appreciated. The waitress looked at me as if I had two heads.

## The Berlin Wall

Getting back to that season, this was the first year that Berlin was in the league. It had always been a second division team. This meant we had an overnight trip. We spent the night and flew back to Stuttgart and were home the next day.

The city of Berlin was divided into East and West Berlin by the Berlin Wall. The Wall became a symbol of the Cold War between the Soviet Union and the United States and their allies. A "hot" war is when there's actual shooting involved; the Cold War pitted the U.S. and U.S.S.R. as enemies in every other way, including hockey. The Soviets had built the wall in 1961 to prevent people in their communist country from fleeing to democratic West Berlin. Every now and then somebody from East Berlin tried to escape to freedom and a better life in West Berlin via the Wall, and ended up getting shot by Soviet guards.

We could literally walk over to the Berlin Wall. We did that after a game one time. We all went out to a bar, and decided at 2 in the morning that we're going to the Wall. We hopped in a cab, the guy drove us there, we walked out. It was a zone where a car goes through. We got out and walked over. The German-Canadian guys told the guys on the other side we were tourists,

NO GUARANTEES | *Don Dietrich*

and we were half in the bag. We were told no pictures. We just wanted to see what it looked like. We didn't spend two minutes there. Saw it — I was like, I don't want to get shot, let's get out of here. I stood back by the cab for the most part.

It was 28 years old but looked older. That's what I remember most. I would have liked to have been there in daylight. It was heavily guarded. The only lit area was where we were. They had guns over there, and I had some paranoia about that. That was one of that last times anybody saw the Berlin Wall standing, because it came down less than a year later, in 1989, as the Soviet Union began to collapse. By 1991 the U.S.S.R. ceased to exist, done in by the high cost of defence spending, corruption, and the sterility of totalitarianism. A new Russia that allowed free enterprise took its place. The West had won the Cold War. But I can say I saw the Berlin Wall when tensions were still there.

On our team, Mike Siltala was finding it difficult at the start of the season. He finally started putting some numbers up. We went to Berlin one time and he got hit into the boards really hard. He wasn't a big guy, about 5-10 and 175 pounds. The thing about Berlin is, at that time it was like New York City. It was open 24 hours. If there was anything in the western hemisphere, Berlin had it. So they were going to have a top-shelf hockey team. They paid for some top players, and some pretty rugged German guys too.

Silly got hit and was bleeding out of his mouth. He'd broken a rib, and his rib had broken through and popped his lung. He was in desperation on the ice. They took him to the hospital. This game was at four o'clock in the afternoon, which meant we could fly out that night, a Sunday. I didn't think anything of it until I got on the plane. I thought, I left that poor bugger in Berlin, at a German hospital by himself — which I knew all about from my knee injury.

I'm on the plane and I'm feeling pretty awful. Sure enough, when I went up and talked to the manager he assured me everything would be fine. I said I should have stayed. He said don't worry about it.

Well, when Mike finally got home he was pretty upset — and pretty upset with me. I don't blame him. I'm sure his experience wasn't the greatest. I felt bad. It didn't matter what I said. He missed most of the season that year. The thing was, I'm on a road trip. I'm handed a ticket, here's the gate, here's the time. He wasn't able to ask me to stay because he was in so much pain and coughing up blood.

On the plane I went through in my mind what I went through for a week in hospital. Even Tony Currie couldn't come and see me when I was in hospital because they were playing every day. And you know what? They brought in another foreigner to take my place. That was the nature of the beast. Silly ended up coming back and playing the end of the season, notching 15 goals and 20 assists over 26 games, more than a point a game. He got another goal in three playoff games.

For my third year I wish I'd had more points. Strangely enough, in 1988-89 Silly and I totaled the same number of points, 35, as I said, though it took me 35 games to his 26. Like him, too, I got one goal in the playoffs.

Now I need a contract for next year. What am I going to do? I'm talking to my agent. He says, "You know, you've got a bad leg. I don't know what we can do." He said there was a team in Switzerland that might come up from the third division to the second division. This was Lyss. I arranged to go down and talk to them.

So I went down and sat with the owner and watched a game. They were at the top of the third division, which would probably be equivalent to senior hockey in Deloraine. Local guys. Going to the second division was a pretty good step. In Switzerland, hockey was No. 1. Soccer was No. 1 in Germany.

So their first division was excellent. Their second division was pretty good too. I impressed them with my ability to speak German and with my off-ice manner. I had proven on-ice stats: Defenceman of the Year, good point totals. They were planning to get a Canadian guy for next year to come in and coach.

We never talked much about money or anything. I told them what I was expecting financially. I was looking in the area of $50,000 US tax free. I knew they could pay. I'd been making $43,000 in my third year. I had increases the three years I was there. It was not substantial, compared to where I thought I should be.

Lyss brought up the matter of my knee, which they said could be a problem. I said I'd played well the last two seasons; there won't be a problem. They ended up sending the contract to Rollie Thompson. But I'd finished my three years, so I was done with him.

I met him and he said, "Geez, it looks like a pretty good deal here. Did you talk to them about money?"

I said, "Yeah, a little bit. We didn't get into particulars about bonuses." I always had team things: 200 bucks per point the team got. At the end of the year, if we had 20 points they owed me $4,000. It wasn't based on my individual efforts but on what the team had done, which I liked. The German guys would get wind of that and like it. I wasn't worried about my points.

There were lots of games where I lost points that I should have had but I didn't make a big deal of it. That happens. In the NHL, they've got guys who sit up in the press box. If they're not sure who gets the second assist they zip it back on the camera and see who touched it. Same thing in junior hockey.

Over there it was left up to the referee and that's all there was to it. If you couldn't talk him into the fact that you deserved a point, you didn't get one. As a foreigner, it was tough to do. One thing about playing in Europe is that you were considered the big bad Canadian. You were supposed to be able to take a punch in the face, or whatever. I think referees would turn their head if something was happening to you. Lots of times you would get into situations where you wondered why there were no penalties. After games I used to have welts from sticks and stuff on my stomach and arms, the backs of my legs. I'm not complaining about it because it was just part of the game. I was aware of that when I went over.

Anyway, this contract looked pretty good. I told Rollie that I was going to sign it and put bonuses in. It was very plain compared to an NHL contract; it's just upstairs [in his house]. I took a bit of pride in it because I had done it; I had done it speaking German.

But Rollie wanted a piece of it — more than I was prepared to give him. I didn't mind that he wrote it up and made sure all the legal mumbo-jumbo was in there. But by no means was I going to give him 10 per cent, or whatever I had given him before. I was willing to give him two or three per cent for writing it up.

So we got into a bit of an argument about that, after I signed it. Lyss was small, about 600 people, half the size of Deloraine. But it was between Bern, which is a huge city, and Biel. An eight-minute train ride either way. But it was second division.

They had talked to me about this Canadian guy who was coming over. He had played at Boston College, played in Switzerland, Holland, Germany and was about 39 years old. He had been a career European player. His name was Dick Decloe, from Ontario. People told me he was a good coach. He'd been a heck of a player: five times he'd scored 50 or more goals in Europe.

## Player/coach

Lyss talked to me about being a player/assistant coach, working with the defencemen. I thought that was a pretty good deal for me. I was interested in getting into that. I was looking into the future. I had a bum leg, and this could be an opportunity. So I signed.

I also knew that Switzerland was not loyal to any foreigners. If you didn't play, you were gone. If you didn't perform, plain and simple you were out of there. And one of the things about being a foreigner at that time was, you had to be a complete player, as I've said. There were guys like John Anderson of Toronto and Hartford of the NHL, who were 50-goal scorers. They were playing with guys who could set them up. They went over to Switzerland and had no success at all. With Anderson, it was probably more what he did in that last 40 feet than what he did on the rest of the ice. There, on the bigger ice surface, those things come into play.

So I was pretty excited. Player/coach. I looked forward to it. Finally Rollie Thompson and I agreed on things, through discussion. He backed off totally. I never paid him anything. I gave him $200 at Christmas that year. He knew too that maybe my career was near its end. He knew what kind of injury I had. We had a good rapport, and we talked candidly. He knew I had talked to other players in Germany to find out where salaries were at.

I was pretty fired up about the next season, 1989 - 90. Nadine had always liked Switzerland. Everybody spoke a little more English. It was a little different culture. Bern had different shopping opportunities and different things there. It turned out that we had a pretty good palace of a place to live in, too. As a bonus, Nicholas came along in May of '89.

# Chapter 13

## MY FINAL PROFESSIONAL YEAR

*"I thought, coaching! This could be good. So I'm excited. Not a lot of money, but you've got to take what's there when you get an opportunity."*

MY 1989-90 SEASON was really interesting, to say the least. We went over to Lyss at the usual time in July. Nicholas had come along in the spring. We've got three kids and a dog now. Nicholas was a lazy baby, and I'll have more to say about that later. When we went over to Switzerland, Tristan was in Grade 1. They had a good private school just outside of Bern, which the team had agreed to pay for, an English-speaking school.

The guy who owned the team was a real-estate developer, and he put us in a palace of a house that he had just finished. We're half-way down a hill, and he's at the top. There were three bedrooms upstairs and a large living room on the level. It was on the edge of town. We had a field of cattle beside us.

Our dog, Max, a golden retriever, usually stayed close. Sometimes Max would take off and go down to the train station. We got a phone call one time from the police, who said they had our dog. They brought him home. Another time he was in a restaurant and the cook was feeding him. The police took him out of there and took him to the station. I went to pick him up, and he was lying behind this desk. He wouldn't come because these guys were treating him pretty well! He got to be pretty well known in our town. I've already mentioned the time the Swiss army bivouacked in our garage and Max stayed with them. We got him about 1987. He would have been about three.

### Knee troubles

I started playing and practising with the guys and my knee started bothering me. I kept doing the off-ice training and got on the ice and started skating and had a few practices and every once in a while it would lock up on me.

And hurt. Then I'd move it and it would snap and away I'd go. I had some concerns about what was going on. But I was afraid to say anything at the time.

To start the season we played against Davos, who had been dropped to the second division from the first. They had picked up a defenceman who was supposed to be the No. 1 guy in Switzerland, a guy named Poulin. This game was really billed as a showdown between him and me.

We ended up beating them 3-2 and I had a hell of a game. Poulin played well too. I was the player/assistant coach who was running the defence, and I developed a philosophy: "When in doubt, put yourself out," so that's what I did. I think I had a couple of points, and this guy had a goal and an assist too. But we held them off. The little rink was packed.

We were really excited. I remember the coach, Dick Decloe, going to the owner and saying, "I told you this was the guy to get." You see they had been interested in this guy Poulin, too.

But my knee was really bothering me. So I went to see a doctor who took some X-rays. He put his thumb on one spot and I just about went through the roof. He said I had some torn cartilage in there and they would have to give me the scope. I knew it wasn't going to be good because in Switzerland they don't wait. They've got special terms in their contracts that provide for insurance to take over payments if you're injured, and they replace you right away. I was scheduled for surgery in two days, and in two days a guy had taken my place.

## *Assistant coach*

He played pretty well; this was an opportunity for him. This was Mitch Lamoureux, a proven American League 50-goal scorer. He could play. It was going to be him and me, but now there's three of us, including Siltala. I get put on the back-burner. A scope takes about 10 days to get over, and this guy was playing very well. So they put me behind the bench as assistant coach. I'm skating and working out with the guys, and this went on for a couple of months. I had a tough time with it because I wanted to play and I knew now that until this guy played poorly, or somebody played poorly, I was out.

I kept a stiff upper lip, and did my best behind the bench. I watched how coach Decloe ran the bench, and he did a really good job. He always told the guys who was up next, and I learned quite a bit from him. He spoke fluent German. Everybody understood.

By about the middle of November Nick was about six months old. We'd have to prop him up with pillows. He wouldn't move or anything. I was at practice one night, and Nadine phones me down at the pub we went to afterwards and said, "You've got to come home." She was changing his diaper and he had a big ball the size of a golf ball, a hernia, a strangulated hernia. He'd been born with it. But it never showed up. She got tickling him and he got laughing, and he exerted himself a bit and up popped this thing.

So he had to go in and have surgery. This is why he was "lazy." He was dealing with pain from the time he was born, so no sense exerting himself. We took him in for surgery, and Nadine was there in the hospital with him. This took top priority with our family. Finally he came home. The doctor said he shouldn't exert himself too much, and he's got a gash from surgery two and a half inches long.

Now, as soon as he comes home, I've got a kid who is just squirming. We can't keep him still. He's pushing and wild. Before he never moved and all of a sudden he's bouncing all over the place. The pain he was experiencing from the surgery was far less than that of the hernia.

From that day on, Nick has been daring and active. All of a sudden we had to baby proof the house. Within a month he's standing and walking, holding himself up, just flying all over the place. Even now he's very active, he does flips, he plays hockey on the edge. He plays forward for the Triple-A Midget Cougars out of Souris, Manitoba. He's 16 as I speak, in December 2004, and he plays with no fear.

Anyway, that was a good outcome. But now I'm worried. Is my hockey career over? It gets into November and the guy they brought in is having some trouble, so I got back in the lineup as a forward. So now we've got two foreigner forwards playing.

## Good numbers

Statistically, I ended up having an incredible year: 24 goals and 22 assists for 46 points in 36 games. I had never scored that many goals in my life. Everything I touched turned to gold. We ended up in the relegation round, which is not a good thing as far as the team goes, but the team probably played 50-some games that year. I maybe missed 14 of them. And then they had a playoff after that which consisted of 20-some games, during which I picked up eight goals and 22 assists.

I was over there for a long time, and it was grinding, day after day. That's why you never wanted to be in those relegation rounds, because it was the bottom two, which we were, and the top two from the third division. We ended up staying in that second division.

Our last league game that we played was against Davos again, but in Davos. At this point the guy who had replaced me had left, and we'd brought another guy in that I had played in Moncton with. Lamoureux had also hit the wall a little bit, but this guy never did get into a game. So that's the pressure of being in Switzerland; they don't waste any time. If you're playing badly, they oust you.

Because the coach, Dick Decloe, knew of my interest in coaching, he let me run the bench by myself in this last game. I didn't play; I stood behind the bench. It was a nothing game, for them and for us. They were finishing at the top, and we were ninth or so, and relegated down. So the game meant nothing in terms of the standings, but it was a good move by him because the guys really played for me.

We ended up beating them. They were responsible for the win; I was the guy who drew up the plan. And it worked. A totally different feeling came over me. I was so happy. I'd never had that feeling in hockey before, a different sense of happiness — not the warrior, tired and sweaty, hurting but victorious kind of happy. I was the general who had strategically put guys out there and it worked, kind of happy. So I was pretty fired up about that, and it gave me a good sense of maybe where I wanted to go in hockey. I'll just never forget that feeling.

At year end, I didn't get any offers. I didn't have an agent anymore because I'd negotiated my own deal and had maybe burned a bridge or two as I'd gone along. So I thought, well, my phone isn't ringing anymore. We went back home to Maine. I got home later than usual, April 28 or 29; we used to be done in February or March.

Lyss was not at all interested in my coming back, even though I'd had a good season, because I had a bum leg. It's just the way they think over there. As a foreigner, you've got to be healthy. You've got to be the total package. I'd lost half a step. There were 14 games I missed, and that's a big for them. You just don't miss 14 games.

I've mentioned NHLers who couldn't make it in Europe. But if you could get in there, you could make some money. However, they had ways to get you out. And of course it spread throughout Europe that I had a bum knee. If I do talk to somebody, they say, "What happened? You missed 14 games."

## Home to Maine

After the scope, I never had a problem, though I was bit slower. They had a point. So I go home to Maine, and we've got three kids now. We had a place with a pond. We had bought a house in 1988 and it was getting small, so we put another level on it and I helped the guy pound nails.

Nadine went back to work. She bartended. There was pretty good money in bartending, in tips. I tried to find some work. In the late 1980s and early 1990s there was a recession. The cost of living was high, and $6 or $5.50 was the minimum wage. I worked for a temporary employment agency where you just went out and loaded trucks or whatever. There wasn't a lot of work there. I had saved some money and put a lot of money down on the house. In that nine years I had probably saved $50,000, and maybe earned $325,000 over that nine years, which is a pretty good living.

We put $30,000 down on the house to bring the payment down. Basically we had about $20,000 to try to live off of and with three kids, two in diapers still, that goes pretty quick. We were sitting at home and it was the end of

November and we'd had a pretty cold fall there. The pond had frozen over. It was about a mile wide and a mile long.

Tristan had shied away from hockey in Europe, being a foreigner and you know how kids can be, but on the pond he'd get all dressed up and we made a little rink out there. My neighbour had a small plow on his Chevy S10 and he'd plow us off a spot. So I'm out there skating with the kids every chance I get.

## Farrish phones

All of a sudden I get a phone call from Dave Farrish. He's coaching in Moncton. I'd been in Moncton with him when we'd played in the Calder Cup. He was an older guy who had played in the NHL, and he took me under his wing a little bit. He said, "You know, I'm hurtin' for D, and we're in Hershey, and I really need you to come and play."

And I said, "Geez, I haven't been doing much in that line. I haven't given it much thought."

"Well, have you been on the ice at all?"

"Yeah, I've been skating on the pond with my kids."

"OK, there's a plane ticket down at Portland for you. Get your ass down here to Hershey." So I go down to Hershey.

"We just need you for the weekend. I've only got three D."

I go in, and it's early in the year and I'm in the lobby waiting for the players to come down, or Dave Farrish to come out. And I'm starting to watch these guys. They're just like titans. I hope he's on my team. Great big guys, 6-4, 220, and young.

Farrish comes down and takes me into the restaurant. "We'll sign you to an amateur tryout (which is 25 games)."

They're not tied to me and I'm not tied to them. We put a dollar figure on the game. He said, "We'll give you $600 a game." Well, $1,200 for a weekend's work, that's pretty good. I got talking to him and he said, "Yeah, I've only got three D." I thought he was exaggerating. He said, "You're going to play."

Sure enough I played. We won that game 3-1. I got an assist in that game, and just played a ton. Tried to hold my own out there, and played well, though out of shape and sweating away. When I got up the next morning I ached so bad. That's one thing I never missed, the pain of getting up. We had to play the next night again. I had the Heat out. I'm taking Advils and everything I can to get loosened up, and we go out the next night and we beat them 2-1 and I had two assists.

Farrish is happy. This is great. He says, "You know what, I'm going to take you back to Moncton to see if they'll keep you around for the year." Moncton was the farm team of the Winnipeg Jets.

So I went back to Moncton and spent two days practising with them, but

Winnipeg wouldn't sign me to anything. They just said get him out of there. Send him home. Well, I was there because guys were hurt and they had call-ups. I'm not in their plans. I'm 30 years old with a bum knee. Even though it wasn't a lot of money they were paying me.

I go home, and I'm sitting at home for about three days and the phone rings. It's Pat Hickey. He's coach and GM of the New Haven Nighthawks. LA is their parent team. I had played with a guy by the name of Murray Bromwell who had suggested that if they had a chance they should grab me. I might fit into their picture.

So I signed another 25-game amateur tryout, based on me making $24,000 a year. I thought, well, the phone isn't ringing. I'm not having much luck in the job market where I am. I'll give it a try.

And Hickey says, "You know, I've got Nick Fotio here as assistant coach." He was a Rangers tough guy. I knew him a little bit. "The AHL has cut our rosters by one. Now we're down to 19 players. Instead of having four lines of three and six defencemen, they have six defencemen and three lines with a spare." They want that spare guy to be able to play defence or forward, or sit out, or come down between periods with evaluations of what was going on.

So I'm excited. Coaching and playing. Not a lot of money, but you've got to take what's there when you get an opportunity.

## East Coast League

So I went there in December of 1990 and had to leave the family at home. That was tough. They sent me to Roanoke of the East Coast League for two games of conditioning. I'd never played anything less than AHL. I had one assist and eight penalty minutes. The old East Coast League — she was pretty rugged!

I ended up dressing for 13 games for New Haven and probably sat out 20 or so. All I was asked to do was stay in shape and be that guy who could be there when asked, and come down and give my two cents' worth.

Lots of times I'd be sitting out and I'd run into different guys. Bob Murray was scouting for the Blackhawks. We didn't make the playoffs. We were actually a pretty bad team. So I went home, and a week later it was announced that Hickey and Fotio were let go. No more farm team in New Haven. They were strictly going to stay out in Phoenix. My in was now out.

But, that was my 10th year of professional hockey. As I stated before, I wanted to play 10 years of pro hockey. And I had done that. But realistically, it was done. I'm probably in that 85 to 90 percentile of players who aren't ready for it to be done. Some guys are ready to be done, they accept it, they're financially set. I wasn't ready at all. That's a whole other chapter, life without hockey.

# Chapter 14

## LIFE WITHOUT HOCKEY

*"I was looking at a $7 an hour. Same with Nadine. Here we are, we're trying to keep the family unit together, we're working 18-19 hours a day, both of us. And still not making it."*

WHEN I GAVE motivational speeches, I put together a tape of some of my highlights of playing in the NHL. I scored no goals in the NHL, but one thing I always used to dream about as a kid was having the announcer at Maple Leaf Gardens, Paul Morris, say my name. He had that monotone voice; he was great. It would be: "Toronto goal, scored by number 27, Darryl Sittler, assisted by number 10, Errol Thompson."

It was funny because when I got traded to New Jersey and ended up playing with them, it was a Hockey Night in Canada game. It was the first night they used a new slow-motion replay device. We scored the first goal on the power-play. I shot the puck, and it looked like I scored. But Doug Sullivan on our team deflected it from the slot, and of course the slow-motion replay showed it clearly.

I got an assist. At that point we were still on the power play because the guy had a double minor. On this video I've got, it shows — and I laugh when I show the kids because I tell them how long I waited for that moment to hear that guy say my name — I was still on the ice when they announced our goal. And of course as Morris is going through it all I'm standing on the blueline, listening. "New Jersey goal, scored by number 22, Doug Sullivan, assisted by number 5, Don Dietrich." Then all of a sudden the puck goes whizzing by me and I thought, "Oh oh! I'd better get playing!"

The Leafs had won the face-off and shot the puck down and I hadn't even moved yet! On the tape you can see how late I actually turned and went back to pick it up. The hair on my back was standing up.

Paul Morris was an institution at the Gardens. He held the job for 38 years, from October 14, 1961 to 1999, working 1,585 consecutive Leaf games. "His dispassionate, monotone voice was instantly recognizable to two generations of Leaf fans," says an article in Wikipedia.

Morris's father, Doug Morris, was an electrician at Maple Leaf Gardens from its opening in 1931. Morris began working at the Gardens in the summer of 1958 while a college student. He quit school and stayed at the Gardens, becoming PA announcer three years later when Red Barber left.

When the team moved from the Gardens to the Air Canada Centre in February 1999, Morris was not given a full-time job at the new building. Instead, he was offered $300 a game to continue as announcer. He finished the season and then retired at age 61. Andy Frost was hired as his successor in September. At the Leafs' 1999-2000 home-opener on October 4, 1999, Morris was honoured during a pre-game ceremony. In the third period, he announced "last minute of play in this period" one last time.

I liked those announcers we grew up with. Whenever I came back home to Deloraine and played senior ball, or went golfing with Dennis Olischefski and others, I'd do a Dynasty Royals play-by-play. All-star guys. Players from the past that I could remember as a kid. I'd have them playing the Canadiens, with Lemaire, and J. C. Tremblay, and guys like that. The guys used to laugh. I don't think I did it very well but of course when you have a couple of beers in you, you think you're pretty good!

Play-by-play man Danny Gallivan had real style, and I used to mimic him. "This is Danny Gallivan high atop the gondola, for this game between the Canadiens and the Deloraine Royals. You can feel the electricity in the air." Then he'd go into the weather. "And the weather in Montreal is partly cloudy, with intermittent drunken spells," which is how I used to say it. "Face-off to the left of Gary Ewen (of Deloraine). It's the Canadiens now. Everybody up. Oh, a Savardian spinnerama, and oh! a cannonading drive but Dryden threw out his glove in rapier-like fashion. It's the Royals now applying lots of intestinal fortitude." He had all those sayings. "And the puck was tied up in big Chartrand's paraphernalia."

Then there was Dick Irvin. Gallivan used to say, "And you know, Dick, I had lunch with Guy Lafleur the other day, and he said he was going to let that shot go." He was always having lunch with somebody.

I don't remember much of Foster Hewitt, except for the 72 Summit Series. They brought him out of retirement for that job. He was the original radio announcer in Toronto, and then he went on to TV and Hockey Night in Canada. "Hello Canada, and hockey fans in Newfoundland and the United States," he'd say, or words to that effect. What many people don't know is that he kept tabs on what was going on in amateur hockey, such as York University hockey in Toronto, and he would go to the rinks to see any up-and-coming players, even in his later years. He'd try to hide by pulling his coat collar up so people had less chance of noticing him. He was elected to the Hockey Hall of Fame in 1965 and he passed away 20 years later, at age 83.

Another man I want to mention is Archie Henderson. Archie played 11 years pro, mostly AHL, with stints in the NHL. He was a notorious bad guy, a tough player, at 6-6 and 225. He was near the end of his career when I played against him in Maine. He was about 34 then. Sometimes I played left wing and he played right wing. I never had a fight with him, but sometimes we'd have these little run-ins.

And then we traded for him. In the dressing room and everywhere else we sat, Archie sat to my left. In our regular rink, he was the stall next to me. In the practice facility, he was the stall to my left. In the bus, he sat in the row in front of me to my left. And I used to talk to him. I'd be getting ready and tying my skates, and sometimes he'd never answer me. He wouldn't even acknowledge that I was there.

I'd say, "How are you this morning, Arch?" or whatever. Nothing. Sometimes I'd say something and he'd just turn and go, "Huh!?" And I'd just jump. I'm thinking, the guy still hates me. This went on for about a month, through games, practices, on the bus, or whatever. I really was getting a complex thinking that this guy must really hate me.

Finally one day at practice I said something to him and he never answered me. I said, "Arch, what's wrong? You don't like me, or what?" He turned to me and said, "What?" He said, "I'm deaf in my right ear." We turned out to be the best of friends.

## The Baron of Bedlam

Archie was a character. He stood out in a crowd. His nickname in the AHL was the Baron of Bedlam. And he had one of the best quotes I've ever heard. He was with Halifax, and we were in the playoffs. It was a game in Maine, and it went to a third period of overtime. They scored on us with about two minutes left, so essentially we'd just about played two entire games. It was one o'clock in the morning. Archie hadn't played a shift the whole game.

Right away the local newspaper guy picks up on that and is over talking to him. "Geez, you didn't play, Archie."

And Archie says, "You know what? I've sat games out before. But I've never sat out two games in one night."

But that wasn't the best part of what he said. He then said, "I'm like a gun in a bank robbery. I don't have to be used to be effective." Which was true. Just knowing he was on the bench made us all think, "We'd better watch what we do out here." It was a very true quote. We didn't want to deal with Archie Henderson.

Archie had other good quotes too. There's a website called the Biofile by Scoop Malinowski that carries a story Archie tells about playing junior:

"I got on a bus when I was 17 to go play junior hockey. And I actually got cut from the hockey team. The next day I showed up at practice with my equipment on and went out on the ice and skated around with the team. The coach skated over to me and said, 'Hey, Archie, I thought I cut you yesterday.' I looked at him and said, 'You did, coach. But that was yesterday.' I went on and played 700 pro games [he laughs]."

One time his wife said to him, "Archie, you love hockey more than you love me." Archie replied, "That's true, darling. But I love you more than I love baseball [he smiles]."

On the same website Archie says the toughest men he ever fought were Barry Beck, Behn Wilson and Bob Probert: Beck was the strongest, Wilson the meanest, and Probert the guy with the most stamina. He'd take your best punch and then knock you down. He ranks Probert #1. During his first two shifts in the NHL Archie fought Behn Wilson twice. Archie Henderson topped 200 minutes in penalties seven times before retiring in 1988. He then turned to coaching.

Henderson lives in Calgary now, where he was born in 1957. For 10 years he scouted for the Washington Capitals. In 2007 he started scouting for the Ottawa Senators. I see him around at the rinks once in a while. Guys used to play jokes on him. We'd be at a hotel and somebody would order a dessert tray to his room. Then we'd all push into the room, eat up and go, "Thanks, Arch!" Meanwhile, he got billed for the food.

When we first moved back here it was my birthday, April 5, and the Wheat Kings were in the playoffs. We went over to the Keg and were having supper with the family, and we were going to the Wheat Kings game afterwards. I'm sitting there and I notice Al Arbour is in there and some high-up guys in the NHL.

I'm sitting there eating and all of a sudden I hear this, "Yup! Don Dietrich. Best darned hockey player I ever played with!" I look up? It's Archie! Hadn't seen him for years. He comes over and shakes my hand and what does he send us? Desserts. But he paid for them. I thought he was going to pay me back!

[In talking to the editor, Archie said they had a lot of fun in those days. "We didn't get rich financially, but we became rich from the experience."]

■　　■　　■

We all found ourselves in the minor leagues for a reason. You've got the five to 10 per cent superstar players, the Gretzky-type guys. Then there are another 60 per cent of guys who are in the right place at the right time. Then there are 20 or 30 per cent on the bottom who can fluctuate in between. A lot of it is being on the right team, and having things work out for you.

At that level, if you've got talent you're going to get up. There were some career minor-leaguers who played 800 to 1000 games, but there would be a deficiency in their game somewhere.

I was in that position too. The average pro career at that time was three to five years. That's why I wanted 10, even though it was six years in North American and four years in Europe. It's short-lived. There are a lot of mental things that you've got to deal with. It's an emotional roller coaster. As my story shows, one day you're here, the next day you're there. It's the same in a game: one shift you score a goal, and the next shift it's your fault when you let a big one in and miss an assignment.

I think at the time, I was probably a little bitter about not getting more of a chance to play in the NHL. But hindsight is 20-20. I've got a son who's experiencing things now, and I find that harder to deal with than when I played. Sometimes I wonder, but when you get to those levels it's a business. It really is. It's about dollars and cents. When I wasn't happy with a situation and wanted to be traded, my agent would say, "If you simply fall out of bed for the next couple of years, you make x amount of dollars."

And I would say, "I don't care about that. I just want to play."

And he would say, "You sure cared about it when I was drawing up your contract. Money was the issue." And he was right to a certain degree.

Today, with the salaries as high as they are, there's more pressure. Even guys that scout have to do a good job. You recommend a player, they dump a bunch of money into him and he turns out to be a flop, you might not be scouting anymore. You've got to really do your homework and pay attention and do your job.

Being over in Europe for four years, I lost contact with guys on this side. I was probably in that percentile of players who weren't prepared for hockey to be over.

*"No doubt about that," says Nadine from the kitchen.*

When I was done, we put an addition on our house that spring. It was 1991. I helped the guy with that. I really dragged my feet, trying to get into something else. It was a tough time on the east coast. They were experiencing a recession in the early '90s. There weren't a lot of well-paid jobs out there.

I tried to hang on to the hockey end of things. I sent letters out. I never got any response back. So in the meantime in early June, I went down to a golf course that had just opened. I applied for a job to work in maintenance. I didn't hear from them for about a week.

They'd looked at my application. I've since found out it was, "Hmmm, professional hockey player, $6.50 an hour. Well, maybe." People didn't think I was going to work for that. But that's what was basically out there. So I ended up being hired and I carried a weed wacker around for about two months straight. That's all I did. Cleaning up the rough, and around trees. If it rained, we were told to go home, and you went without pay. So I used to work in the rain.

We had some money saved, but with three young kids, and two of them still in diapers, it goes fast. Nadine was working two jobs at that time, Stable Oaks and Olive Garden, bartending. And she was teaching modeling.

We'd put a lot of money down on our house to get our mortgage payment reasonable. Any house you were buying was $100,000 plus. We'd bought it in '88. But we weren't making it. We were still dipping into the savings. We got through the summer, and it wasn't working out well. I was wishing I was still playing. But I wasn't working out or anything. I'm 31.

I wasn't prepared for it to be done. I started drinking more, smoking cigarettes more. We had a fourth of July party, and I got pretty tanked up. We had a boat then and I'd do this "Canadian water skier" shtick. I'd stuff a pillow under my T-shirt and go out and take off on the water and the crack of my butt would be showing. Of course I'd be half in the bag. My brother-in-law Dave was over and we're playing volleyball and he went to jump up and his feet went out from underneath him and he came down splat on the ground.

I know Tristan used to be quite disgusted with me. I had to get up at a quarter to five to be at work at 5:30 to start mowing. I think that night we went to bed at about 2 a.m. I had a couple of hours sleep and got up and headed down to work and stopped at a convenience store on the way in and bought myself a muffin, a big coffee and a pack of cigarettes.

I went into the maintenance shed where we worked, and was a little bit late. Some of the guys were already in there, and were sitting and having their coffee. The shed was just filled with cigarette smoke.

*On that fourth of July [Nadine adds] Tristan got mad at him, and went in the house and started crying because he was drunk. Tristan would have been nine or 10.*

Tristan never liked me drinking.

*No. And that's when he went in the house crying.*

Right, and this adds to what happened in the maintenance shed. I had a pang of conscience about what had happened with Tristan. I'm hung over, there's all this smoke, and that was it. I took the cigarettes out of my pocket and threw them in the garbage. And I vowed from that day on that I wouldn't have a drink or a cigarette again.

*You also had a scare. They found something in your throat. And once you found out you were OK, you started smoking again.*

I did, didn't I.

*Yes. And I got so mad at you, because, like anybody who finds out they're OK, you started smoking again. Then, you stopped smoking. And I give you tons of credit for that. It is an addiction, and I was very proud of him that he did quit.*

I had these polyps on my throat. They went in and chopped a bunch of them off. Now I don't even drink an occasional beer. One's too many. Because then 24 wouldn't be enough.

*He had a problem with alcohol.*

When I look back on it now, I drank way too much. I was an alcoholic. I was by no means a bad drunk or anything, and neither was my Dad. I don't go to AA meetings or anything like that. I just quit. I'd get plastered, and then I'd start bumming cigarettes from people. That's just the way it went. In those days it was common. It wasn't brought out as a problem until later years when you had John Kordic who died of a cocaine overdose in 1992, at age 27. He also used steroids and drank to excess.

You see, we were all small-town farm guys. Drinking was part of the culture. We never went to the golf course here without a cooler of beer. You never played ball without stopping afterwards and having beer. Small town, to an extent, means alcohol. And I don't mean to say bad things about small towns. Remember the Craig MacTavish incident? MacTavish, of the Edmonton Oilers, drove drunk and killed a woman and was imprisoned in the U.S. for vehicular homicide in 1984. That was when you didn't get off for being an athlete anymore.

Financially too, it's tough. Cigarettes and alcohol were things I couldn't afford. I really couldn't. So that summer went by. I only had a seasonal job. The guy liked me, this Chuck Welch. But he couldn't keep me on full time. So I ended up working at a place called Jordan Foods. We loaded trucks by hand. They went to all the little ma and pa stores and delivered food: frozen steak, everything that was boxed. They were packed, tight, individually, from the last load to the first load. The left side had to be heavier because the road was crowned. I started at 8 o'clock at night. I'd never worked a night job before.

I get in there and I'm totally lost. They've got a guy who reads the stuff off; he's called the picker. We set it on pallets all the way around. He calls the number, they put it on a roller and down it comes. The worst job I ever had in my life. I get hired for $7-something plus night shift differential and overtime. It turns out that it's not bad money. But these guys are all over me because I'm an ex-hockey player.

There's one guy in particular, an older guy, who is nasty. We'd go out with these pallet jacks. I'd go and pick up the next truckload that we'd have to do and if I didn't set it right out of the way so that he could get by he'd start yelling at me and giving me heck. I wasn't used to that. The first night I'm there I'm overwhelmed. The other guys were younger than me and had done it for three or four years. They were throwing 100-pound meat boxes down this roller thing.

I was out in the colder area where the cooler was. We'd finished a truck and I wanted to go and get another sweatshirt on. So I went into the change room and came back. These guys thought I was quitting, because that's what usually happened. I said, "No way. They weren't going to get to me." So I learned how to load the trucks and ended up doing a pretty good job. But I still hated it. And I had run-ins with this older guy.

They had alleyways where they picked stuff off and this guy used to help the second-shift guys when they were behind, do some picking. So I went back down to pick up a pallet load. It was in a big warehouse. I purposely set my stuff right in his way. He stopped. And I confronted him. I just told him, "This is going to stop. Otherwise we're going to settle it right here, right now."

And he got down off of his forklift, a big gruff guy.

I said, "Just remember one thing. You beat me up in here, you'd better make sure I'm either dead or knocked out, because I'll run over you in the parking lot with my truck."

And he backed off and didn't say anything. He could see I was serious. He never bothered me again. We stayed away from each other. So that made it a little bit better, and I worked my way in there with those guys. They used to make it look like they were picking up this heavy box, and it would be empty. They'd throw it to me and I'd go to grab it. They'd fire it way up in the air and all have a big laugh.

So I started doing stuff like that back to them. We ended up being one of the faster groups of guys. I'm pretty good at memory recall and so I used to remember numbers and things and how to pick them. I learned to stack trucks really well. The first couple of trucks I did spilt on the driver. So when he came back, he gave me heck.

Then I got some bursitis in my left shoulder. I was off work for a little while. And when I came back, one night I was on a break, and I had left a drink out in the truck. I went to get it and who was out there but Chuck Welch. This is about February.

"Don," he says, "there's some new people bought the golf course. I can have a full-time assistant and I want you to be it."

I said, "You've got it."

He said, "You'll be salaried" — and it wasn't much; it was $17,000 a year — but he said "you'll have to get a spray-applicator's licence for pesticides and stuff like that. You can start next week."

So I said fine, and went back in to see the shift manager. I gave him my two-week's notice. He wanted to know why.

I told him my old boss has offered me an assistant superintendent job at the golf course. I'd only worked for him for five or six months. He didn't seem too impressed.

The next day I came in and the plant manager was there. He called me into the office and said, "What are you doing?" I said I have another job. It's out-doors and I like that. It's different every day from what I'm doing here. I said working nights is terrible. It was hard because Nadine had three jobs and we still had kids at home and I'd work all night. She'd work all day and into the night. Jacob is four or five, Nick's two or three, and they need attention. We can't afford baby-sitters or anything like that. It was a rough transition.

*We always had family. My sister was a big help. And my mom. And we did have a neighbour who the kids would stay with at night.*

That two-year period after hockey was tough. When I got done at this place, the plant manager was upset. "Gee, we had plans for you. Not many people come in here like you did and work." I asked him what he meant.

"Well, you'd be a good guy to drive truck and deal with the public. Sales, or something like that."

I said, "I like this other job." I just didn't like the place. But I did it or tried to do it as best I could.

This golf course job would be a little more money. I started there at Sable Oaks Country Club in February and worked through the spring. Nadine worked at the Merriot, which was part of the country club. She bartended there a couple of nights a week. What happened was, they needed a doorman at their bar. So I ended up being a bouncer as well.

Sometimes I'd go right from working at the golf course to there, till two or three in the morning. And now that I'm the assistant, I have to make sure I'm at the course, and that all the equipment is gased, oiled, checked, so I'm there half an hour before anybody. There were lots of nights when we functioned on two or three hours of sleep. When we finally had a couple of days off we'd just sleep.

We had a tough time. We went through the money saved. We needed the help of Nadine's mom, her sister, the neighbour down the road. We had a period of time when we were on food stamps. We were getting assistance, to have heating oil for our house. But not once did our kids ever know that we were in that position. I think that's something that we pride ourselves on.

Given the past that we had, we'd been living pretty well. Then, within a year and a half, we're struggling. We lost our boat, had to sell it. It was a tough time.

*In Europe, we'd been used to having money. People say, you're a hockey player and you were a model. They think you have tons of money.*

Everybody knew Nadine, and knew me, because we were in a small-town area. Of course I never told anybody back here what was going on. We used to have a lady that lived down the street, who used to leave groceries at our door. That was a tough pill to swallow. No matter what I was doing, I was looking at $7 an hour. Same with Nadine. Here we are, we're trying to keep the family unit together, we're working 18-19 hours a day, both of us. And still not making it.

The cost of living was so high. Our mortgage payment was $600 a month. And we'd put $30,000 down on the house. We paid cash for our car. I was driving an old beater of a truck, a 1980 Chevy, straight six. We didn't have health insurance. If the kids were sick, they went to the doctor. If Nadine and I were sick, we didn't go. It was $45 a doctor's visit. But as assistant superintendent, I was under their plan. So add $600 a month to it as well.

We slowly got out of it and were doing all right. But there was that adjustment period. And I repeat: I sent out resumes. I wanted a scouting job, I wanted to stay in hockey. Nothing available. I phoned people. I phoned Kelly McCrimmon in Brandon, a good friend of mine, GM of the Wheat Kings who later became owner. He said, "What do you want?"

I said, "I want to stay in hockey."

"What have you been doing for the past two years?"

"Working at a golf course, and I loaded trucks."

"Well, your problem Don is that you're a young guy with a young family. If I'm hiring a full-time scout, that guy's going to be gone 30 days a month. I know that you with three kids aren't going to be there all the time doing that job."

So they hire a 26-year-old who's had two or three years of pro, or somebody whose kids have all grown up and they're retired. Then, as the salaries rose in the later '90s, how can somebody justify hiring you when you haven't been in hockey for five years? I still clung to the hope that somewhere down the line I'm going to get back into hockey.

When I talk about character people, Kelly McCrimmon is definitely one of them. He and I roomed together, and I respect him a lot. I played two years of junior with him. You always knew where you stood with him. He went to the University of Ann Arbor, Michigan, on a scholarship. Took business. He came back and ran the family farm for a while, then got into coaching in senior or Tier II and continued on, ending up where he is now.

To this day, when I deal with things with my son, I can phone Kelly. He's somebody that was there for me when I was taking chemotherapy. They told me there was nothing more they could do. I went over to see him one time and he literally broke down and hugged me. He told me: "If you need an MRI in the States, I'll pay for it." He's a straight-forward guy. I love him. Like I said, my best friendships were forged in junior hockey.

Some of the guys I called I'd met in pro and they stayed in pro, having kissed the right butt or whatever. Now it was, "What are you phoning me for?" I can understand it now that I see where they're at. I've been out of hockey since '91. It's 2005 — 14 years.

I am doing a little scouting, for the Spokane Flyers. They know my health isn't the greatest. They ask me to look at some kids and I do that. Or look at an age group and I do that. I've probably been to about 18 or 19 games. It works around Nicholas and his Triple A too. And I don't make any money at it. My expenses are paid and that's it. It's something else that keeps me busy right now.

Sometimes when things aren't great you tend to forget them — and forget them very quickly. My first two years out of hockey weren't great. I'm glad Nadine was here to help piece them together. I try to be positive, but that's tough to do sometimes.

# Chapter 15
## DIAGNOSED WITH PARKINSON'S

*"He kept saying, 'I have Parkinson's disease. That's just part of me, but it overwhelms the rest. I might be a good gardener, but people never talk about my flowers. They always talk about Parkinson's'."*

IN THE SPRING of 1993 I was asked to be the assistant superintendent at the golf course. I was responsible for workers now, and making sure jobs were done. I liked it. I learned to use a back hoe, front-end loader, drive a dump truck, even a bulldozer, when we were doing course repairs. Every day it was outside and every day it was different.

We'd start at six in the morning and work till noon, and everybody had certain jobs. We had no coffee break or anything. We had about 300 golfers a day, so we used the morning to get ahead of them as much as possible. The afternoons were easier.

The biggest thing about 1993 would be the first discovery that I maybe had a problem. We had ice buckets that we filled to take ice to the coolers. I was out with one of the kids we hired, and I'm filling this water cooler with a scoop. The boy says to me, "What's wrong with your arm?" What he was seeing was my right arm flailing away a bit behind my back. I'm right handed. Yet I was scooping ice with my left.

A Parkinsonism is when you're doing something, and you can't control the other side of your body. Anyway, I should have been scooping ice right handed. And as the rest of the day went on, I stopped and looked at my hands. I had calluses on my left hand, none on my right. My wallet was in my left pocket, as was all my change. What had happened was, I had lost the fine-tuned skills of taking my right hand and getting it in my pocket. It was troublesome. So was turning a screwdriver. I couldn't do it with my right hand. Unconsciously I had adjusted to that.

I got in the car to drive home. I drove a 1984 Grand Jeep Grand Wagoneer. I always drove with my right hand on the wheel and my left elbow out the window. Now I notice I'm driving with my left hand; my right arm, tense, is on the arm rest. I have some concerns, but I don't say anything to anybody. I make mental notes and notice that anything that's fine-tuned, such as fixing a sprinkler head, I do left-handed.

I went through the summer of '93 wondering and dealing with that. I said nothing to Nadine. I had to wait 90 days before my health insurance would kick in, which it did that summer. I finally went to Nadine in the fall and talked to her. She had noticed that it was true, and urged me to see a doctor.

## Saw a neurologist

So I went to a neurologist in Portland, Maine. This lady doctor said we may have to get a CT scan, which was going to cost $2,200US. She suggested some medications, which were for Parkinson's. When she mentioned that word I'd try to change the subject. I tried one of the medications, and it just made me sick. Really sick. She said it could take a month to take effect, without any other real explanation.

I went back to her after a few weeks and told her I didn't like its effects. "Well," she said, "it's not so bad. Just thank God you're not a brain surgeon." And that's the way it was left. I noticed as the winter wore on that I had more rigidity in my right arm. It was tense as I drove in traffic.

In the spring of 1994 my parents phoned and said the ice cream shop in Deloraine was for sale. They thought we might have some interest in doing that. We were just getting back on our feet again. Nadine was working as a real estate agent and having some success. I was at the golf course, which was owned by a man named Friel. He owned a number of others as well.

Nadine's mom had run ice cream places, and Nadine had worked in them. We thought it might not be a bad deal. We flew to Deloraine in March, and it was thawing. Things looked pretty good. And we talked to people on council here about the possibility of me being a recreation director. Not only the business was for sale; this house was too. It was part of the deal.

Nadine liked the fact that the kids could walk down the street, safe. We thought Deloraine would be a good place to raise the kids. We were pretty set where we were in Maine, so we thought we'd make a low offer, and if they say no, fine. If yes, we'll move.

They accepted our offer. Now we've got to get back here! This was early April, and we've got a house that has to be rented, and a big move to make. We have to give notice at work. We have to get the ice cream shop going for the summer, to make a go of it.

My mother-in-law decided to retire at that point and come with us. She worked at a factory that made engine parts for cars. Through the winter of

'93 she had moved in with us at our place in Maine, at the lake. Having her in the household was good, as she helped with baby sitting. And she had a knee replacement that year, so we were helping her.

I'm pretty excited too about the possibility of getting a rec director position. We packed up a 40-foot U-Haul and we packed my mother-in-law's car to the max and we had two dogs and three kids. We rented out the house.

## Nadine's Diner

The drive was OK — the U-Haul had a governor on it that kept the speed to 55 mph — and we arrived here May 28. We were shooting for getting open for the fair and races weekend, the third weekend in June. Nadine's Diner, our new business, opened then. It was a good weekend, and we were just swamped. I ended up washing dishes, and Nadine took over the front section herself. We served mainly fast food. My mom, mother-in-law and sister worked also, and a couple of girls.

We got through that weekend and made up a schedule; we were all going to take turns being at the diner. On the Wednesday after the weekend these two guys walk in. One of our staff is looking after them. I see them from the back.

The girl turns around and points to me. This guy comes up to the counter and says, "Are you Don Dietrich?"

I said, "Yes."

"I'm so-and-so from Immigration. We've had a report of illegal aliens working in here." They were referring to my wife and mother. We had taken every step we could to make sure everything was done right. They knew the circumstances; we had faxed paperwork through. But yes, we were breaking the law, because they needed work visas.

But he was treating me like I had 10 Mexicans in the back. He said they cannot be in here. We applied for the work visas. We had to hire the girls on a more full-time basis, and I was over there a lot that first summer. The rec director job never panned out.

I asked the Immigration official, "Why are you here?"

He said they'd had a phone call. Someone had reported us. Dad was very upset at that. To this day I don't know who it was. By October, they were issued papers so they could work. I threatened to go to the *Winnipeg Free Press* with the problem, and that got some results.

Stress makes my Parkinson's worse. I'd be working there and Nadine and mom would come in, and they'd notice I'd be doing everything left-handed. My right would be curled up under my chin.

Dad was an alcoholic. He wasn't happy with what had happened to us, so he was drinking a lot. He was probably drinking 40 ounces of vodka daily. I found that taxing, because he'd phone me at work, and there's only so much you can do.

One night in November he admitted himself to hospital. He was going to try to dry out. I was in the diner doing some cleaning after hours and got some ammonia in my eyes. It might have been on my gloves and I was sweating, and I wiped my eyes. It was stinging so I went down to the emergency and was sitting there. They had rinsed my eyes out and around the corner came Dad.

## Talked with Dad

My wife says things happen for a reason. Dad sat and we talked. That was the first time since I'd been home for about six months that we had a really good conversation. It was like old times. I was so pleased. He'd been in before, but he couldn't beat alcohol. I thought, this time he's going to.

We'll never know, because we got a phone call the next morning. While sitting on his bedside reading a newspaper, he'd died of a heart attack. Dad had a business in town here for 45 years, a garage, and so it was a big funeral. He had actually sold the business a few months earlier. Bill Astle bought it, and he'd been there since he was about 15. Dad had only a few months of retirement.

Our kids really only got to see him for about six months. He died Nov. 23, 1994. So they never really got to know him. I'm sure if he was around today, he'd be following these guys around all over the place, the boys and their hockey. Tristan's got a four-wheeler out there; he'd make sure he had a place to keep it warm and work on it. He was a good man.

Until you think about it, you don't think that alcohol has an effect on your life. But it does. I mean he used to come home after work at 5:30 and pour himself a quadruple rum and by six o'clock you didn't want to talk to him. That's where he went and put out the rest of his frustration.

But I knew never to call home after 5:30. So I probably missed a lot of things and a lot of opportunities. I miss him. I feel cheated, sometimes, that the boys didn't get to know him better. They didn't really see the real grampa Dietrich, the one that cared so much.

Nadine and Mom said I had to see a doctor, so I went to see Dr. Tomey. I'd skated a couple of times with the old-timers, and really had no problem. Everything seemed to work all right.

In 1995 he referred me to a Dr. Young in Winnipeg. There is no X-ray or blood test that proves you have Parkinson's. They do a series of other tests. While sitting in his waiting room I see some older people that are really wiggling around, or can't move, or have a blank look on their face. I'm hoping I don't have what they do.

## *You've got Parkinson's*

"You've got Parkinson's disease," he tells me after various tests. But he suggested I see this other doctor for a second opinion. "He's the best movement disorder specialist in Western Canada. Then you can decide what you want to do."

So I saw Dr. Doug Hobson in May. In his waiting room, everyone's got Parkinson's. Around the corner comes this big guy, he's about 6-9. He's just marching, and flailing around. When I got in to see Hobson, he told me the same thing: I had Parkinson's. I liked him. He was straightforward.

Back in the waiting room the big guy walks up to us and says, "You two are too young to be here." Nadine got talking to him and his wife, and his name was Leo Kristjanson. He was diagnosed with Parkinson's Disease at 48. I was 34. He was the president of the University of Saskatchewan. He'd won the Order of Canada. Tons of things. He was bigger than life, yet he focused on me. And what a sense of humour he had.

He was sitting there and got talking, and he had dyskinesia pretty bad, which is constant movement, and to me he brought some reality to what was going on. But he was also somebody I could question; he had it at a relatively young age too.

He kept saying, "I have Parkinson's Disease. That's just part of me, but it overwhelms the rest. I might be a good gardener, but people never talk about my flowers. They always talk about Parkinson's. 'How are you doing?', this or that."

To my regret, Leo passed away about a month ago, late in 2005. He choked. Parkinson's causes problems swallowing. He choked on some food.

When I left that place, I still thought to myself, "I don't have Parkinson's." I walked out of there and went back to work at the Deloraine Golf Course. I was given some meds. With working there and the Diner, I got pretty tired.

I expected to play hockey with the senior team that fall. I was going to do everything. Maybe I was in denial. It was the middle of the summer, maybe the end of July that I came home, and I couldn't get out of the truck. That was the big wake-up call.

# Chapter 16

## THE ROYALS AGAIN — AND CANCER

*"I'm an ex-professional hockey player and I always knew who my enemies were. I said, 'You tell me what I've got so I know what I'm going to fight. I'm not going to roll over and die'."*

I COULDN'T GET out of my truck. My brain was telling my muscles what to do, but the phone lines were down. I just sat there for a long time, 10 minutes or more, trying to move, but not moving.

That was the first time I had to deal with a symptom of Parkinson's that disrupted my daily routine for an extended period of time. I sat there trying to open the door. I could see it in my mind, but just couldn't do it. This time nothing was working.

That's when I realized I should address my medications properly and document things, as to what was working and what wasn't. I had more frequent trips into Winnipeg to see Dr. Hobson. So I addressed things better through that summer of 1995.

Yet I still had it in my mind that I wanted to do everything I could. That's when I decided I was going to play some senior hockey with the Deloraine Royals. I worked at the rink as well. I still took medications. I'm 34 now.

### Skating was a release

For some reason, when I got on the ice you wouldn't know anything was wrong. It was like a release. I since have found out that adrenaline had something to do with producing the dopamine that I didn't produce normally. With Parkinson's patients, they either produce too much dopamine, which causes dyskinesia, or not enough, which doesn't keep the phone lines firing.

When I hit the ice, my passion would kick in, and I had adrenaline which allowed me to function properly on the ice. All of a sudden I find a place where I feel human again. I'd been away from it for quite a while — '91 had been my last year.

I remember the first time I played an exhibition game at Pierson. We'd had some practices. Clark Tweed was the coach. My whole outlook on it all was, I'm not getting any younger. Maybe I could play a third-line centreman, play a little bit and contribute, see how the year went. If I couldn't do that I wouldn't.

I was sitting on the bench watching the guys out there and they're playing for keeps. It's rough. There's some scrapping. I can tell that everybody's pretty fired up. It made the hair on my back stand up, because here we are playing, and not one of us is making a dime. We're playing for the love of the game again, and it just excited me even more because all of a sudden I'm thinking, "This is what the grass roots of the game are all about."

So I played that year and ended up playing quite a bit. I played defence, and ended up making second all-star team in the Southwest Hockey League. We lost out to Boissevain in the first round of the playoffs, and it was pretty intense. I started to find that near the end and after games I was having trouble the next day moving, or getting things done. Remember I'm no spring chicken anymore, I'm 34. I've got three years of junior and 10 years of pro behind me. There's wear and tear on the body.

It's funny, because I had gone to some sportsmen's dinners in Brandon with the Wheat Kings. You run into some old players. I met up with Doug Wilson one time, and the first thing he asks me is, "How's the body holding up?" And he had no idea that I was having trouble with Parkinson's. He played for way more years than I ever did. But that's the first question they ask.

I thought, well, I made it through the year, did what I wanted, I shouldn't push it anymore. I'd upped my medications somewhat, so I knew the disease was progressing. I was still very aware of what was going on.

## Chris Nielsen

I sure enjoyed the season, and we had some great guys on the team: Jamie Olson, Dan Dekezel, Jason Wickham, Ricky Maddess, Jason Rommelaere, Lyle Spence. That season we brought some Southwest Cougars in to play with us, and one of them was Chris Nielsen. As a 15- or 16-year old kid he was fantastic to play with. He certainly had the gift of the game. You knew he was going to go on.

One time we were playing Foxwarren, which had a good team. The game decided who would get into the playoffs. Chris Nielsen set me up with just a bullet of a pass, and it was just like something that would have happened in pro. There were guys between us. I put my stick on the ice and he and I made eye contact so I knew it was coming. I had a wide open net, and that made it 6-5 and we ended up winning.

Chris went on to play in the NHL, AHL, and in Germany. He threaded that pass underneath a stick and through a couple of guys, and it came hard. I was pretty pumped up about that goal. It put us into the playoffs, and we had to play Boissevain, the first-place team. We'd never beat them the whole year. The series went five games and we did beat them once, at home. They were good. They came at you.

That year too, I got every defenceman's nightmare, the Most Sportsmanlike Player award! I don't know if they felt they had to give me an award, but that's what I got. Looking back, as a 16-year-old I got Rookie of the Year in the Southwest Hockey League. A difference of almost 20 years, full circle.

Things with the Parkinson's would get worse. I'd go in about every three months to Dr. Hobson. It's 1996 now. I worked at the golf course in the summer and helped out at the restaurant if I could. And I got involved with coaching minor hockey. I coached the Royals one year. It was pretty shaky. We would go to Boissevain or Pierson, the top teams in the league, with about 10 guys. I got a little upset that year because I wanted commitment and I had three kids playing and we would go to Boissevain with 10 guys to get beat 15-0. At the same time I was running minor hockey practices. That let me see how my kids were doing.

The great thing was, I became a fan of the game again. Through all the years of junior and pro, you're constantly criticized. So I could only ever see the things that were done wrong on the ice. I'd go to an 8-and-under game at the rink and see a kid do something and think to myself, "Why is he doing that?" I started to learn to go to a game and a boy would do something really good, and I'd appreciate it. So I started to see more of the positives instead of the negatives. I became a fan of the game again. Full circle here too.

I worked in the fall for Don Butler at the anhydrous depot on the edge of town. I had read some things in Ben Kroeker's *Deloraine Times & Star* about Canada Customs jobs. So I went — I think it was '97 — to write a test. You can't study for it or anything. There were about 50 of us in the Boissevain Arena, and it was tough. When we were done lunch, about 10 people never came back. I carried on, but failed it.

About nine months later, in '98, they offered the test again. I drove to Emerson and wrote it there and passed it. Immediately following it I got an interview — but failed that. There was role playing, and other different things. So I went through the summer working at the golf course.

In the fall of 1999 there was a notice in the paper about teaching assistant jobs. I thought this would be good. They had a student there who needed a Kindergarten Cop type of guy. Me. I got the job. It was mid-November, because I was going out on the ice with some kids that afternoon. I came home for lunch, gobbled down a bowl of broccoli soup real quick and I went, "Oh boy, I ate that too fast."

## *A hardness in my belly*

I held my belly and thought, "What the heck is that?" I started poking it a bit and thought, gee, I had a bowel movement today. I shouldn't feel a hardness there. I poked away at it and it wasn't sore or anything. Then I called my mom over, she's a retired RN. She checked it and said, "You'd better head over to the clinic."

It was closed so I went to emergency. Dr. Bertus Badenhorst was there then. He started poking at it and it got pretty sore. He ran some tests and the blood test came back fine. But he said, "Can you come back tomorrow morning, first thing?" So I came back at 8 o'clock. He handed me an envelope with Dr. Sonny Dhalla's name on it. He said, "You take that to Emergency, I've already talked to them there. I want you to go and see this guy. Something's not right."

We packed up and headed into Brandon on Wednesday — we found it Tuesday at 4 o'clock in the afternoon — and sat in the Emergency room. I went for an ultrasound and had some X-rays done. They apparently could see this mass in the ultrasound, but they didn't tell me what was going on. This was 3 p.m. and I'd been there from 10. Five hours in my little emergency room cubicle.

All of a sudden an admitting nurse comes in, fires a band on my hand and says we're taking you up to fifth floor. That is over on the other wing, where they prep you for surgery apparently. My mom knew this, I didn't. Nadine was with me and she called my Mom.

They came in and I was lying in bed wondering what's going on. Nobody's giving me any answers. Then two surgeons came through the door. One was Dr. Dhalla, who was a stomach-bowel specialist, and a urolologist, whose name I don't recall. They said they'd found a mass inside me the size of a softball. "We're adding you to the schedule tomorrow."

They put me in a room, the nurses came in and gave me an IV, stuff that cleans your system out, that instantly gives you the runs. I remember sitting there and hearing the two nurses outside remark on the importance of my surgery. There were quite a few people in front of me — 900 and some were in front of me. And I was getting added to the schedule.

They had me scheduled for 5 o'clock Thursday. But Dr. Dhalla had a break in his surgery schedule. I was out with my IV pole watching the sports channel at 11 o'clock and all of a sudden this nurse says, "Back in your room. We're wheeling you down."

I had the surgery. They found and removed that mass. They took six inches of the small intestine on each side of the mass. They also went through everything else, kidneys and such, took my intestines out and went through them all, and then put me back together again.

I just had to wait to see whether it was cancerous or not. I was in there for 10 days and I wasn't told anything. The longer it went — you know, you think the worst. Dr. Dhalla was an extremely busy surgeon. I'd hear his name being called. He'd come to see me about 6 in the morning, briefly. He'd rip the tape off, look at the wound, and leave it for the nurses to do back up again and decide when they would take the catheter out of me. They'd ask if I was passing any wind before they let me eat; that way they knew if my bowels were working.

## 'Sorry. We're so busy'

No word. Nothing. I'm getting up, walking up and down the hallways and trying to stay as mobile as I can. The nurses are extremely busy. I used to buzz them, because they wouldn't let me walk by myself. I remember the first time. They put the catheter bag on my IV pole. And the nurse would walk with my pole. This one poor girl, she was just running one day. You could tell they were short staffed. She comes running and gets me set up on the pole and out the door I go. At that point my Parkinson's is acting up a bit because I'm not on maybe the proper meds. So I've kind of got the old Tim Conway shuffle going, you know? This nurse grabs the pole and is taking off down the hall and I've got this catheter in and I can't keep up to her! I'm just about skiing behind her. I'm going, "Wait wait wait wait wait!" She turns around and just starts laughing. "I'm so sorry," she said. "It's just that we're so busy."

I said, "If you could just leave me alone I'll get down the hallway on my own."

She said, "Well I can't."

I said, "Well, I can't keep up to you. So we've got to come to an accommodation." But it was a funny situation.

Anyway I waited for 10 days. Finally Dr. Dhalla came up. Nadine and I were in the waiting room working on a puzzle. He looks at me, walks up to me and goes, "We're going to pack your bowel and send you home." I know he's not noted for his bedside manner, though he's a great surgeon. I'm thinking, "What?"

He says again, "Yup, we'll pack your bowel and send you home."

I'm looking at him and go, "What do you mean?"

He goes, "Oh. Wrong guy. You'd better come with me."

We go down to the room. The nurse who was with him was on the floor quite a bit. I think she was the head nurse.

And she was crying. That's when he told me what I had.

He said I had leiomyo sarcoma. I said what's that? He said, "It's one of the most active and deadly cancers there is." To get the C word is pretty intense. I immediately started crying. Then the old hockey player in me whelmed up and I could hear all my coaches in the past saying, "If you get knocked down on the ice, get up off your ass and get into play." Play the game of life. Don't swing your stick in anger and take a penalty. That's the way I felt.

I looked at him and said, "I want out of here. Everybody on this wing here is dying. I've got people who will take care of me at home. I want out of here."

He said, "That's fine. You can pack up and go home."

Then I basically asked him, "What is this disease?"

He said, "I'm just a surgeon. I take them out." He patted me on the back and said, "You have a good rest of your life."

I can say that's harsh, but when you deal with it every day, how is the right way to handle it? I needed to see an oncologist, a cancer specialist. And I couldn't go to see him because I needed at least a month after surgery before I was even going to be administered any type of chemo or anything. In the meantime I found out through the nurses that they had biopsied it there. That's what they thought it was but they'd never seen it before, this leiomyo sarcoma. So they sent it to Winnipeg. Same result, but had never seen it before it's so rare. So they sent it to Vancouver.

The same cancer came back in my liver two years later. When they needed to check a certain drug that may work for me, they still had the initial tumor in Brandon. So without going in and taking a sample from my liver, they took a sample of the tumor and saw if the drug worked against it. But that's why I had 10 days of sitting there wondering. I knew it had to be bad, the longer it took. If it's all clear and you get the green light, they're going to tell you that within a couple of days.

## Prognosis not good

So I had to wait a month, and that's when I started looking things up on the Internet. The prognosis wasn't very good. There weren't many people who lived past five years. A lot of them were dismembered, or had things removed, so on and so forth. You can't believe everything you see on the Internet, but that was the only thing I really had to access. I had a month that I had to sit here. I've got the spelling of it and I'm trying to look it up, and there isn't a lot there but anything there is, is not very good.

I waited to see an oncologist, and I go in to see this Dr. Lorne Brandes in Winnipeg at CancerCare Manitoba at the Health Sciences Centre. Again you're in the waiting room, and everybody there's got cancer. He comes in, and he's checking me out, wondering why it occurred, family medical history and so on, and I had lots of questions. My sister had ovarian cancer and she beat it, so I was cancer aware.

Dr. Brandes had an experimental drug that he was willing to give me, but I had to take it with my first chemotherapy because that's when it had its greatest strength. It was a drug he actually had invented. So we might as well do it. The only trouble that he had was that he had never actually administered the drug to anybody with Parkinson's. So he wasn't sure what it would do to me. There were sheets I had to sign waiving all rights of legal recourse should they administer the drug and I croak or whatever.

I kept saying to him, "Tell me realistically what I've got in terms of time."

Finally he said to me, "How come you're so cancer sensitive?"

I told him that my sister had cancer. Not only that but I'm an ex-professional hockey player and I always knew who my enemies were. I said, "You tell me what I've got so I know what I'm going to fight. I'm not going to roll over and die."

He welled up emotionally a bit, which kind of caught me, my wife and my mother who were with me off guard. He's got a tough job because everybody he sees has cancer. He's got to tell them. He looked at me and said, "Don, you're a 37-year-old man with three kids. The best prognosis I can tell you is you come in every 21 days for treatments and we take it from there."

I just went, wow. So I looked at him and said, "What's the longest guy you've had with this. How long has he lived?"

"Well," he said, "I've got a guy in here right now who's working on four years."

And I said, "You've had others?"

"Yes. Not many. They didn't do that well."

I said, "I understand from the Internet that the longest guy's been five years. I'll be here for 10."

He looked at me as if to say, OK.

"Yes, 10 years. What do we do next?"

He said, "I think we wheel you down and administer the first chemo. You seem strong and healthy enough and we might as well get it going."

So every 21 days I went in and over a three- or four-hour span was given this DPPE, an experimental drug, and three or four different chemo drugs as well.

This experimental drug gave me unbelievable hallucinations. I don't remember half the things I said. I can remember my wife and my mother telling me that I'm laughing because the pictures were going up and down the wall in the room I was given. I remember being given the drug one time and the chemo nurse, just her face came right over top of me and she's going, "Mr. Dietrich, you have to shut up!" They told me later I was laughing and making jokes and stuff. You're supposed to be quiet. My wife said something about me seeing Pamela Anderson, too!

I went through that for six months, and it seemed to be pretty good. I had no problems. I went back to work. I worked for Canada Customs before that. I was told by Dr. Brandes that I would come in every three months for a CT scan, blood tests and chest X-rays. He said you'll probably do that for the rest of your life.

Then, on a routine three-month checkup, almost two years to the day, I went in and had spots on my liver. Four spots on my right lobe and two spots on my left. That was June of 2001. Dr. Brandes said your liver's infected; there's another experimental chemo drug and I think we'll try you on that. I went into Winnipeg and was on that drug for seven days, eight hours a day, straight. I was administered these two chemo drugs, slowly.

The first day I was in there I got sick right away.

# Chapter 17

## DEALING WITH CANCER

*"Now I just worry about today. I just get through today. But it took chronic illness — Parkinson's disease and cancer — for me to realize that. I should have been like this the whole time. I'm a better guy. I'm a better person for having the illnesses I've had. I am the luckiest man in the world."*

I WAS GIVEN a chance to take an experimental chemotherapy through Dr. Lorne Brandes, who was my oncologist. He was also the man who invented it. I had to go into Winnipeg every 21 days, to CancerCare Manitoba in the Health Sciences Centre. It was called DPPE, and I had only one shot at it. I couldn't take the standard chemo and then take it afterwards; it had to come first.

What this drug did was increase the effects of chemo by 15 to 20 per cent. But it also increased the side effects. So I would be hallucinating, and I had to stay one or two nights in the hospital each time, depending on how I handled it.

At that time the Cancer Foundation building at the Health Sciences Centre was going through some renovations, so it wasn't a good setup. There were people getting chemo in the waiting rooms; it just wasn't really comfortable or an easy place to do it. Anyway, it was pretty tough. But I took that experimental drug.

### Beaten the odds

Whether that's why I've beaten the odds, who knows? I tend to lean towards a combination of my attitude, my luck with these drugs, and family support. Again, it appears I was in the right place at the right time.

The effects on my family were considerable. Each of our sons is different in terms of how they handle things. Tristan, our oldest son, is pretty even keeled. It takes a lot to rile him. He's a very smart man. He has the ability to research things and find out answers and he doesn't wear his emotions on his sleeve.

My middle son, Jacob, takes the burden for the rest. He's the worrier. He would blame himself for what's happened to me. Nicholas, my youngest, was mad — just mad at the world. He had a chip on his shoulder because something was going to take his Dad.

My wife — I have no idea how she made it through all this stuff.

*I believe in my guardian angels [Nadine says]. There was something there to help me, because I had to be strong for my kids and for Don. I still see a psychiatrist to this day, to help me cope with things, and I'm not ashamed of that. I was so concerned for Don, and the kids, that when the whole thing was over and he was in remission, that's pretty much when I broke down. You're in total shock when this whole thing is happening. I had to be his support and the kids' support. As far as breaking down, I was very stressed. I still battle to this day with anxiety and panic attacks.*

*People have asked me, how did you do it? Here I was, going to be on my own, and I'm young. This was my soul-mate who I had planned on being with the rest of my life and they told us he was leaving. I had to take care of him. When you're so wound up with being a care-taker, you don't have time to think. When everything settled down after his second bout, that's when I had too much time to think. To this day I have to stay busy. You block it out and worry about things when they happen. When the doctor says six months to a year to live, the first time, you don't believe that. It could still come back. I believe my husband lives on borrowed time. That's why he goes in every six months.*

*His doctor has never said the cancer is gone. He has never said the word remission. My husband is living on borrowed time. Tristan's a big help. But you try not to say too much because you don't want him to worry. Being able to talk to somebody outside the family, the psychiatrist, is a big help. The second time it came back, his oncologist said there is nothing more we can do. His doctor looked into it because we wouldn't take no for an answer. We brought this radio frequency ablation to his attention and he found a surgeon who would try it on Don. I do believe in my guardian angels. They did try that surgery on other people, and Don is the only survivor.*

The hardest thing I had to do was phone my mom and tell her what I had and the prognosis. I was still her baby. She had her daughter go through ovarian cancer. Now me. I broke down when I had to tell her. You talk about strong people; that's mom. I had Parkinson's too. I used to be very active. Some days, I have trouble getting around. I'm sure that's hard to take and hard to watch. Like I said, I don't know how they do it.

I went through that chemo and things seemed to be fine. Nothing was showing up in that area of my small intestine. And so I went back to work at Customs.

What had happened was, I got a phone call about April, 1999. I had written the test and passed it but failed the interview, and thought that was the end of it. All of a sudden I get a phone call; they want me to come to Boissevain for an interview. And I'm in about the last two months of taking my chemo. So I walk in there loose. I'm beyond caring. I'm sick. I walked in there just as loosy-goosy as could possibly be, and passed it. I was told I had to take training starting at the beginning of July. I did, and ended up working for Customs from that point on.

Again, the interview process was foreign to me. As a hockey player I'd not been through it — sitting around a table with a tie on with people asking you questions. In the process of looking for jobs after hockey, I was always really honest, which was costing me jobs. The guy would say, can you do this? And I'd say, I don't know. I've got three kids. Some people laugh at some of the things that I say, but it's true. I'd never been in that situation.

## At Cartwright

I got on with Customs and got through that chemo. When I got done, Dr. Brandes told me, "You're going to come in here every three months. You'll get at CT scan, blood test, chest X-rays, the whole bit." He said the cancer would come back in my lungs or my liver. I said, "I've got a job. I will come in every three months, and we'll go from there."

I worked over at Cartwright to start with. I transferred over to Lyleton, and worked there two years almost to the day. Then I went in for one of my routine CT scans. We were just getting things back to normal: my Parkinson's was under control, I was having no problems at work. We worked three 14-hour days and then had four days off. Once in our 56-day cycle we got nine days off. So I never took any vacation and worked lots of overtime. We were getting ahead on the money end of things.

I went in and I got a phone call from Dr. Brandes. He said you have to come in, you've got spots on your liver. I couldn't believe it, because I didn't feel bad. Just like I didn't feel bad the first time. And as it turns out with your liver, if you think of it being like a loaf of bread, it there's one good slice in there and 20 bad ones, you still function. Now I'm thinking, well, be positive. This is why he wanted me in every three months. We'll get this early. We should be all right.

In the meantime I've been researching on the Internet and talking to different people about my cancers and certain things these people have been doing and I'd write things down. We went in and it was before the summer started in 2001, the spring. So it wasn't quite two years along that this came back.

He said there was a drug being used with some success on this type of cancer at the University of Ohio, and we're trying to get it approved up here. He wanted me to go on that. I'd be in there for seven days in a row, eight hours a day, to receive the two chemo drugs.

That in turn put me out of work. The Customs people allowed me a leave of absence. I was going for my full-time status when this all happened. And I would consider myself a good officer. I liked it. I liked that job probably more than I did hockey.

I can't tell you how many pedophiles I turned around. Different types of people. There are certain rules and regulations. And we can be bona fide tax collectors. That was my job. I worked at a one-man port where I was by myself. I liked that. I was the boss. And I got paid well. I felt pretty lucky to have that job. I always wanted to do a good job. I did lots of undercover stuff that I can't even mention — things of value. It was challenging. Every day was different. You never knew who was coming down the road. I had some pretty bad guys that I would turn around.

I just had a knack for sensing who they were. I paid attention to the people who trained me, and I study body language pretty well. If you're right-handed and you're recalling something, if it's the truth, you may look to your right. If you're lying and you're right handed, you're going to look to your imaginary side and think, what story am I going to make up? That movie The Negotiator, with Samuel Jackson brought that out.

Usually those guys were too friendly. Everybody's nervous to a certain degree coming to a port. When they're too friendly and they're coming with a car full of their worldly goods, they want to get up here. I don't think the Customs officers get enough recognition.

So I ended up going for this treatment and they put me on sick leave. When I went in this time they gave me chemo for seven days and when I came out of there I was hurting pretty good. On the second day I got sick. And within five minutes my doctor was right down there. I said to him, "You must have sprinted to get here from your office."

## Tumors out of control

"Well," he said, "this drug is pretty intense." I got talking to this one nurse and she was saying each bag I get is $5,000. So I'm getting $10,000 a day, seven days a week, of a chemo drug that, as I found out, wasn't stopping anything. I went in for MRIs now, a three-dimensional view of the tumors, and they're doubling in size every three weeks. They're out of control.

I go in to see Dr. Brandes in August and he pretty much tells me there is nothing else they can do. There's no sense wasting time being sick on chemo. At this point I've got no hair, I've lost every hair on my body. Sick constantly. I'm taking injections for white blood cells. Sometimes there was too much in there so the bone marrow areas in your hips and chest were expanding and just pounding. Very painful. Throwing up all the time.

I was sitting here at home one day and Chris Nielsen, 18 years old, phones me. He tries to give me a bit of a boost. The maturity of the kid like I said is second to none. All of a sudden I'm sitting here one night, a Wednesday night, men's night golf, he shows up. He says, "C'mon, we're going golfing."

I said, "I can't."

He said, "Just come out and get in the cart. I'm taking you to the golf course and I'll buy you a steak."

So I get in his truck and he takes me out there. I'm sure he'd been talking to Nadine or somebody. I went out there and we got going around a bit, and he said, "Why don't you hit a ball?"

I said, "I don't think I can. I'm in a lot of pain."

He just looked at me and said, "Don, sometimes you've got to play with pain."

And I thought to myself, "Right on." I was at the point where I was starting to feel sorry for myself. And this kid just completely boosted me. I hit some balls, and it hurt. But I did it, and I thought, you know what? I'm going to beat this. It just got me back on track.

So I went in and at that point I had different things. There was a chemo drug that they made for leukemia patients that was not approved in Canada, but if I had a positive enzyme in my tumor, I could use it. They had saved my tumor from two years earlier. This drug could actually stop the growth rate of my leiomyo sarcoma. It would be $2,000 or $3,000 a month for me to take this. In the meantime, I didn't test positive for the enzyme. But my doctor had campaigned to get it approved in Canada and it was, within a month. They were giving it to leukemia patients right away.

You hear horror stories about the medical system, but I can't complain about the way things went for me. Again, I leave there in August, and pretty much have been told to get my affairs in order and have a good rest of your life. I went home and stopped in and talked to Kelly McCrimmon, a good friend. Hadn't seen him in a while, and he offered to pay for any MRIs or anything if I went to the States.

Kelly's not a real emotional guy. But we were outside the Wheat Kings office on the ramp in the Keystone Centre, and he hugged me. And it really caught me off guard. I hadn't hugged him back. He stood away and he was crying. At that point I went to hug him back, I said, "Aw, Crimmer," and he pushed me away, and was looking around to see if anybody's looking!

Every time I went in to see Dr. Brandes I had something that I'd seen on the Internet. And he'd just shoot it right down. Like I said, he doesn't have an easy job, every patient he sees has cancer. Some he can give good news to, some he can't. I remember bringing certain things in and he'd just laugh, or put them in the garbage, and I'd look at him.

## 'I'm dying here'

One day he threw something away and I was pretty upset. I told him, "You know, I'm dying here. I'm trying everything I can. I just want a little bit of something back. Like, 'Good try,' or a pat on the back, or whatever." I don't think anybody had ever talked to him like that. We're actually pretty good friends now. I think he showed a bit of compassion. A lot of his patients left the world on him, and I kept assuring him that I wouldn't.

I went home and got a phone call September 10th. Dr. Brandes says I want you to come in. There's something I need to discuss with you. So Nadine and I got up early and drove in and at nine o'clock were sitting in his office. We sat there about two hours and 45 minutes in the back room, nothing happening. I can hear people scrambling around in the waiting room area. He came in and says, "Well, there's a liver specialist here at the Health Sciences Centre, Dr. Jeremy Lipschitz. He wants to take a look at you. And you can go and see him right now." He gave me some hope.

We walked out of there and they've got TV screens in the waiting room. I see this airplane flying into the side of the World Trade Center. Of course it was September 11, 2001, a bad day in history, but a great day in Don Dietrich's history, because this Dr. Lipschitz told me he wanted to try to zap the tumors with what's called a radio frequency ablation — which I had read about on the Internet. Radical new surgery that zaps the tumor itself, and leaves the tissue around it healthy.

After the MRI he looked things over, and my right lobe had four tumors which were taking up a lot of my liver. I had two tumors on the left side. He warned me that in the surgery they open people up and sometimes find cancer that they can't see in an MRI or CT scan, and then they just stitch you back up again.

It was November that I had this surgery, almost two years to the day that I was first diagnosed. At that time I was helping to coach a bantam team. I coached a bantam game in Pierson that night, and drove from Pierson into Winnipeg for 6 a.m. We all drove in, Tristan, Mom, my wife. Mother in law stayed here with the two younger guys. My middle son was playing in Pierson.

Again, we're all dealing with this. We're not sure what's going to happen, what's going to go on. I went in for the surgery and remember being in there a long time. When I woke up the recovery nurse was there, and I asked her, "Did they do something with my liver?" That's all I wanted to know.

She said, "Yes."

Then I slept. I remember waking up and seeing my sister, my mom and my wife and Tristan, standing there. They had worried looks on their faces. I'd had these shunts put in because what they'd found out was that the whole right lobe of my liver was done. So they sectioned it off, cut it. Part of the tumor on the right side was growing into my left lobe, so they shaved it. Then they zapped the other two tumors with this radio frequency ablation. They had to take parts of the tumors to make sure what kind of cancer it was, so they had put shunts in all my arteries and I was puffed up like the Michelin man. I must have been about 270 pounds and was all ballooned up. I waved at the family to let them know that I was OK, but really out of it.

That was on a Thursday night. I know I was in a room with about five people, and they changed me to a different room with just one person. The nurse was trying to lift me up, and she dropped me. The nurse was upset because she said, "I've lifted guys your size before." But she didn't realize I had all this fluid in me. I mean I was heavy.

## Liver regenerates

The liver is the only organ in the body that regenerates. Mine completely regenerated. I still have remnants of the two tumors on the left, but for some reason they're shrinking. No explanation why — they shouldn't be, but they are. He did five liver resections that year, and I'm the only one that's alive. Whenever I go in and see Dr. Lipschitz, he shakes his head with a smile on his face. Dr. Brandes says the same thing, and each credits the other with what goes on.

I was taking Parkinson's meds, filtering that stuff through my liver. I had to alter my medications so much after the surgery because I was taking too much. I had dyskinesia so bad. I was wiggling around, and I had a scar across my belly. The pain from the stitches was intense. When I came home, I ended up going into hospital here and the doctor put me in a room and knocked me out, so I could finally sleep. But Parkinson's wasn't anything I worried about to that point. It was secondary.

Support here in Deloraine has been great. The first bout that I had, the town did a fund-raiser for me. Marty Murray has given me some money from his golf tournament. At different times I've had support that I'm overwhelmed with. It's tough to face people with cancer. What do you say? Lots of times just a pat on the back was all I needed. Not to that point did I realize just how many people are affected by cancer, even in our small community.

You want to talk about support, this community had a benefit hockey game for me. I said at the game and I'll say it again here, having both Parkinson's disease and cancer, a lot of people say you really got the short end of the stick. But I'm a pretty fortunate man because of the support of the community that I've got. I'm pretty lucky.

Just the family alone that I have. My wife — she pushes. Sometimes you need that. She had a big-time role in all this. My kids — I still don't sleep. I walk around in the middle of the night and look in at everybody, and say,

"You're not taking me away from this now." I'd stretch every day for every hour I could get. Anytime anybody drops that C-word on you it's a shock. To go through it two times is indescribable.

When I played hockey when I was younger, every day I lived that day. Tomorrow, I couldn't have cared about. I knew that I had a paycheque. There was always going to be another game, another year, another contract. I just lived for the day. Then all of a sudden I got out of hockey and started worrying about the future and what it held for me. I didn't like the way I was. Then I got these diseases that I had to deal with. At some point or another, I gave all my worries to God. And I'm not a Christian or a church-going guy. I don't need a church to believe in God but I believe in God. I've had my conversations with Him. Again, I'm back to living in the day. I live for today. Before, if I had a flat tire I'd come home angry and kick the door open, swear and moan. Did it fix the tire? Did it change anything? So why be that way? Now I just worry about today. I just get through today. But it took chronic illness — Parkinson's disease and cancer — for me to realize that. I should have been like this the whole time. I'm a better guy. I'm a better person for having the illnesses I've had. I am the luckiest man in the world.

I told them I'd be here for 10 years. It's coming up nine this year, 2007. I always laugh and say, heaven doesn't want me and the devil's afraid I'll take hell over. I've got nowhere else to go!

# Chapter 18

## PARKINSON'S SURGERY — AND STRANGE HAPPENINGS

*"I could hear my old coaches say, 'Get up off the ice!*
*Get back into the game!'"*

IN 2004 I went in for one of my three-month checkups. We went through my CT scan, chest X-ray, blood test. There is a lot of anxiety attached to each visit, and I'd had enough. More accurately, my family and I had had enough. So I proclaimed to my oncologist, Dr. Brandes: "I want to quit cancer." He looked at me. "I mean, I don't want to have it anymore. I've been coming in here two years, nothing is going on. I don't want the stresses of tests every three months. I'm fine."

Dr. Brandes matter of factly told me I would continue to come in because I am someone who has beaten the odds and they will continue to monitor me in case I can help somebody else who may come in with the same thing. Do we approach it the same way? Do the same type of treatments? So they had to keep an eye on me and learn from my case. When he put it to me that way it meant quite a bit.

■   ■   ■

"Don is an inspiration to his doctors," Dr. Brandes said. "There are some patients who are just role models for all of us, including their care givers. I would definitely put him in that category.

"Here's a guy who not only has cancer problems, but he's battling to keep going with Parkinson's disease, which is likely a result of his hockey career. So he's not just battling one serious problem, he's battling two serious problems. He's shown tremendous valour in both circumstances. It's a wonderful story."

"I'm a big fan of Don's," Brandes continued. "He's a spectacular person. He's also got a spectacular wife and mother, for that matter. They are a tremendous family who show remarkable courage in the face of adversity."

■   ■   ■

*Every six months we're in for a CT scan [Nadine says]. You need to know what it's like.*

*Around the house it gets very tense, because we are so dreading those words, "It's back." I never want to hear those words again. We go through that every six months. He's got one coming up this week. You hold your breath when you talk to your doctor. Hopefully he says the words, "He's clean." A lot of people can relate to that. We are not alone.*

*I don't know how he does it, stay happy. I'm not the one who has to worry about whether I'm going to be alive next Christmas. I watch him every day. I watch his body giving up on him, the Parkinson's. And I don't know how he does it. I would probably lose it. His Parkinson's is getting worse. I am very amazed at how he handles the situation. With the Parkinson's it is a progressive disease. It doesn't get better; it only gets worse. I can't imagine what's going through his head. He I think is being strong for us. I am very proud of him.*

*Things are stressful around here a lot. But we have a bond that we will always have for each other. My heart breaks for him. I see him getting worse each day. I don't know how he can be so strong. His hockey has to have something to do with the way he is. He's the man of the household and things are tough because he isn't able to work. That has to bother him too. Stress brings on Parkinson's. I don't know how he does it. He is an amazing man and I love him with all my heart.*

*I look at him some days and my heart just breaks. I am a care-taker. I have a problem dealing with the fact that I can't make him better. I can try to make things easier, but I can't take that Parkinson's away from him. And that bothers me. He is very courageous. He was always so physically fit. Now he watches hockey instead of participating in it and that has to break his heart. I know he would love to be out there with his boys on the ice. He can't do it, and it's sad.*

■   ■   ■

The Parkinson's affects me more than the cancer did. But Parkinson's isn't deadly. Therefore Dr. Brandes talked me into going to Cancercare Manitoba and I volunteer any services I can, such as golf tournaments that I go to. I also volunteer with the Parkinson's Society of Manitoba and I sit on their board of directors as, right now, in 2006, their only rural representative.

While the treatment for cancer was going on, I had surgery for Parkinson's. They installed deep-brain stimulators, DBS it's called. This was in 2004. They give you a local anesthetic to cut you open; then they drill a hole through your skull. They put in a pilot tube with the stimulator, and then pull the tube out. They can go 14 or 15 hours per side.

One thing I wondered about but never asked was, how are they going to stop the drill from going into my brain? I could picture him standing above me with a foot-long Makita drill and going in. I hear the drill fire up, like an air gun at the body shop. Then I feel the pressure. And I'm in a panic. He goes for about a minute and a half, and you can smell the burnt bone. My heart monitor is going at a rapid rate. He says, "Are you OK, Don?"

I said, "No!"

"What's the matter?"

"How are you going to stop that drill bit from going into my brain?"

He hangs the drill so I can see it. It had a stopper on it. When it got to skull depth, the stopper froze it.

When the stimulator for my right side was installed, it made a great difference. I totally relaxed for the first time in 10 years. The rigidity left me. For a week or two after the surgery you have the "honeymoon effect" — no Parkinson's. I was able, for example, to eat peas that night with a fork, with my right hand. Before, I couldn't even have balanced peas on a soup spoon. Now I could also write well. And the stimulators weren't even turned on.

A week later they did my left side. The tremor left my hand immediately. Two of 10 cases are complex, and I'm one. It is a progressive disease, and the stimulators are not a cure. Still, I'm better with them than without them.

I'm still on long-term disability because of Parkinson's.

■   ■   ■

Dr. Doug Hobson of Winnipeg is Don's Parkinson's specialist. His full title is movement disorder neurologist at the Movement Disorder Clinic at Deer Lodge Centre. "Don stands out," he said. "His physical fitness level at the start, his coping skills, his ability to rise to all challenges before him, and that gleam out of his eyes … always with a grin, as he plans his next strategy to deal with a strengthening opponent. His willingness to help educate others and his never-ending dedication to family stand out too.

"He is blessed with a family support system that, without question, shares his trait of stubborn resilience. Nadine, as I have directly found out, is his equal in the stubbornness category (I have never considered this a fault). They have worked together to overcome their many challenges, each taking the lead when necessary.

"The goal is 'the best life possible,' " Hobson continued. "Don and his family have managed this despite over the years having to face far more challenges than most. These include tremor, muscular spasms, involuntary twisting of limbs, experimental medication trials, deep brain electrode implantation, loss of career, metastatic cancer, chemotherapy, partial liver resection, life threatening blood clots – and Larry Robinson's slap shot.

"It is a particular pleasure when you realize your patient has taught you something about life."

◾   ◾   ◾

## 'It will come out'

I had something really weird happen to me the first day I found my cancer. It happened that night. I had something in the bedroom. Maybe I was dreaming, but it was a nuisance that was trying to wake me up. The only thing it would tell me was, "It will come out." Just, it will come out. I took it to mean, it will come out OK in the end. I woke up that morning telling Nadine what had happened. She said, that's your guardian angel. The cancers, in a sense, have "come out" with the surgeries.

Something also happened the night I spent in the cancer wing after the first surgery. The Grim Reaper or somebody I swear tried to get into my hospital bed. And I shit myself – literally — and ran out of the room. I sat in the nurses' station the rest of the night. I told them I couldn't sleep. Beyond my family, I've never shared this story with anyone before. The Grim Reaper was trying to get into my bed. I was pretty drugged up, so maybe I was hallucinating. But it was so real to me that I soiled myself.

I sat here at home taking chemotherapy one time and was in that hot tub out there and I swear that Dad was sitting beside Genny, with his arm around the dog. She sits out there on the deck and usually has her back to me and through the cloud of mist at night, I looked at her and I swear Dad was sitting there with his arm around her. He didn't say anything to me. I told Mom, and everybody here. Is he watching over me? That's something he would do. At the time I had been told to get my affairs in order.

I've had a lot of people say a lot of prayers for me, which definitely helps. Like I said I'm a lucky guy.

I attribute a lot of my attitude to my hockey or sports background. When I first was told I had cancer, I could hear my old coaches say, "Get up off the ice! Get back into the game!" Guys like Johnny Olson, Ivan Wilson, Dunc McCallum, Bruce Stevens, Bryan Tyerman, and Bob Caldwell. They also taught me a lot of life skills, as did my parents.

## No guarantees

In life you need something to drive you to do things. Whether it was hockey or baseball, whatever I picked up came easily to me. And when that gets taken away from you through illness, you start to analyze things. The great thing I liked about sport was, each time you participated there were no guarantees.

You didn't necessarily win or do well. You had to make it happen. Life isn't guaranteed either. You have to make life happen.

I was fortunate. I got to live a dream — 10 years of pro hockey. I'm lucky to have done that. But I intend to be here for 60 or 70 years. I'm 46 now. The third period is about to begin.

# Epilogue

ON MAY 8, 2006, Don had another cancer surgery. Dr. Lipschitz removed a tumor near Don's pancreas. The pancreas itself was left intact. This was Don's third cancer surgery (after those on his small bowel and liver), five years after his last one.

Don's recovery was complicated by blood clots. He was ill and out of breath from clots in his lungs. His left foot was purple from clots. His recovery was also complicated by an infection at the incision. Don was put on intravenous antibiotics.

At home in Deloraine, the swelling at the incision continued. Dr. Nell of Boissevain lanced and cleaned the infected area, which drained for more than a month. As a result of these complications, Don didn't feel good until September 2006.

His Parkinson's remains a challenge, and he has increased his medications. Through it all, Don and Nadine remain busy with family. They attended son Tristan's graduation as a water technician. He is now employed by a firm in Chicago. This year son Jacob is slated to return to the Lethbridge Hurricanes of the WHL. Nick graduated from high school. He is also trying out for the Hurricanes, and hopes to play on the Western Hockey League team with his brother.

The four dogs, one cat (Jinx) and Iggy the iguana are doing well, as are Don's mother and mother-in-law. His sister, Donna, in July 2007 was again dealing with cancer. It re-appeared on her thyroid and at time of publication she was waiting to hear about options for treatment.

Don can be reached at hockeytonkman_2000@hotmail.com.

*Brad Bird, Editor*
*August 2007*

BRAD BIRD WAS born in London, Ont., on Jan. 27, 1959. Though raised in Toronto, he lived most of his adult life in Manitoba near Boissevain, where his Metis grandfather, Frederick Valentine Bird, was a doctor for 62 years. The son of a military pilot and stay-at-home mother, Brad played road and pond hockey for hours. Bobby Orr, Dave Keon and Darryl Sittler were among his boyhood heroes.

Over a 25-year career in journalism Brad has reported for and/or edited various publications including the *Winnipeg Free Press, Opasquia Times, Western Producer* and *Deloraine Times & Star*, winning six awards. He has toured and reported from war zones in Western Sahara, Kosovo and southeast Turkey. His first book, *Nickel Trip*, recounts the experiences of his father, Clayton Bird, a bomber pilot in the Second World War. His second, *Me and My Canoe*, tells the story of his 6,000-kilometre paddle across North America with Mark Bergen. *No Guarantees*, about the hockey career and life of Don Dietrich, is his third literary effort. In 2005 Brad walked and ran 1600 kilometres across Manitoba in winter, often camping out, to raise more than $10,000 for heart and stroke research. He also ran as a candidate in Brandon-Souris riding for the Green Party.

Brad and his wife, lawyer Karen E. Stewart, have five cats. They divide their time between Parksville on Vancouver Island and Brad's home at Lake Metigoshe on Turtle Mountain, Manitoba. There he likes to canoe, fish and visit friends — Dave Wall, Ben and Gerrie Kroeker, the Blacks, David Neufeld, Ernie Goodon, Don and Nadine Dietrich, and others. Brad can be reached at birdbrad@hotmail.com.

ISBN 142513072-0